FOR ORGANS, PIANOS & ELECTRONIC KEYBOARDS

E·Z PLAY TODAY

32

SONGS WITH
4 CHORDS

T0084973

ISBN 978-1-5400-0561-8

HAL•LEONARD®

7777 W. BLUEMOUND RD. P.O. BOX 13819 MILWAUKEE, WI 53213

E-Z Play ® TODAY Music Notation © 1975 HAL LEONARD CORPORATION
E-Z PLAY and EASY ELECTRONIC KEYBOARD MUSIC are registered trademarks of HAL LEONARD CORPORATION.

Visit Hal Leonard Online at
www.halleonard.com

Registration Guide

- Match the Registration number on the song to the corresponding numbered category below. Select and activate an instrumental sound available on your instrument.

- Choose an automatic rhythm appropriate to the mood and style of the song. (Consult your Owner's Guide for proper operation of automatic rhythm features.)

- Adjust the tempo and volume controls to comfortable settings.

Registration

1	Mellow	Flutes, Clarinet, Oboe, Flugel Horn, Trombone, French Horn, Organ Flutes
2	Ensemble	Brass Section, Sax Section, Wind Ensemble, Full Organ, Theater Organ
3	Strings	Violin, Viola, Cello, Fiddle, String Ensemble, Pizzicato, Organ Strings
4	Guitars	Acoustic/Electric Guitars, Banjo, Mandolin, Dulcimer, Ukulele, Hawaiian Guitar
5	Mallets	Vibraphone, Marimba, Xylophone, Steel Drums, Bells, Celesta, Chimes
6	Liturgical	Pipe Organ, Hand Bells, Vocal Ensemble, Choir, Organ Flutes
7	Bright	Saxophones, Trumpet, Mute Trumpet, Synth Leads, Jazz/Gospel Organs
8	Piano	Piano, Electric Piano, Honky Tonk Piano, Harpsichord, Clavi
9	Novelty	Melodic Percussion, Wah Trumpet, Synth, Whistle, Kazoo, Perc. Organ
10	Bellows	Accordion, French Accordion, Mussette, Harmonica, Pump Organ, Bagpipes

CONTENTS

Back in the U.S.S.R.

Registration 4
Rhythm: Rock or Jazz Rock

Words and Music by John Lennon
and Paul McCartney

Flew in from Mi - a - mi Beach, B. O. A. C.
Been a - way so long I hard - ly knew the place
Show me round your snow peaked moun - tains way down south.

Did - n't get to bed last night On the way the pa - per bag was
Gee it's good to be back home Leave it till to - mor - row to un -
Take me to your dad - dy's farm Let me hear your ba - la - lai - kas

on my knee Man I had a dread - ful fight ⎫
pack my case Hon - ey dis - con - nect the phone ⎬ I'm back in the U. S. S.
ring - ing out Come and keep your com - rad warm. ⎭

To Coda ⊕
1

G7 Bb7 C7

R. Hey You don't know how luck - y you are ⎧ boy. Back in the U. S. S.
⎨ boy
⎩ boys.

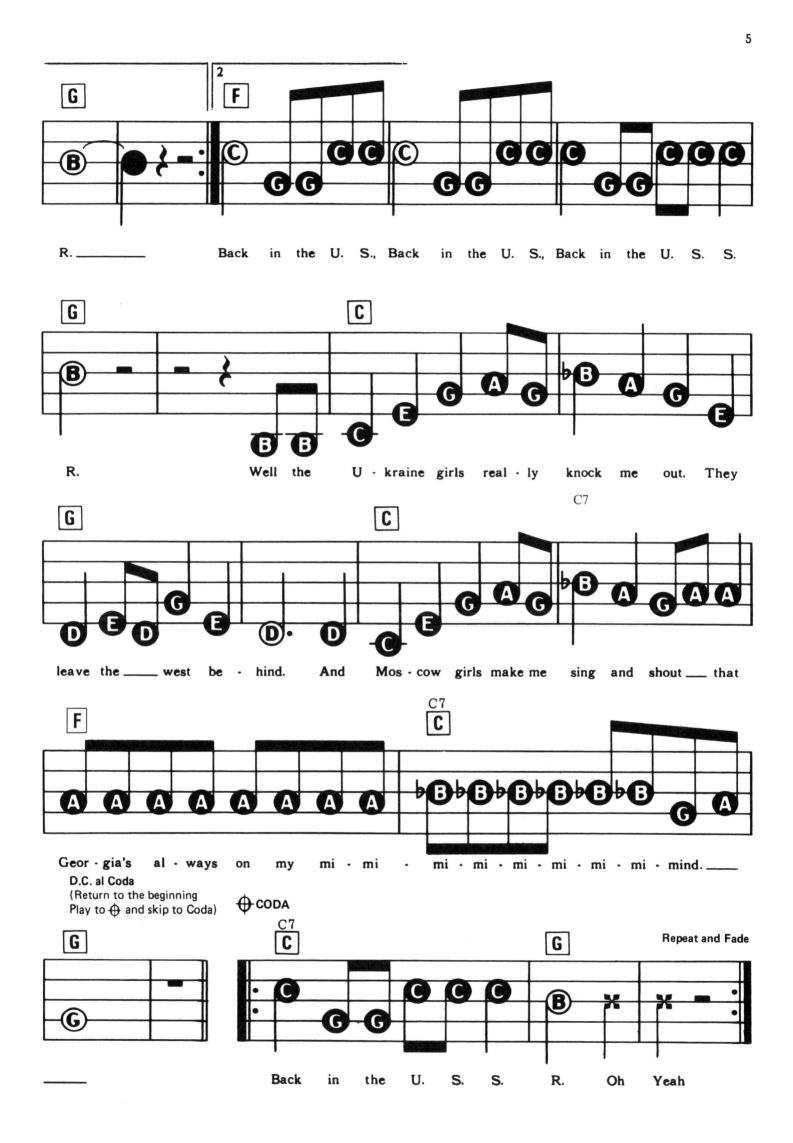

Blowin' in the Wind

Registration 4
Rhythm: Ballad or Fox Trot

Words and Music by
Bob Dylan

C   **F**   **C**

G   G   G   A   G   F   G   E   D   C   E

How	man - y	roads	must a	man	walk ___	down	be -
How	man - y	years	can a	moun -	tain ex -	ist	be -
How	man - y	times	must a	man	look up		be -

G7

F   **G**

G   G   A   G   F   G   E   F

fore	you	call	him a	man? _____	Yes, 'n'
fore	it's	washed	to the	sea? _____	Yes, 'n'
fore	he can	see ___	the	sky? _____	Yes, 'n'

C   **F**   **C**

G   G   G   A   G   F   G   E   D   C   E

how	man - y	seas	must a	white	dove ___	sail	be -
how	man - y	years	can some	peo -	ple ex -	ist	be -
how	man - y	ears ___	must	one	man	have	be -

G7

F   **G**

G   E   F   F   E   D   E   F

fore	she	sleeps	in the	sand? _____	Yes, 'n'
fore	they're al -	lowed	to be	free? _____	Yes, 'n'
fore	he can	hear	peo - ple	cry? _____	Yes, 'n'

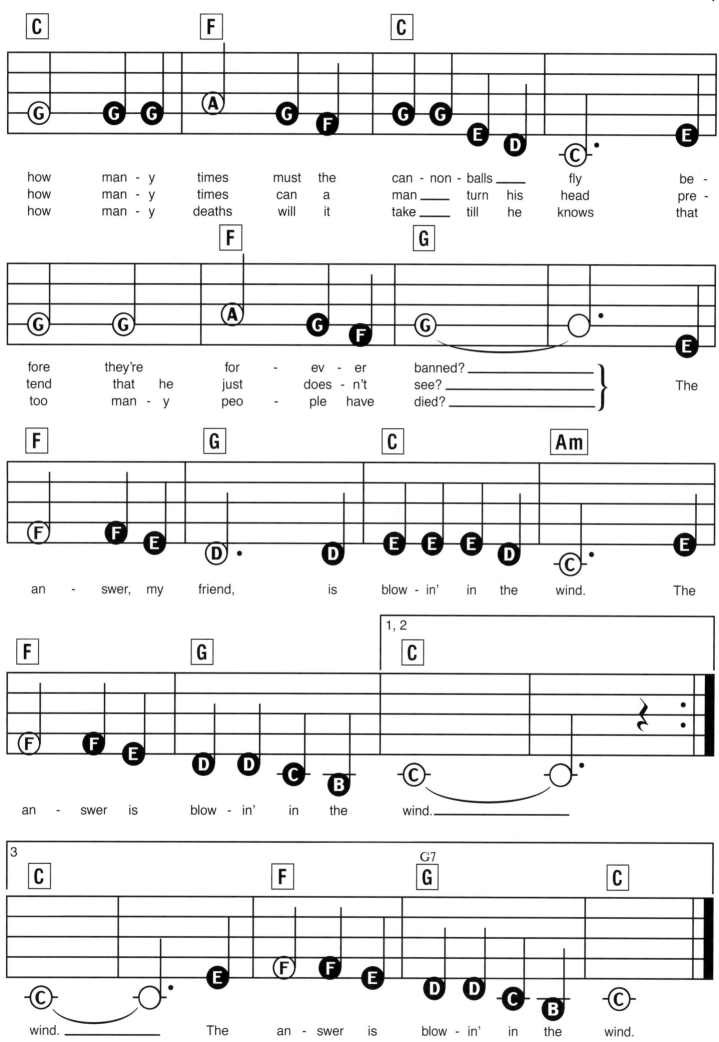

Blue Moon of Kentucky

Registration 1
Rhythm: Swing

Words and Music by
Bill Monroe

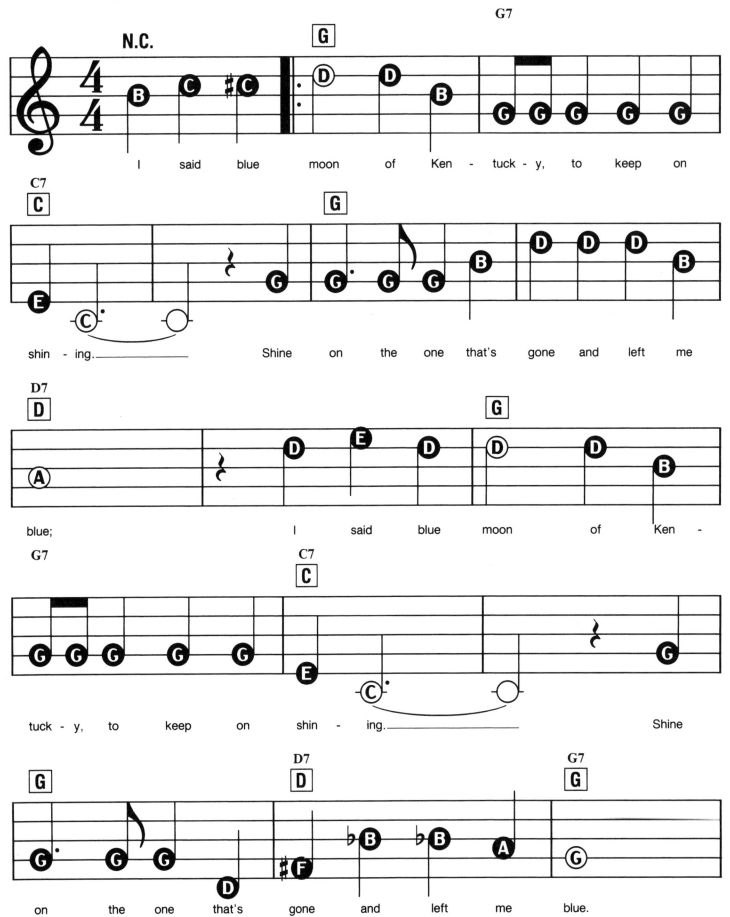

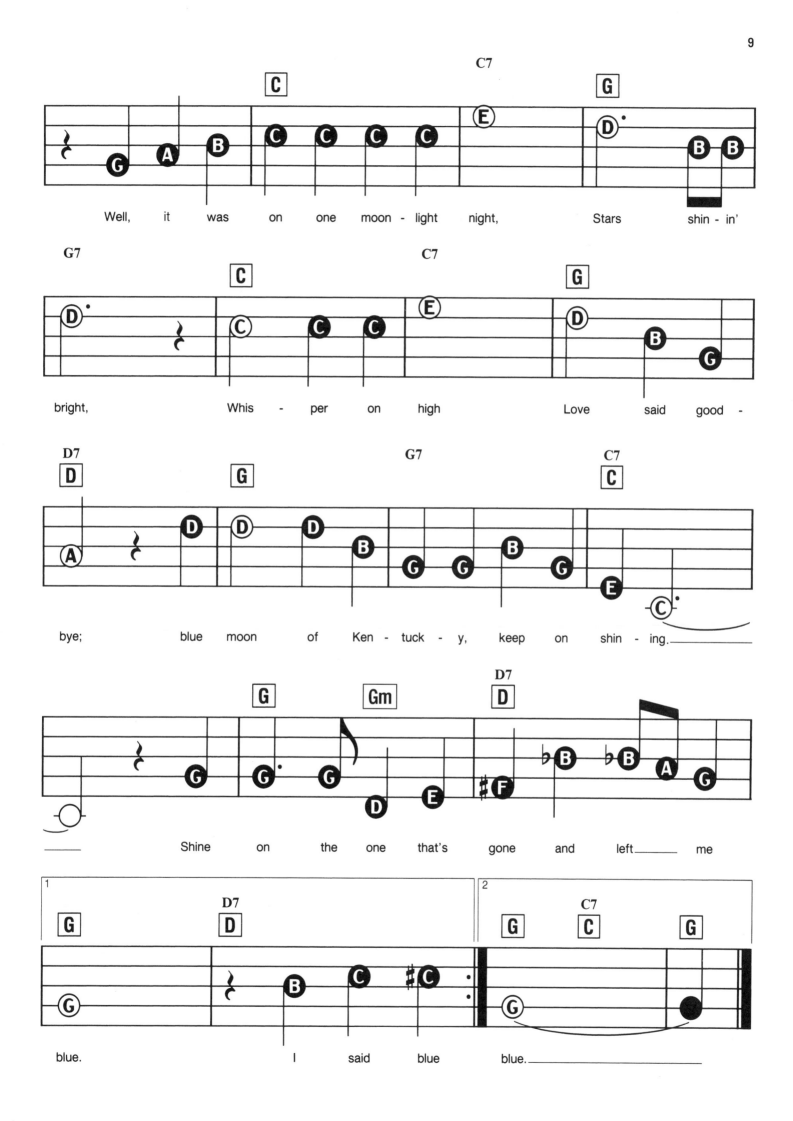

Brave

Registration 2
Rhythm: Pop or Rock

Words and Music by Sara Bareilles
and Jack Antonoff

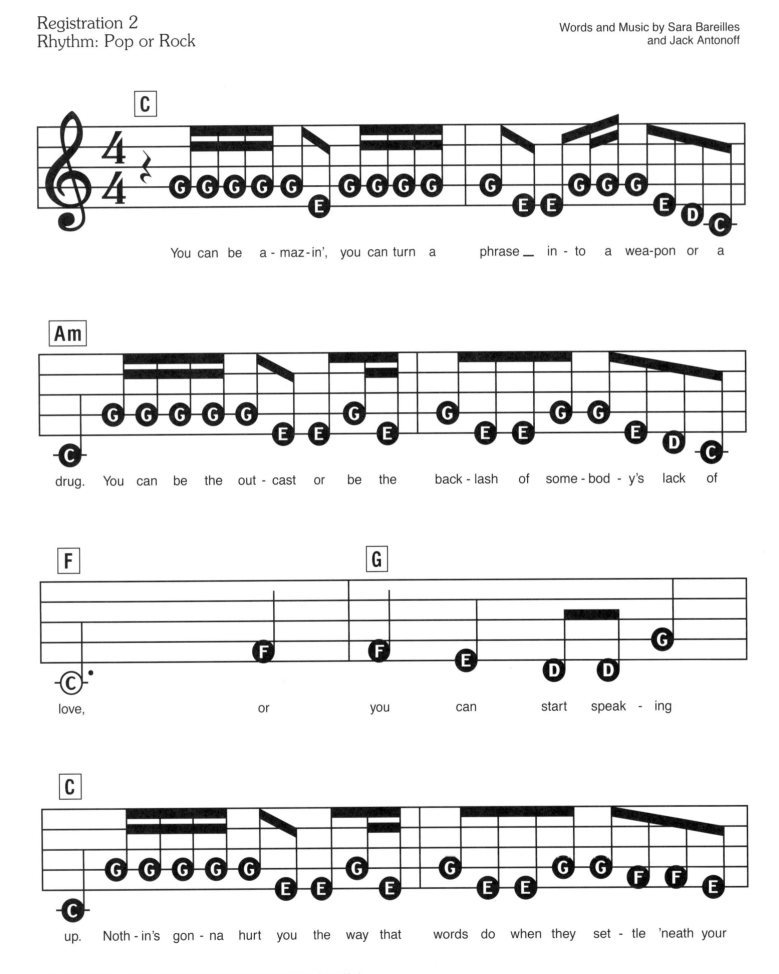

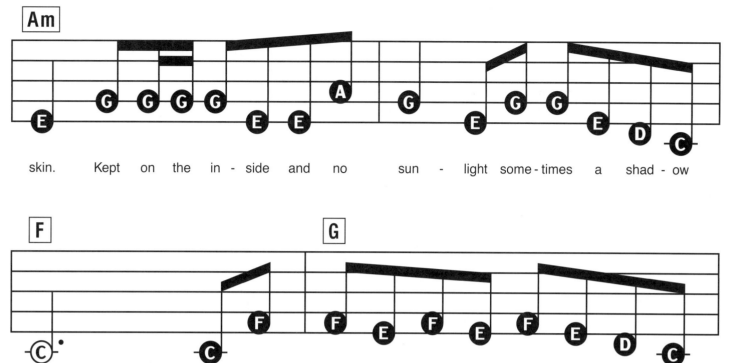

skin. Kept on the in - side and no sun - light some - times a shad - ow

wins. But I won - der what would hap - pen if you

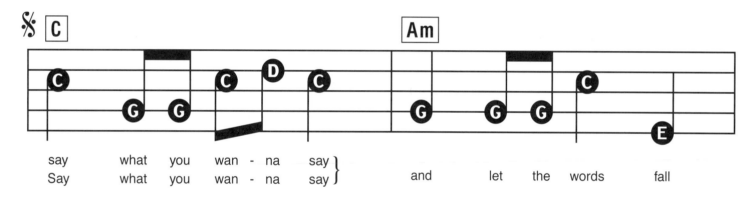

say what you wan - na say }
Say what you wan - na say } and let the words fall

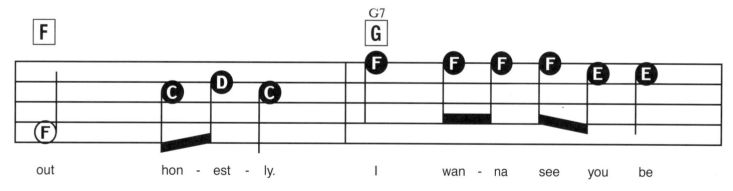

out hon - est - ly. I wan - na see you be

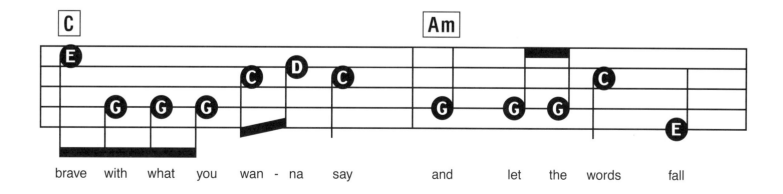

brave with what you wan - na say and let the words fall

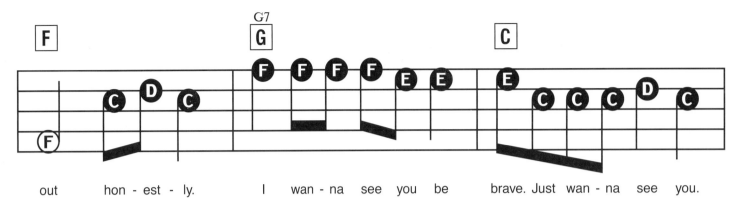

out hon-est-ly.   I wan-na see you be   brave. Just wan-na see you.

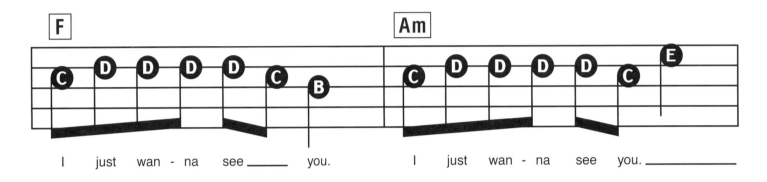

I just wan-na see _____ you.   I just wan-na see you. _____

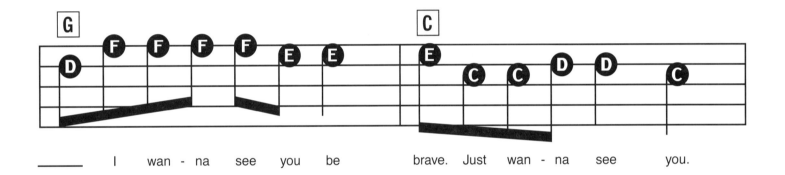

_____ I wan-na see you be   brave. Just wan-na see   you.

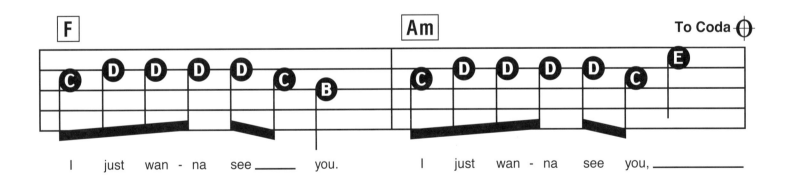

I just wan-na see _____ you.   I just wan-na see you, _____

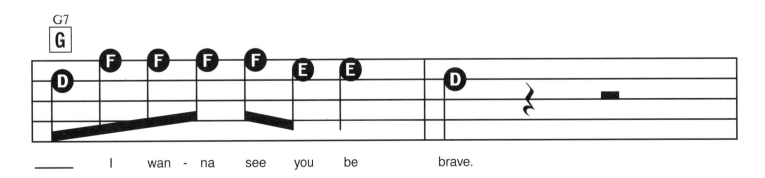

_____ I wan-na see you be   brave.

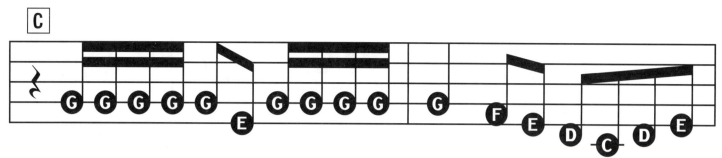

Ev - 'ry - bod - y's been there, ev - 'ry - bod - y's been stared down by the en - e -

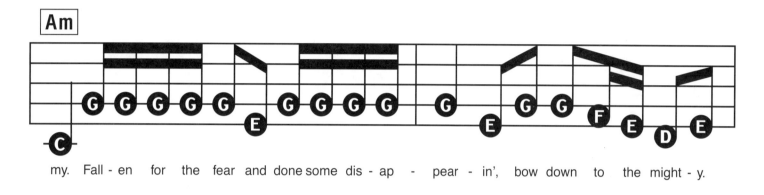

my. Fall - en for the fear and done some dis - ap - pear - in', bow down to the might - y.

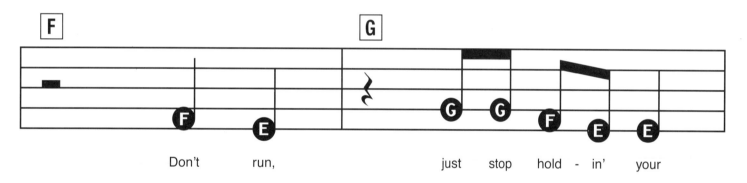

Don't run, just stop hold - in' your

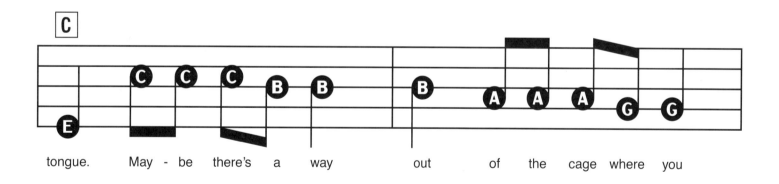

tongue. May - be there's a way out of the cage where you

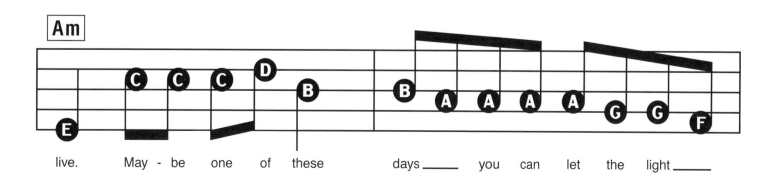

live. May - be one of these days_____ you can let the light_____

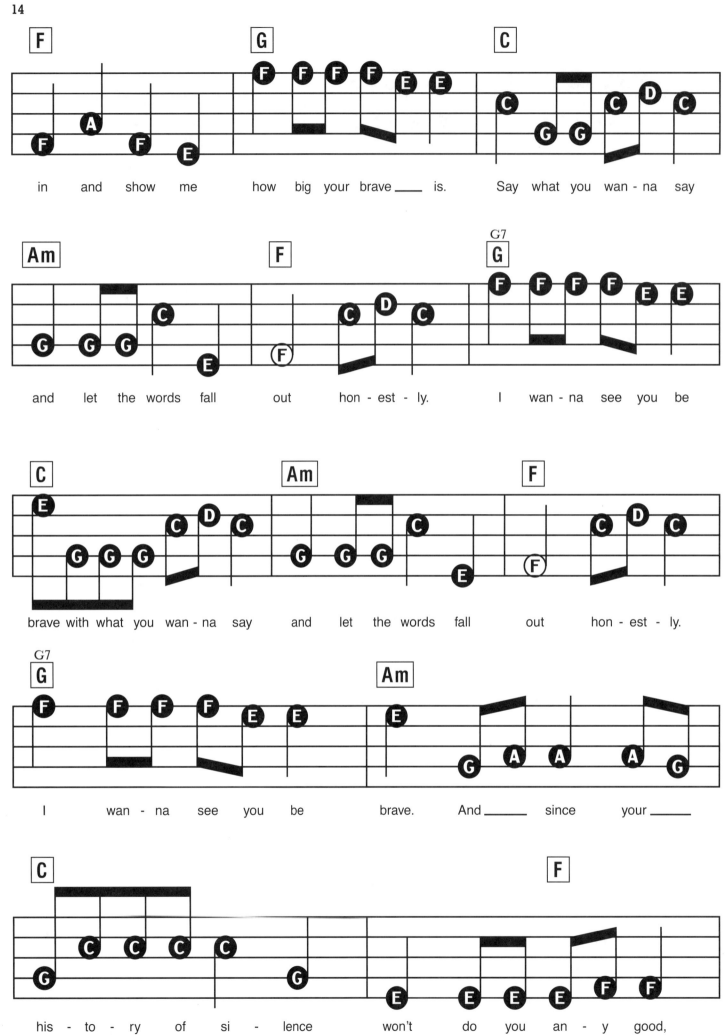

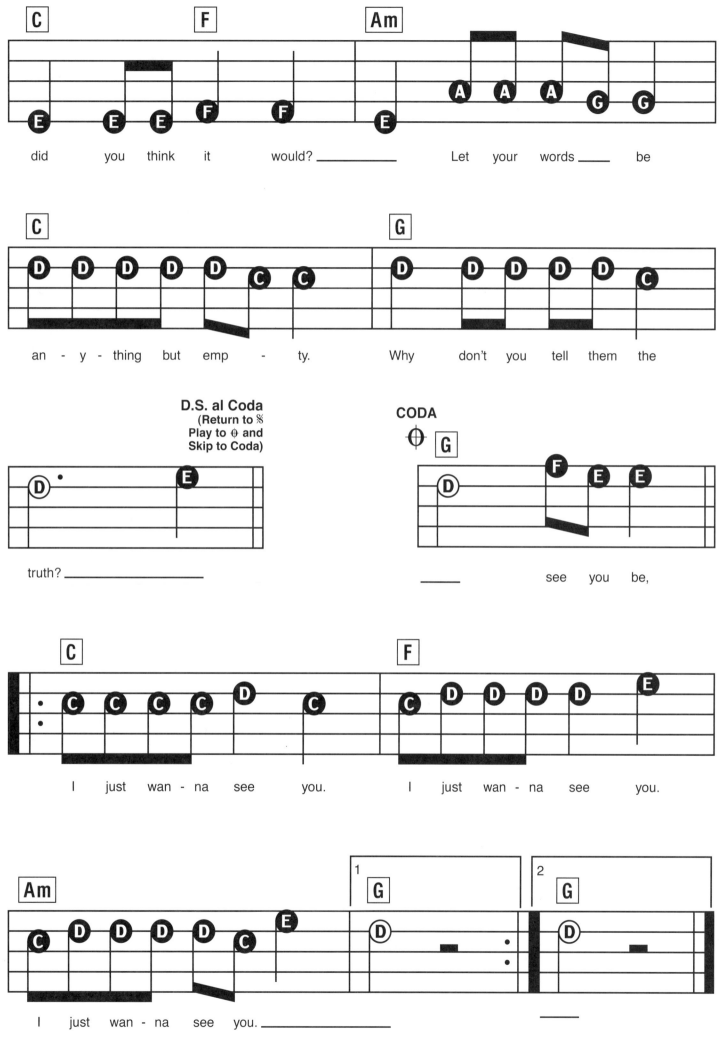

Breathe

Registration 7
Rhythm: Country Pop or Ballad

Words and Music by Holly Lamar
and Stephanie Bentley

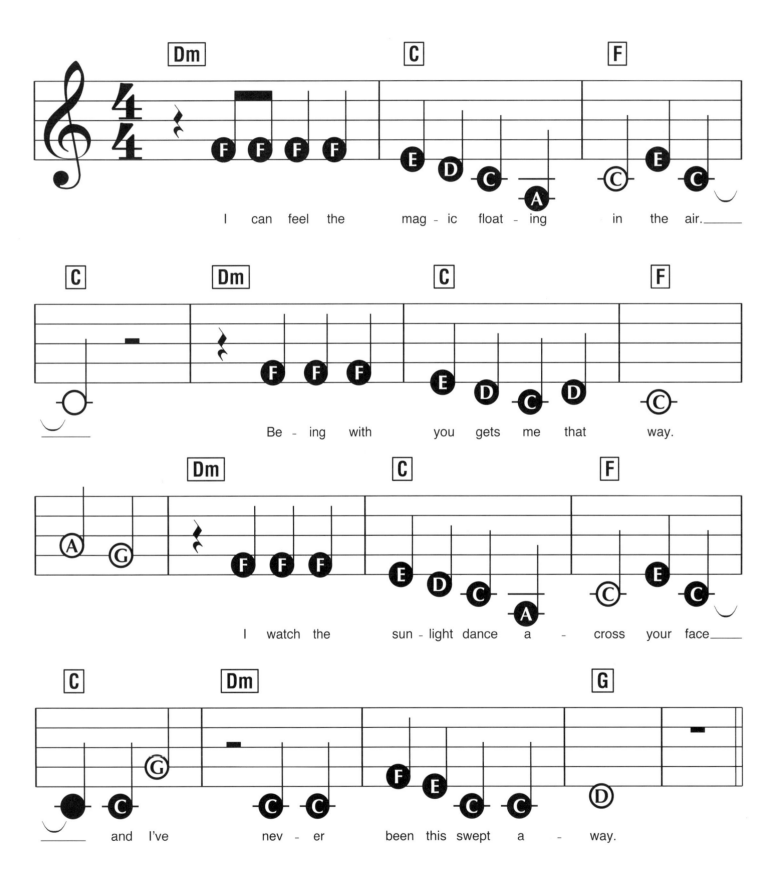

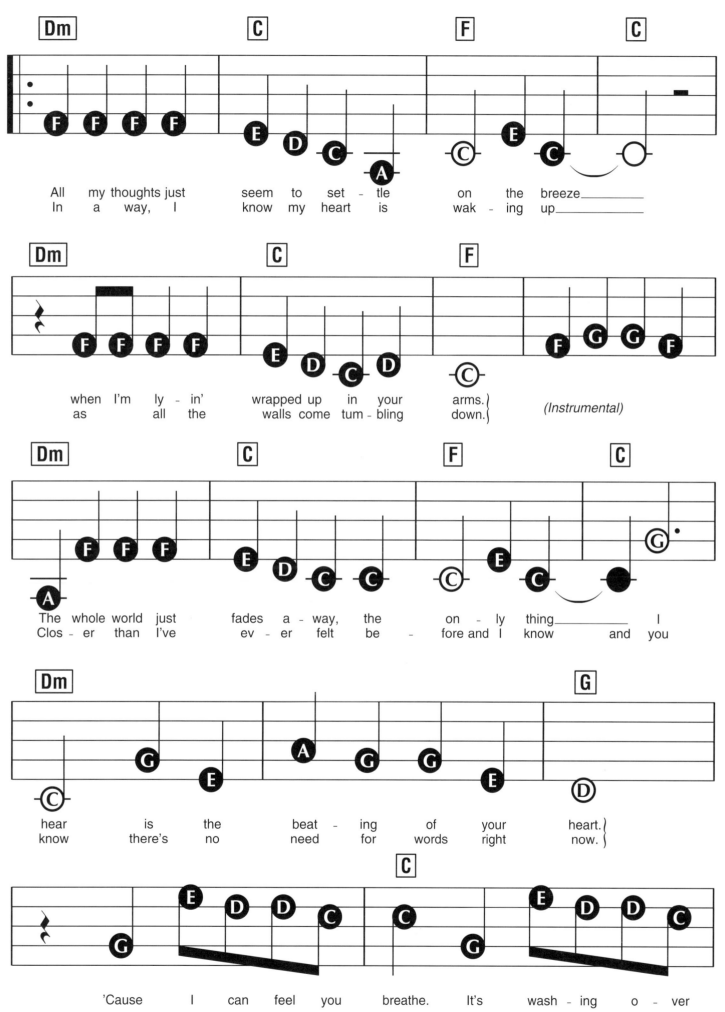

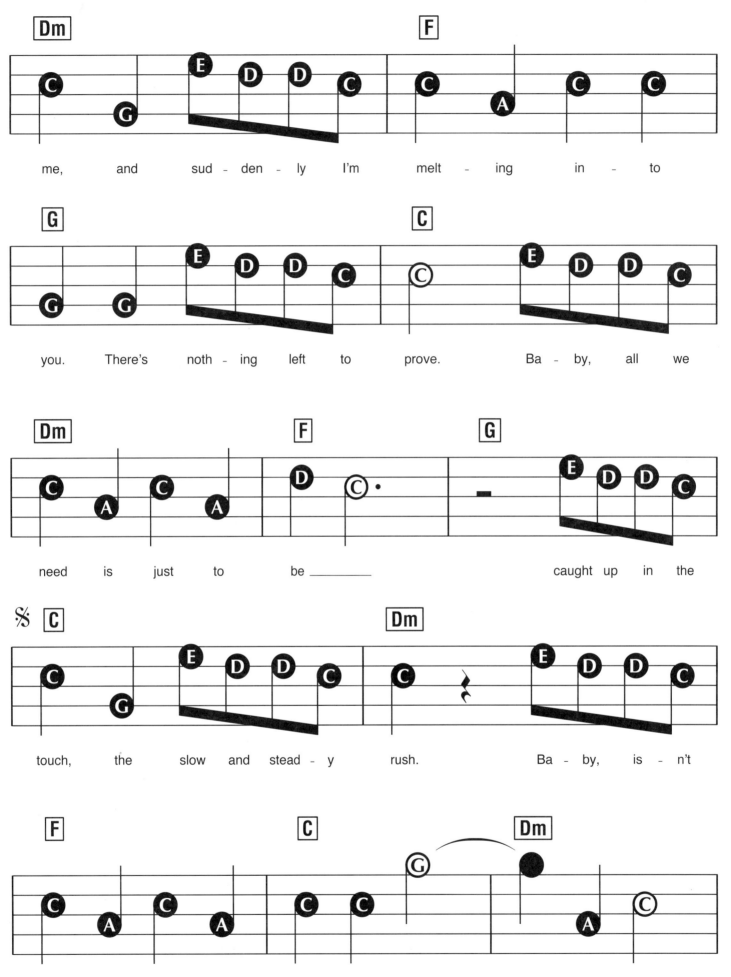

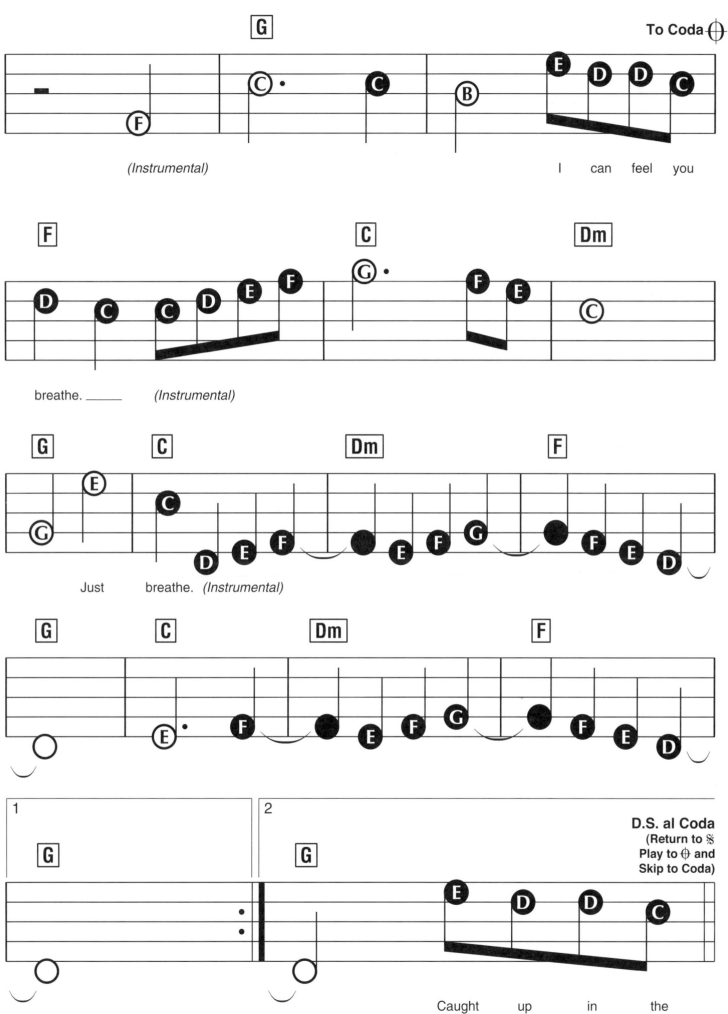

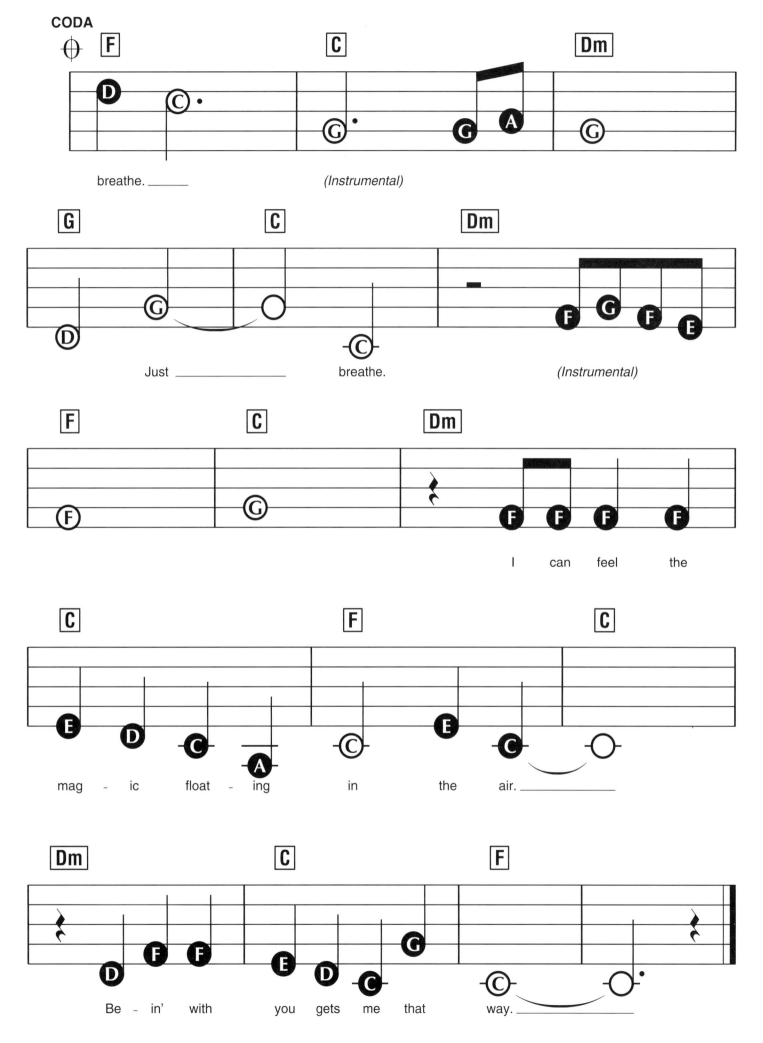

Candle in the Wind

Registration 8
Rhythm: Ballad

Words and Music by Elton John
and Bernie Taupin

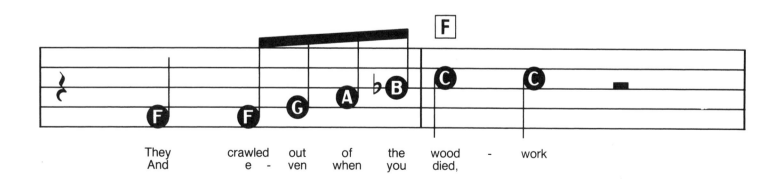

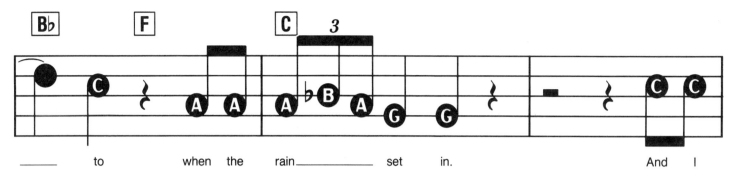

to when the rain_____ set in. And I

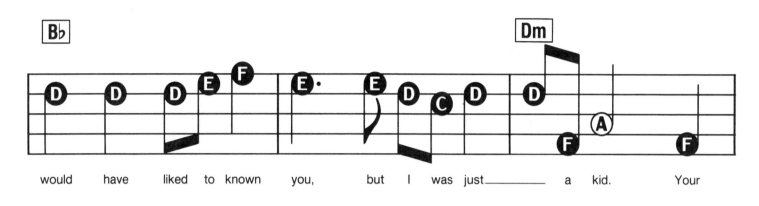

would have liked to known you, but I was just_____ a kid. Your

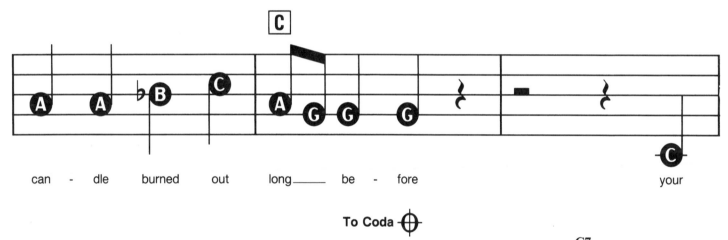

can - dle burned out long_____ be - fore your

To Coda ⊕

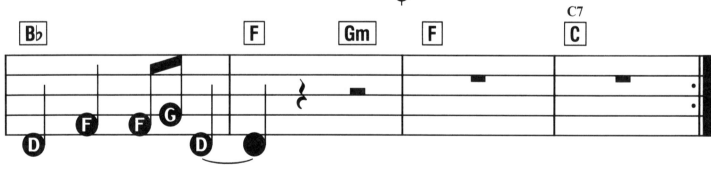

leg - end ev - er did._____

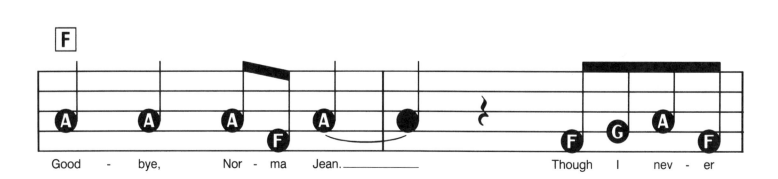

Good - bye, Nor - ma Jean._____ Though I nev - er

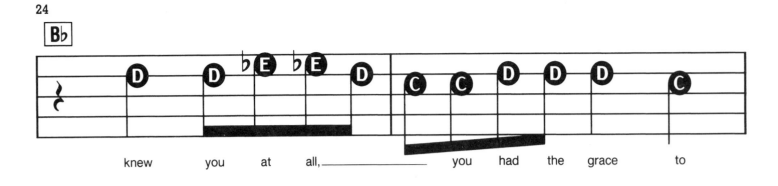

knew   you   at   all,_____   you   had   the   grace   to

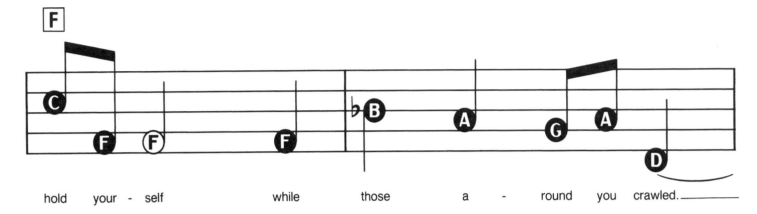

hold   your - self   while   those   a - round   you   crawled._____

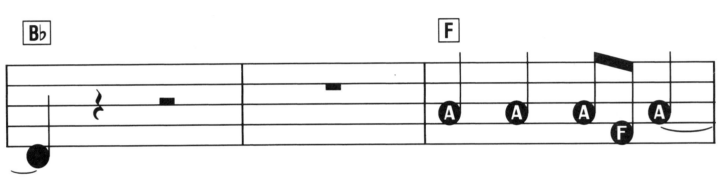

_____   Good - bye,   Nor - ma   Jean,_____

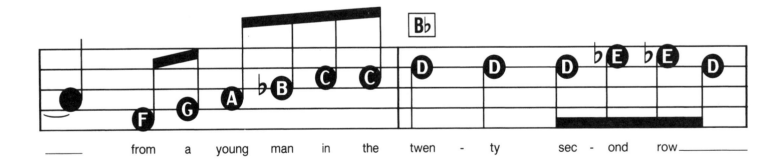

_____   from   a   young   man   in   the   twen - ty   sec - ond   row_____

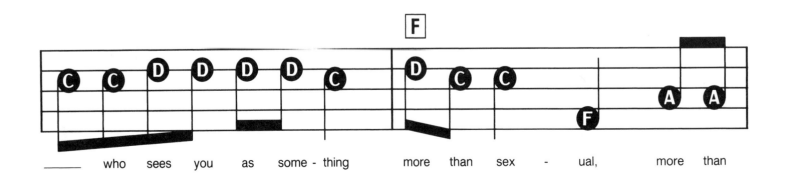

_____   who   sees   you   as   some - thing   more   than   sex - ual,   more   than

D.S. al Coda
(Return to ⅛
Play to ⊕ and
skip to Coda)

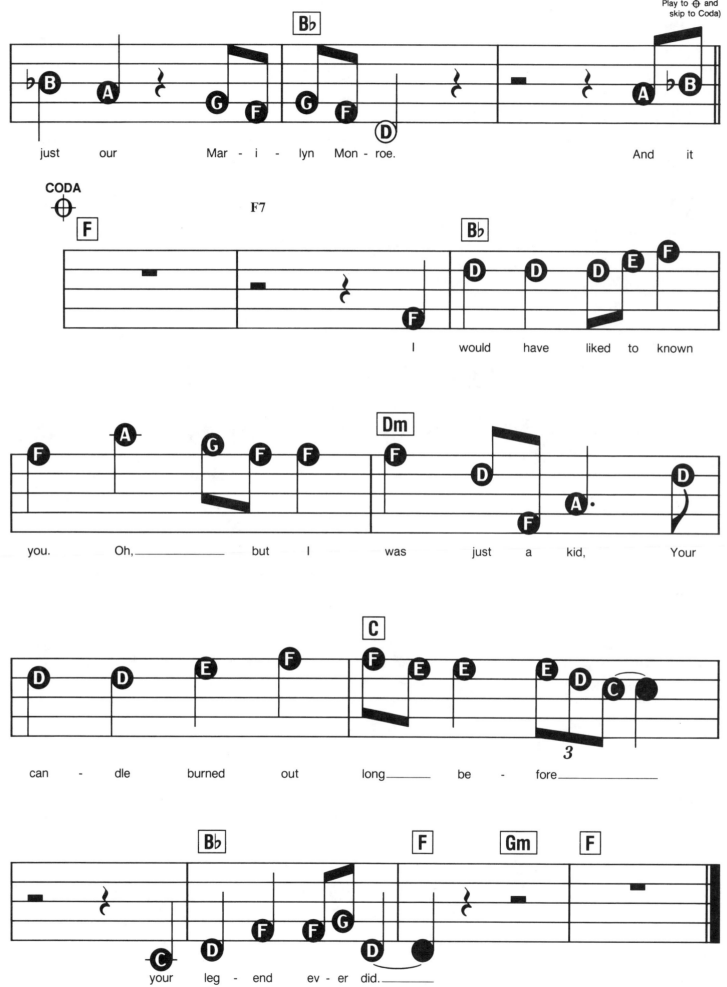

Call Me Maybe

Registration 1
Rhythm: Pop or Rock

Words and Music by Carly Rae Jepsen,
Joshua Ramsay and Tavish Crowe

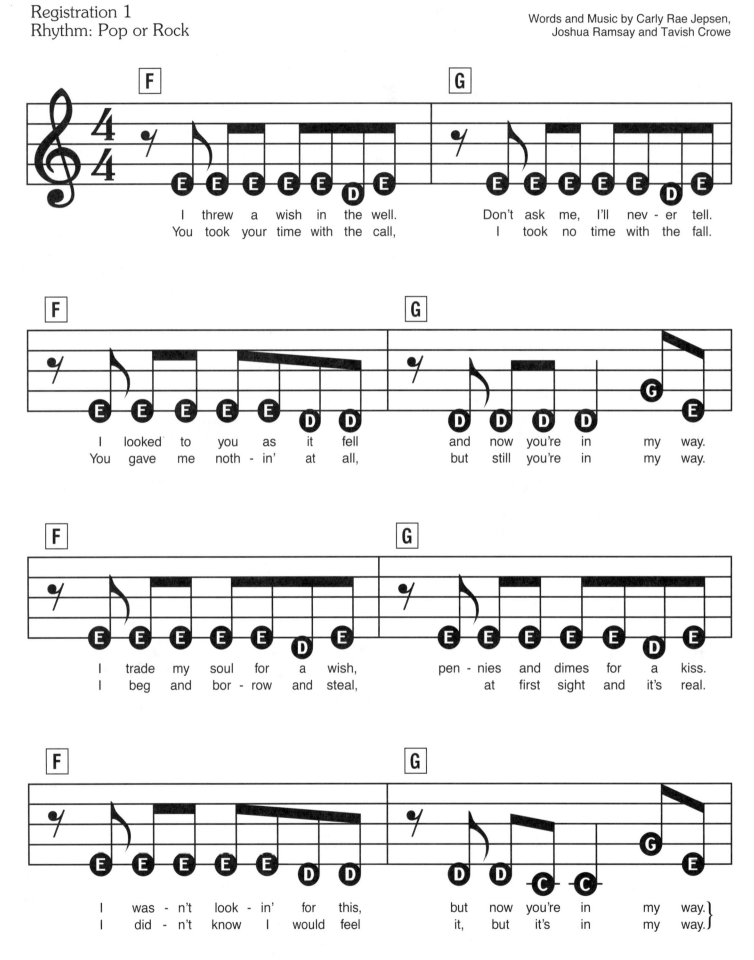

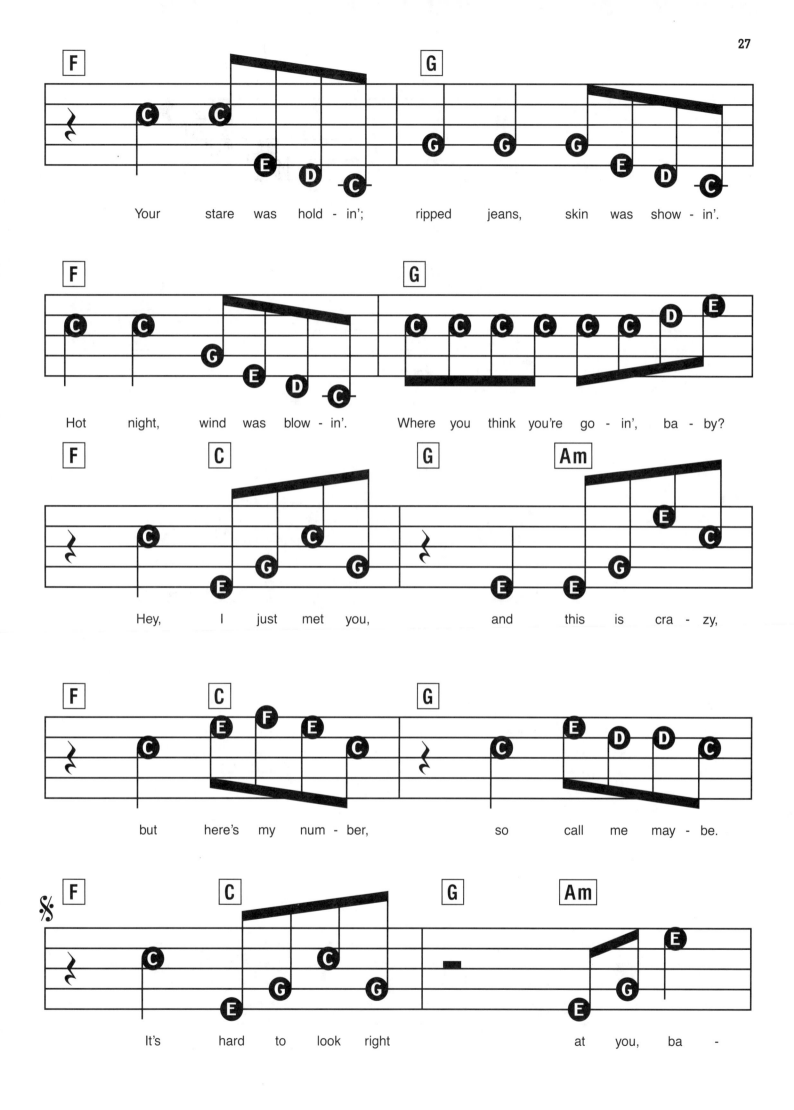

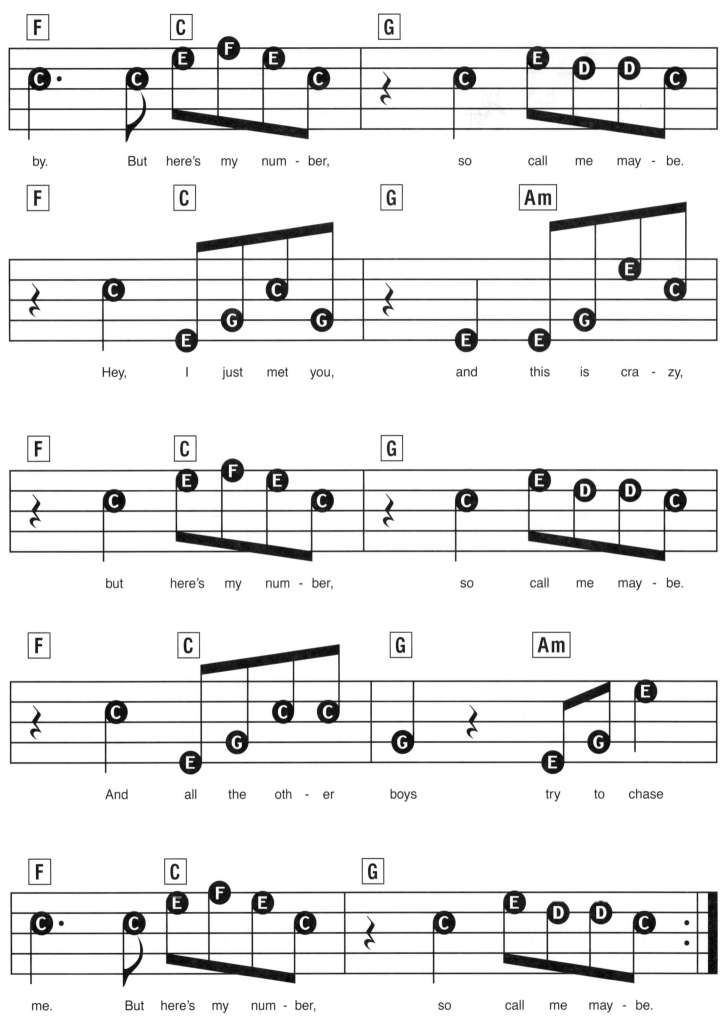

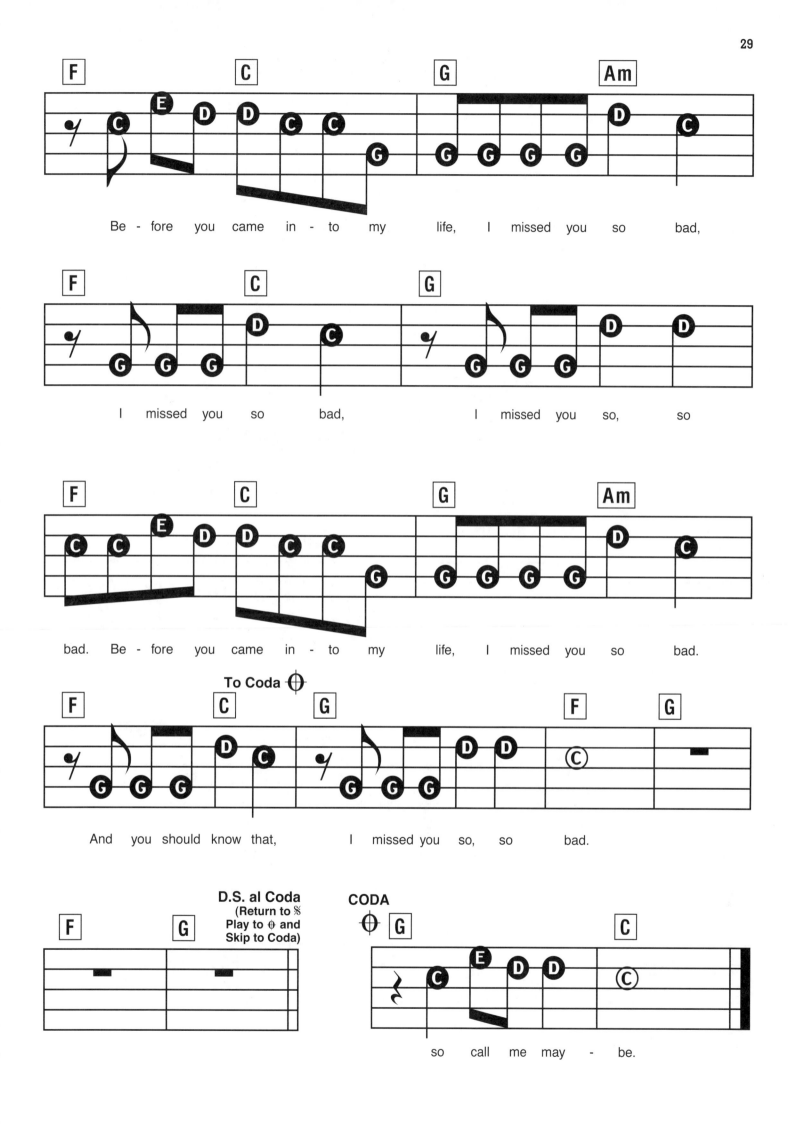

Careless Whisper

Registration 1
Rhythm: Rock or Jazz Rock

Words and Music by George Michael
and Andrew Ridgeley

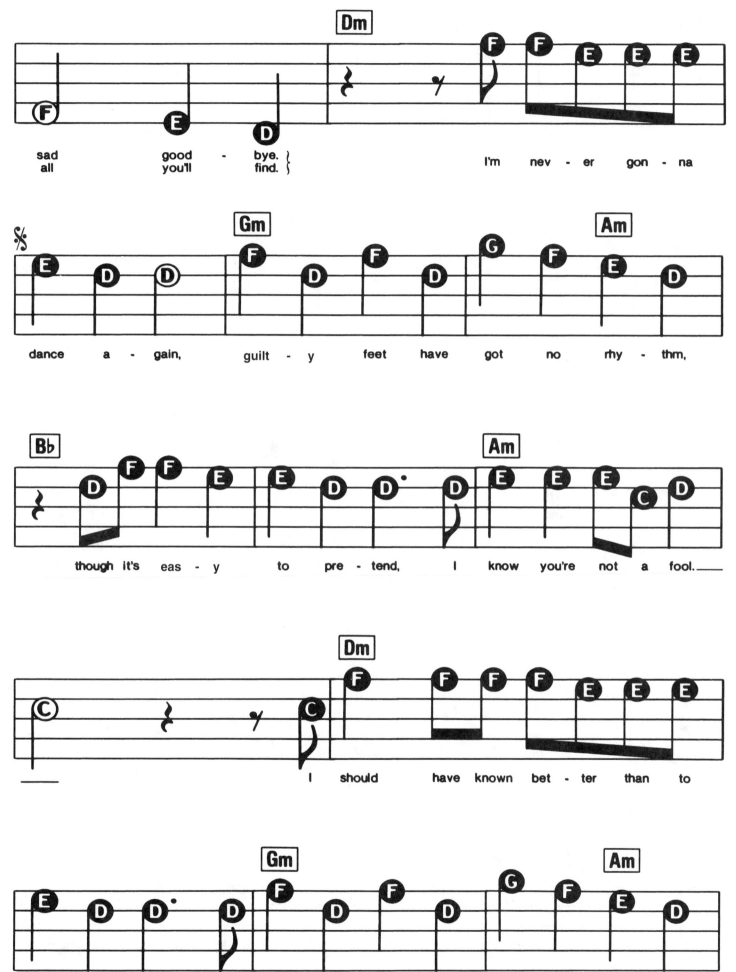

To Coda ⊕

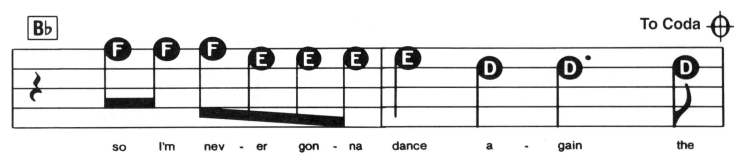

so I'm nev - er gon - na dance a - gain the

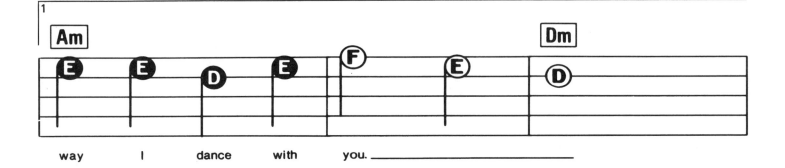

way I dance with you. _____

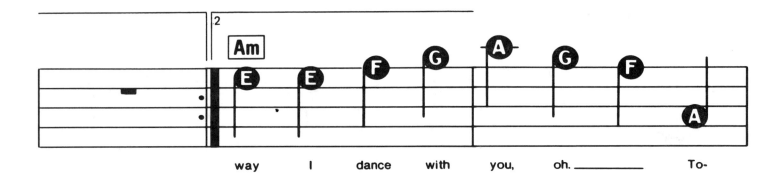

way I dance with you, oh. _____ To-

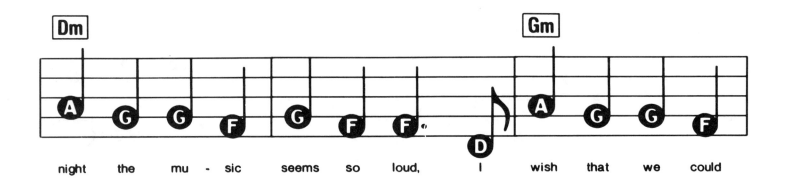

night the mu - sic seems so loud, I wish that we could

lose this crowd, may - be it's bet - ter this way, if we'd

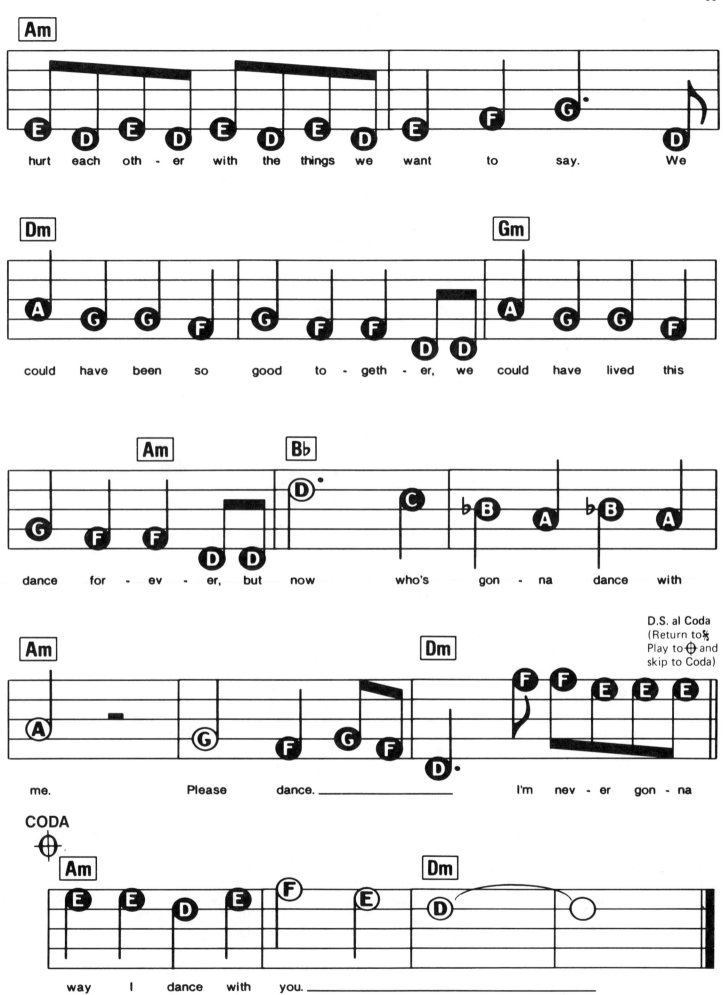

Cecilia

Registration 9
Rhythm: March or Rock

Words and Music by
Paul Simon

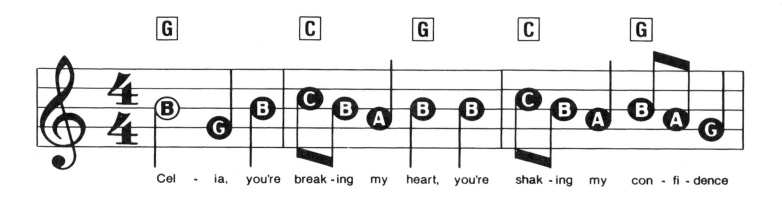

Cel - ia, you're break-ing my heart, you're shak-ing my con-fi-dence

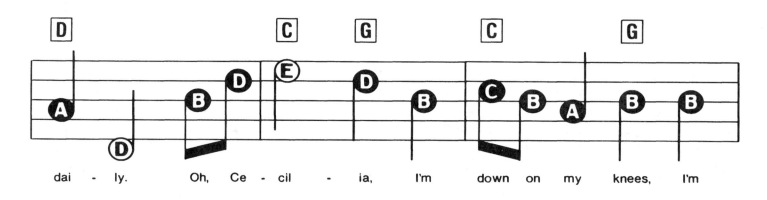

dai - ly.   Oh, Ce - cil - ia,   I'm   down on my   knees,   I'm

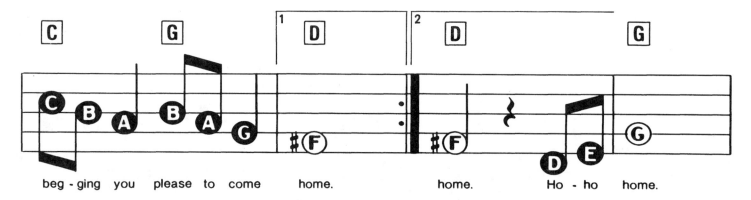

beg-ging you please to come   home.   home.   Ho-ho home.

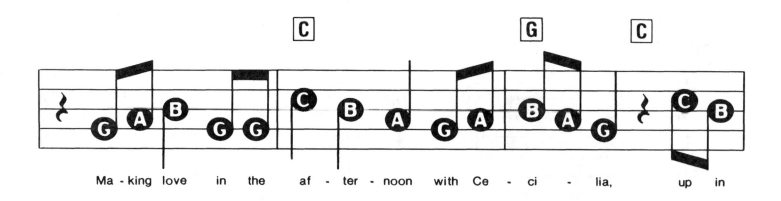

Ma - king love   in the   af - ter - noon   with Ce - ci - lia,   up in

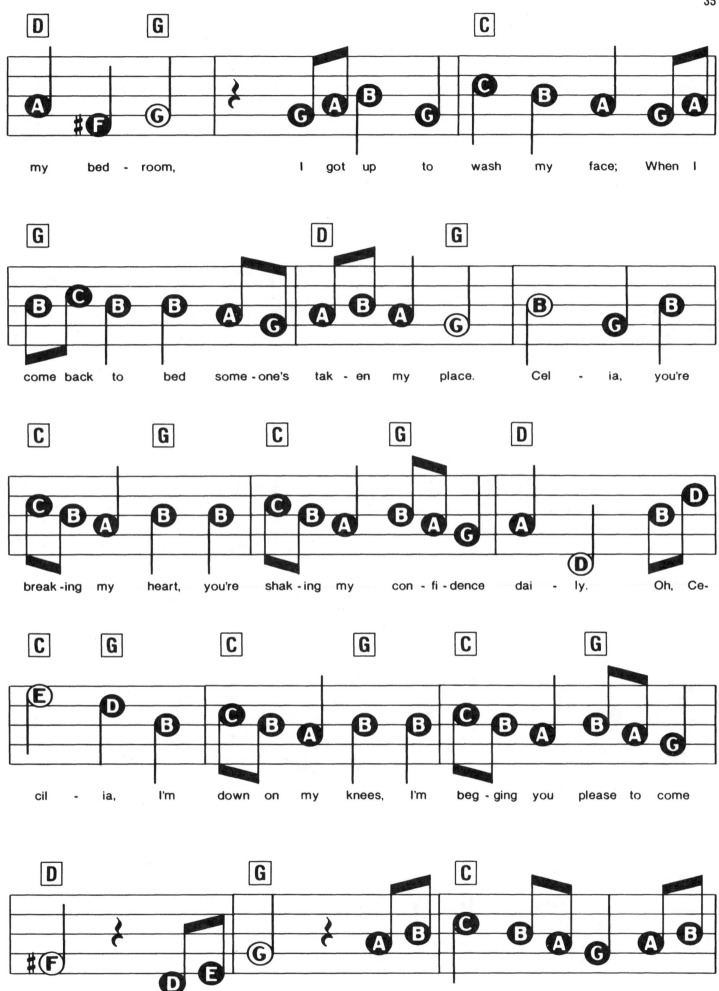

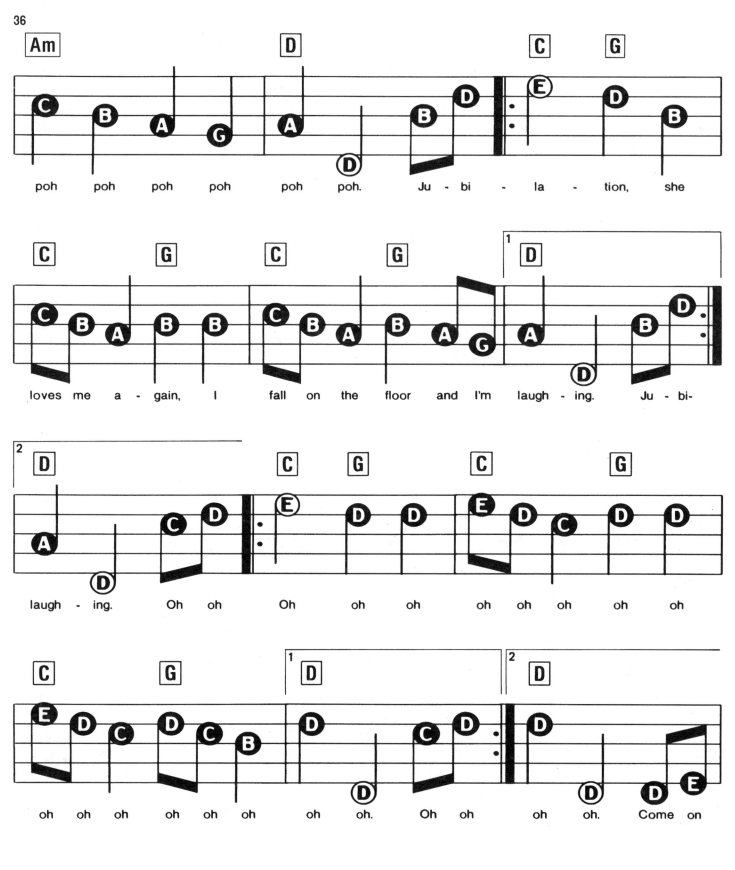

poh poh poh poh poh poh. Ju - bi - la - tion, she

loves me a - gain, I fall on the floor and I'm laugh - ing. Ju - bi-

laugh - ing. Oh oh Oh oh oh oh oh oh oh oh

oh oh oh oh oh oh oh oh. Oh oh oh oh. Come on

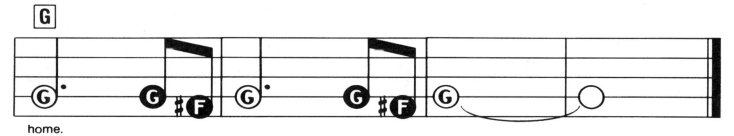

home.

Despacito

Registration 4
Rhythm: Calypso

Words and Music by Luis Fonsi, Erika Ender, Justin Bieber,
Jason Boyd, Marty James Garton and Ramon Ayala

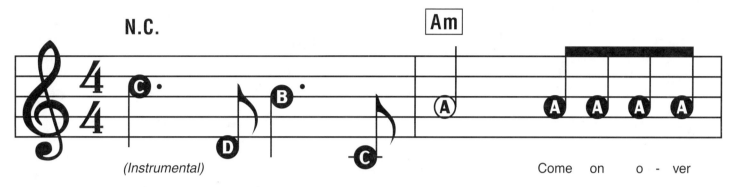

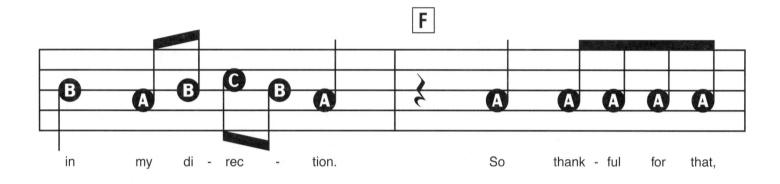

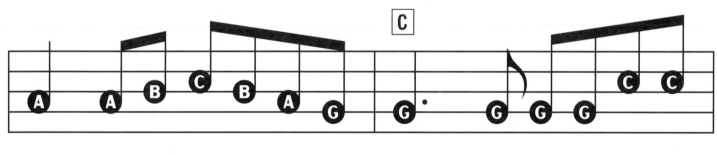

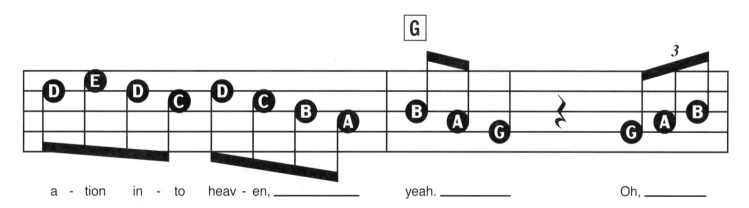

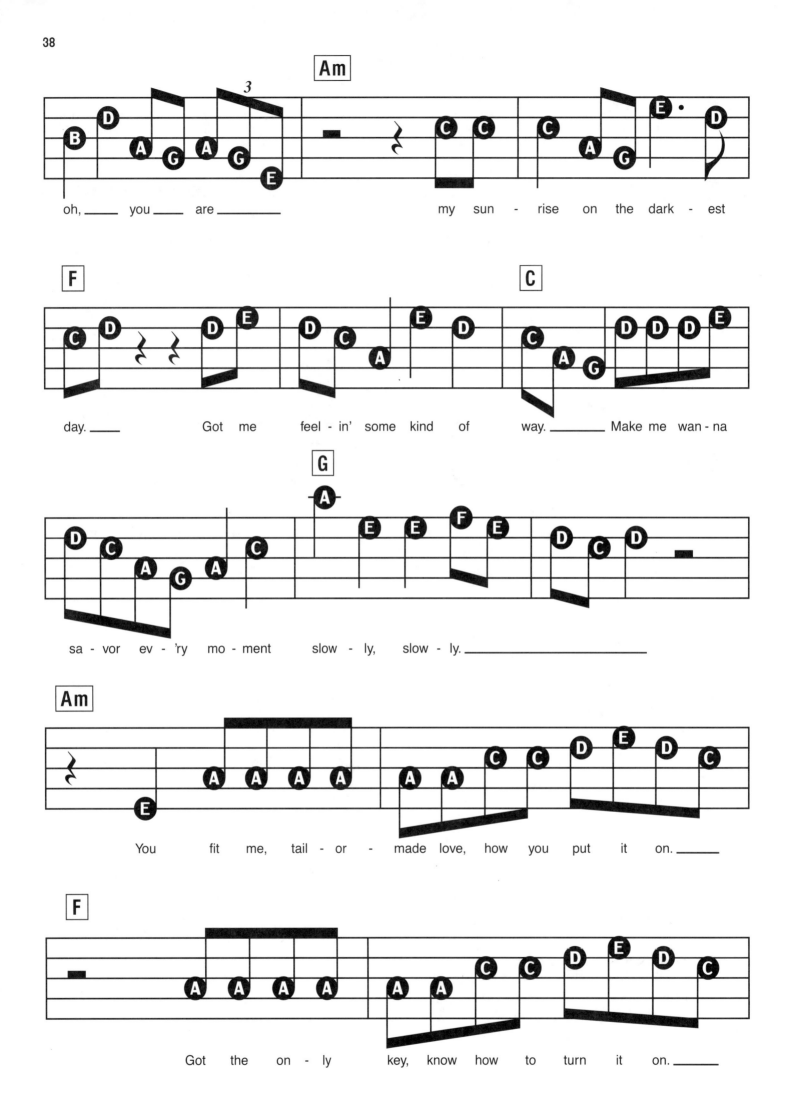

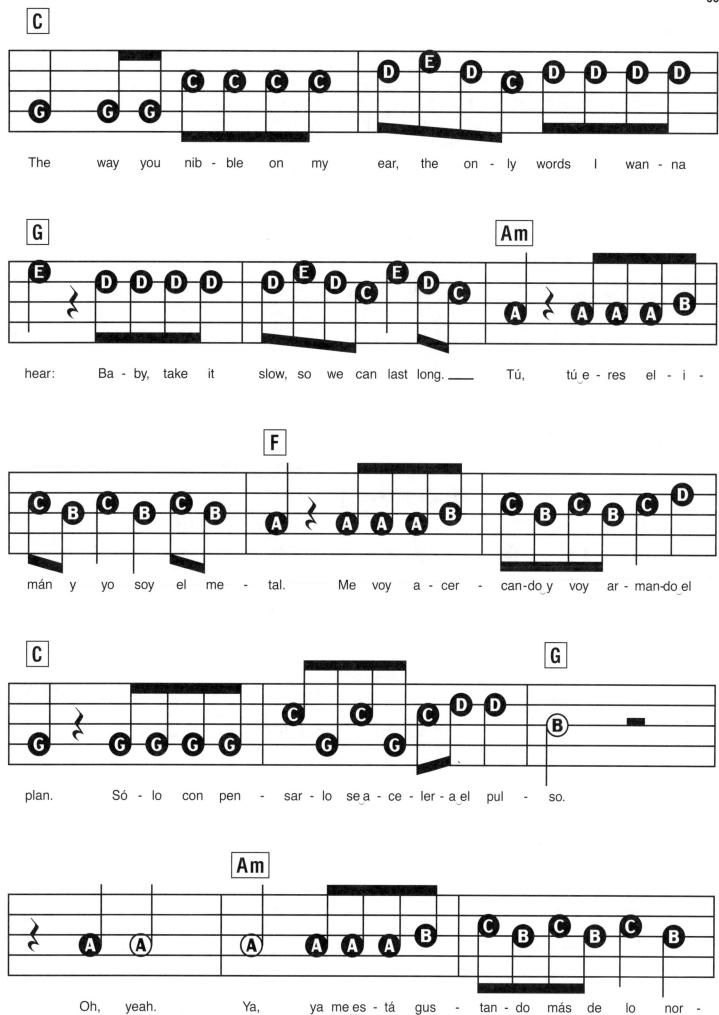

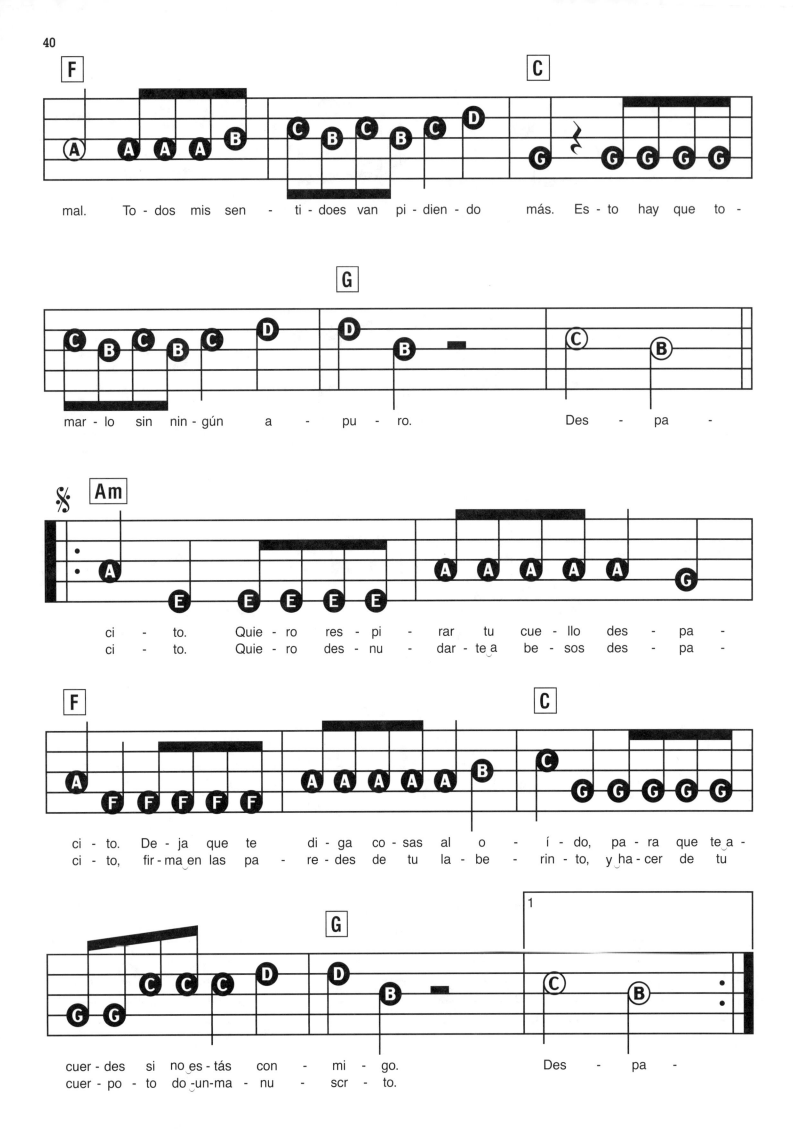

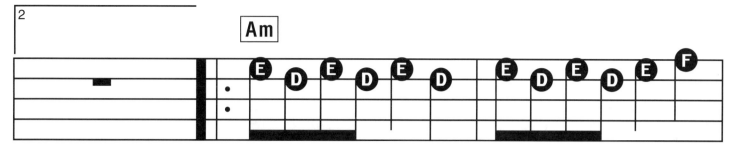

41

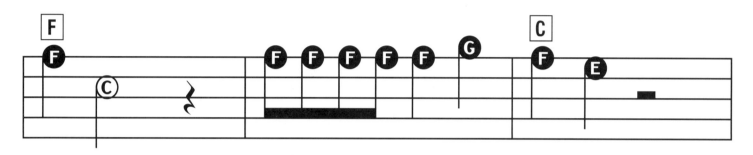

Quie - ro ver bai - lar tu   pe - lo, quie - ro ser tu
Dé - ja - me so - bre - pa - sar tus zo - nas de pe -

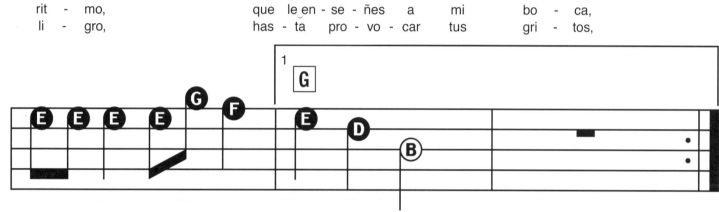

rit - mo,   que le en - se - ñes a mi bo - ca,
li - gro,   has - ta pro - vo - car tus   gri - tos,

tus lu - ga - res fa - vo - ri - tos. _____
y que ol - vi - des tu a pe

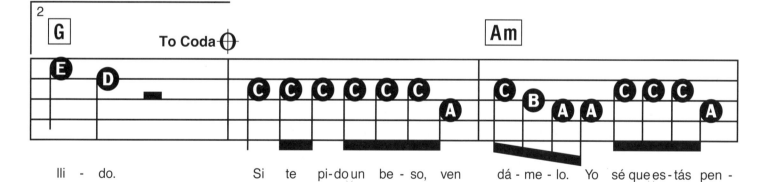

lli - do.   Si te pi-do un be - so, ven dá - me - lo. Yo sé que es -tás pen -

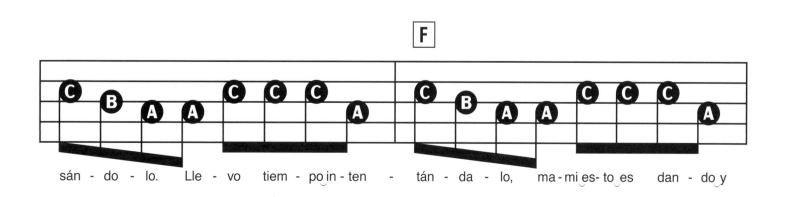

sán - do - lo. Lle - vo tiem - po in - ten - tán - da - lo, ma -mi es -to es dan - do y

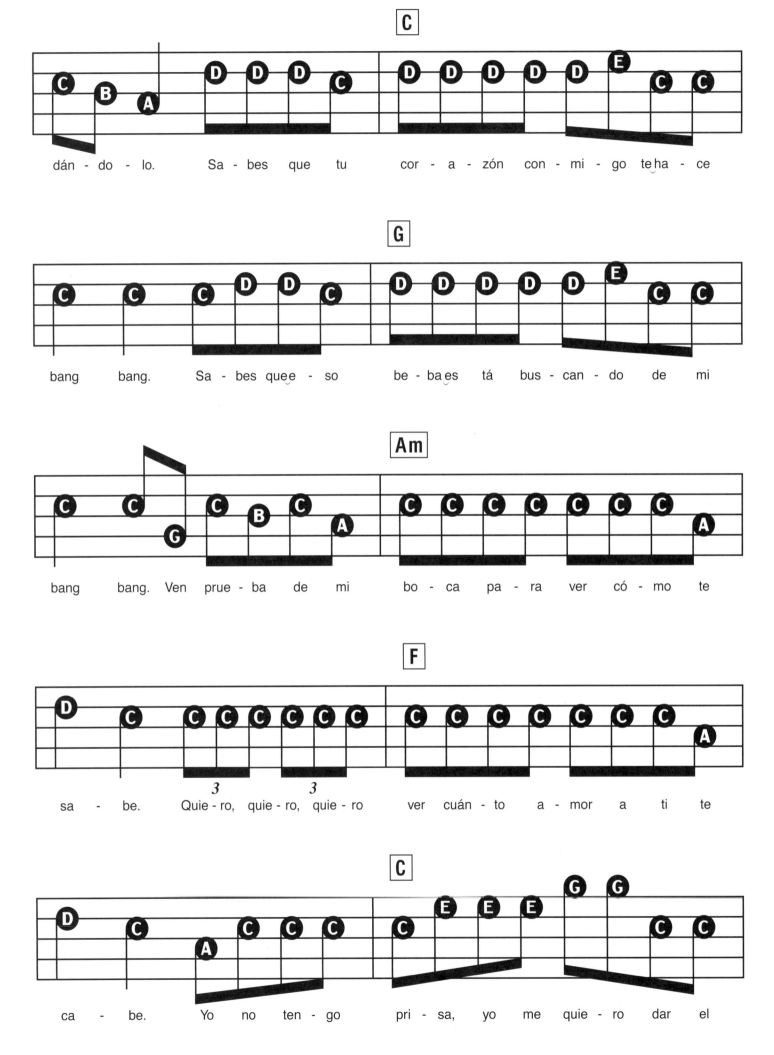

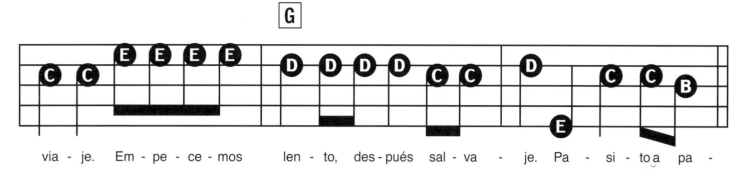

G

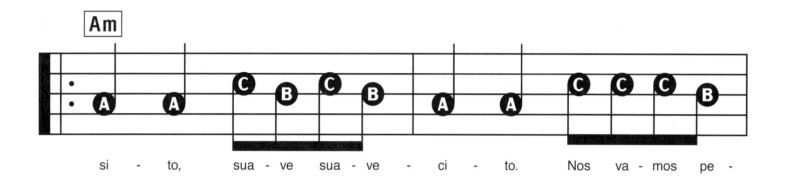

viaje. Em - pe - ce - mos len - to, des - pués sal - va - je. Pa - si - to a pa -

Am

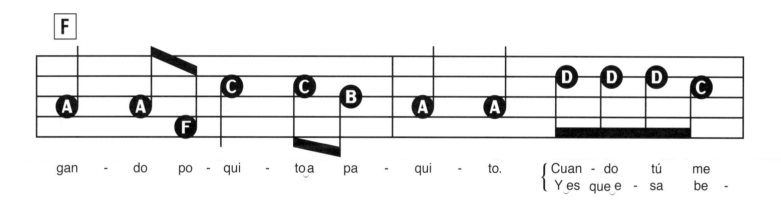

si - to, sua - ve sua - ve - ci - to. Nos va - mos pe -

F

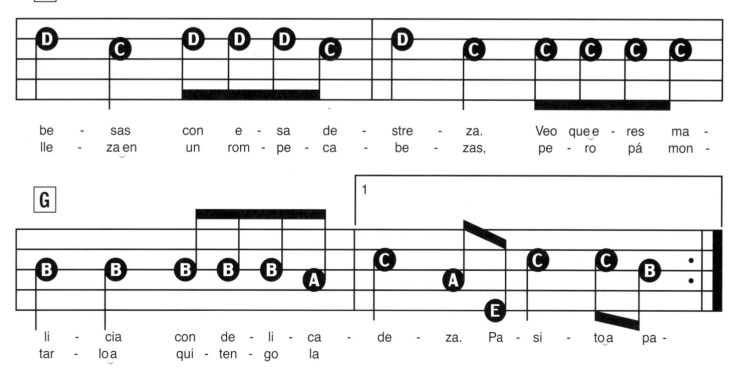

gan - do po - qui - to a pa - qui - to.
{ Cuan - do tú me
{ Y es que e - sa be -

C

be - sas con e - sa de - stre - za. Veo que e - res ma -
lle - za en un rom - pe - ca - be - zas, pe - ro pá mon -

G

1

li - cia con de - li - ca - de - za. Pa - si - to a pa -
tar - lo a qui - ten - go la

44

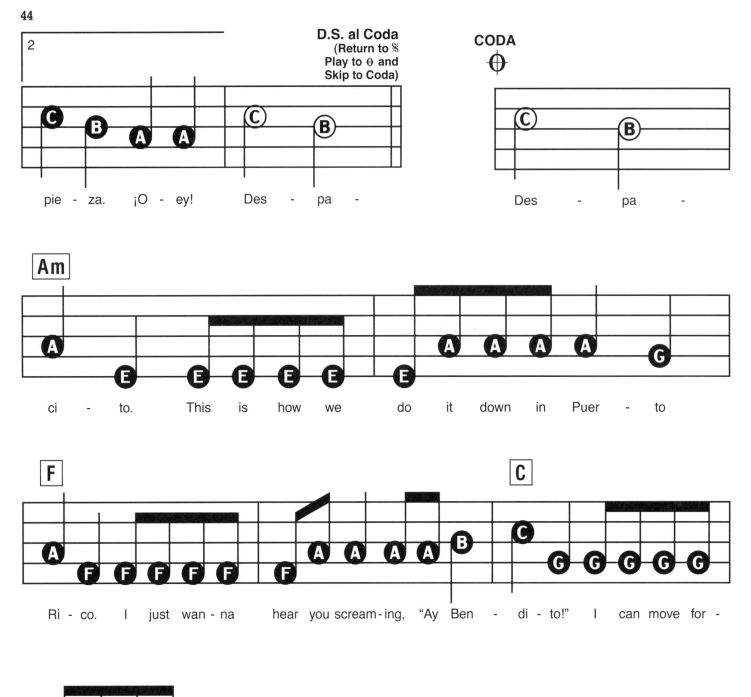

D.S. al Coda
(Return to %
Play to ⊕ and
Skip to Coda)

CODA

pie - za.   ¡O - ey!   Des - pa -

Des - pa -

Am

ci - to.   This   is   how   we   do   it   down   in   Puer - to

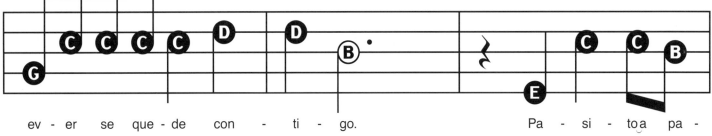

F   **C**

Ri - co.   I   just   wan - na   hear   you   scream - ing,   "Ay   Ben - di - to!"   I   can   move   for -

ev - er   se   que - de   con - ti - go.   Pa - si - to a   pa -

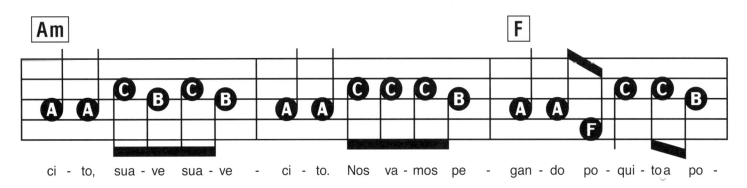

Am   **F**

ci - to,   sua - ve   sua - ve - ci - to.   Nos   va - mos   pe - gan - do   po - qui - to a   po -

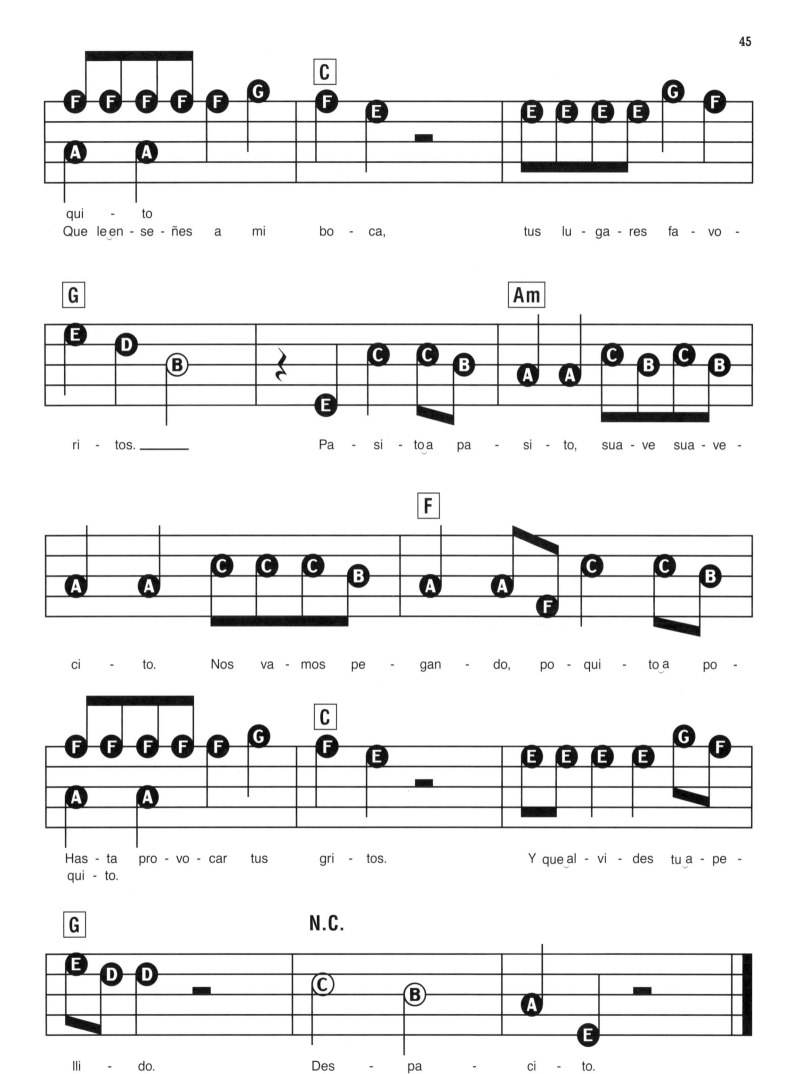

Fly Like an Eagle

Registration 9
Rhythm: Rock

Words and Music by
Steve Miller

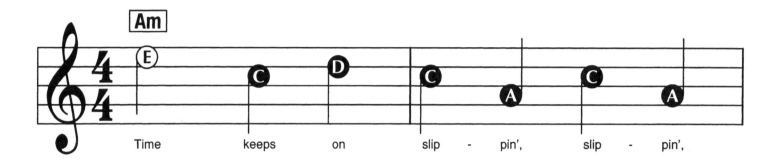

Time   keeps   on   slip - pin',   slip - pin',

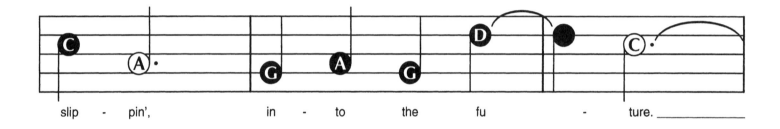

slip - pin',   in - to   the   fu   - ture. _____

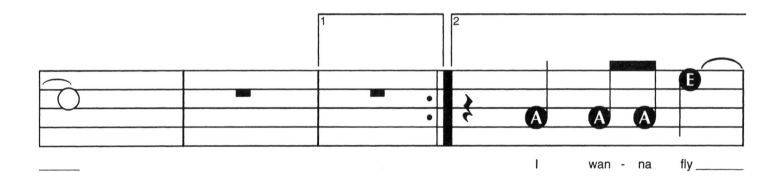

_____   I   wan - na   fly _____

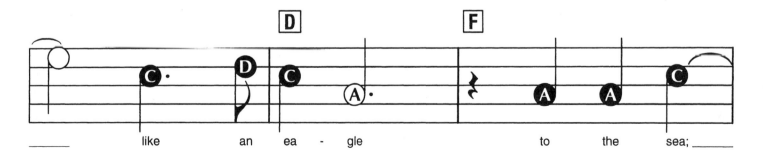

_____   like   an   ea - gle   to   the   sea; _____

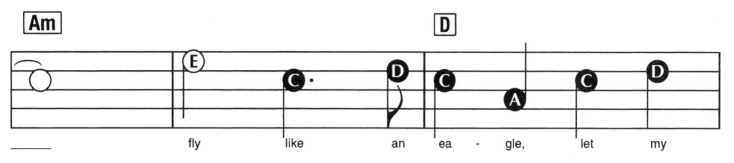

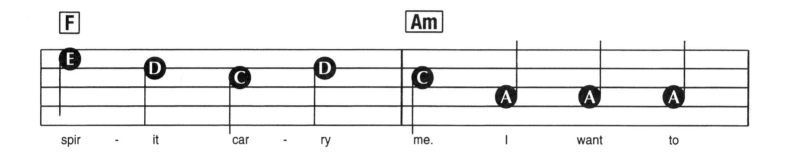

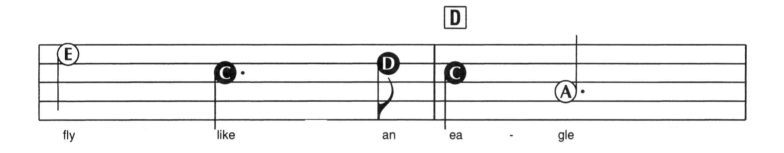

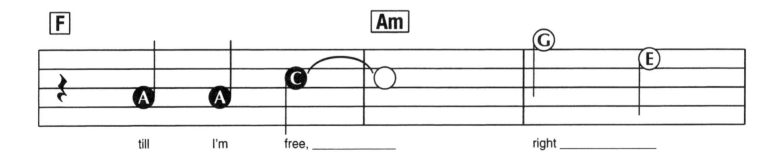

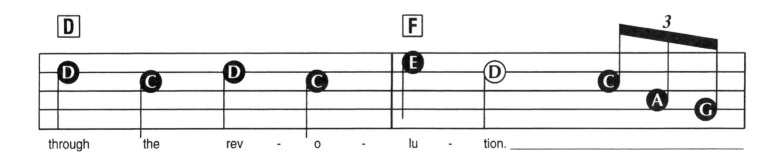

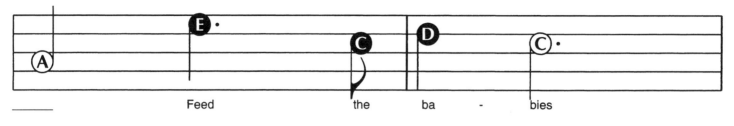

Feed　　　　the　ba - bies

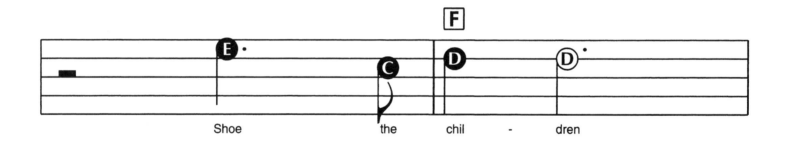

who　don't　have　e - nough　to　eat.

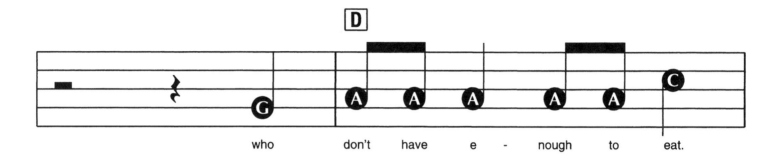

Shoe　　　　the　chil - dren

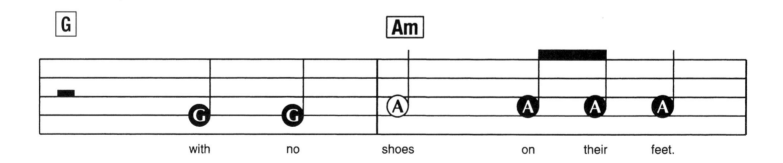

with　　no　shoes　on　their　feet.

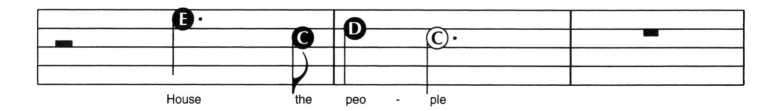

House　　　the　peo - ple

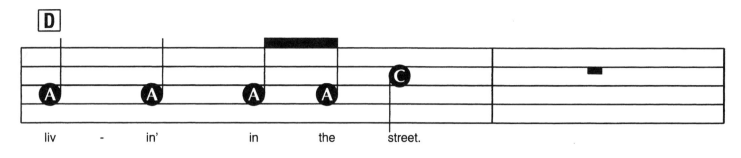

liv - in' in the street.

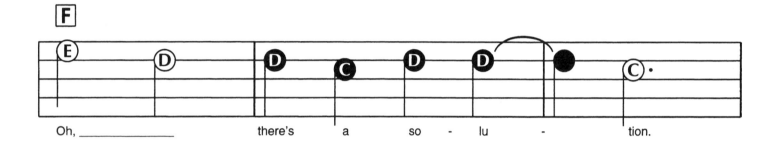

Oh, _____ there's a so - lu - tion.

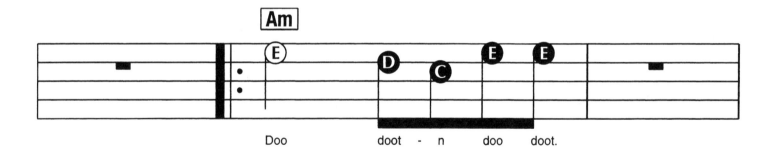

Doo doot - n doo doot.

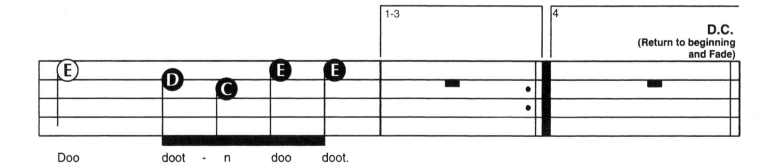

Doo doot - n doo doot.

Fun, Fun, Fun

Registration 7
Rhythm: Rock

Words and Music by Brian Wilson
and Mike Love

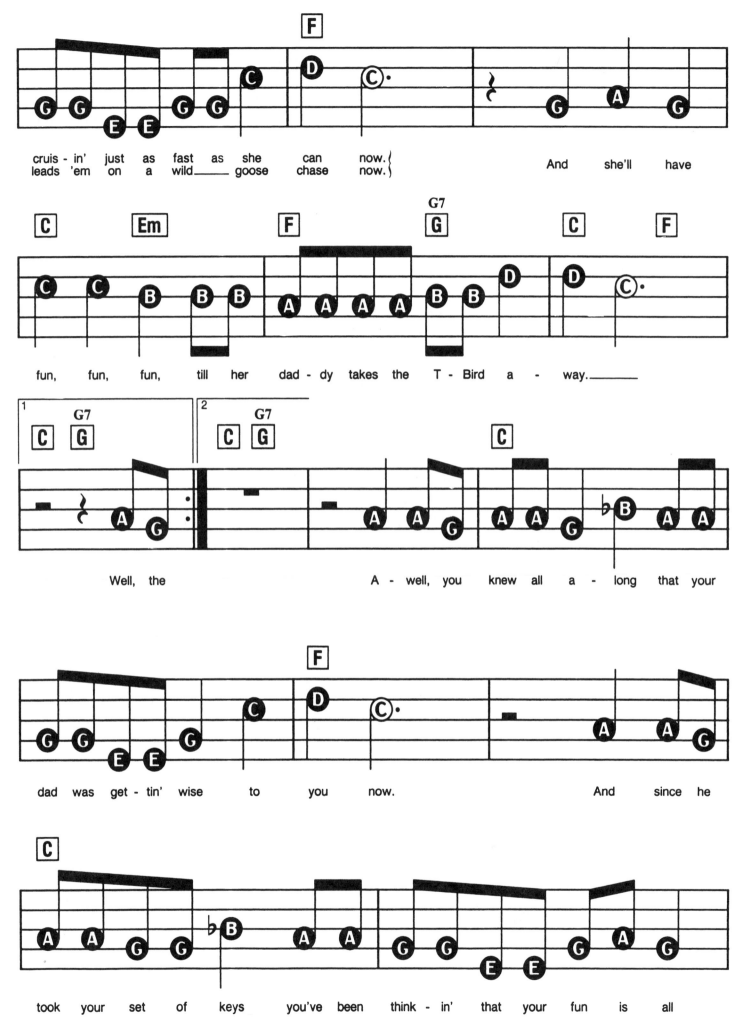

52

Good Riddance
(Time of Your Life)

Registration 4
Rhythm: Folk

Words by Billie Joe
Music by Green Day

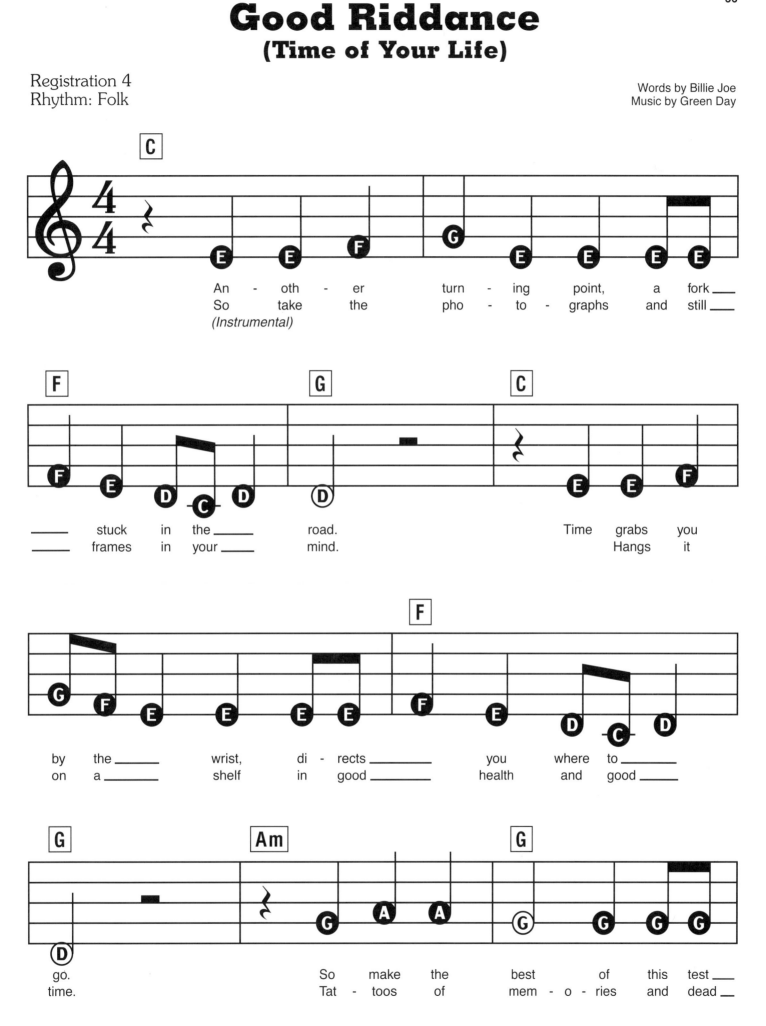

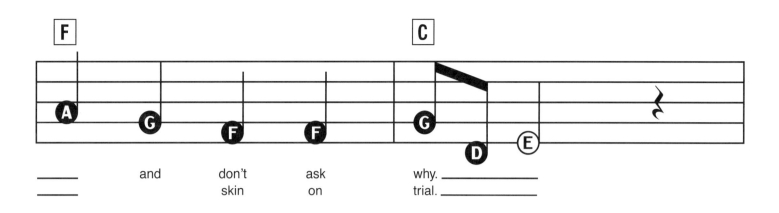

_____ and don't ask why. _____
_____ skin on trial. _____

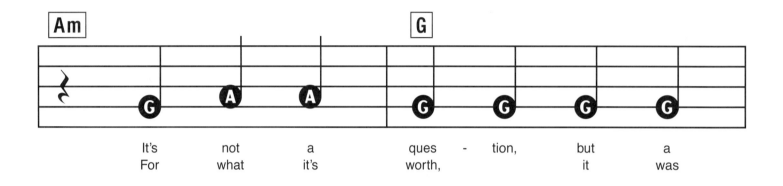

It's not a ques - tion, but a
For what it's worth, it was

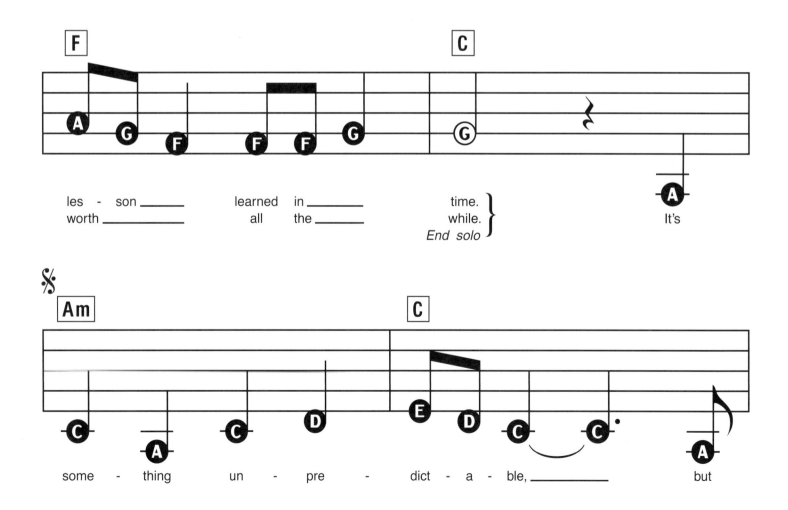

les - son _____ learned in _____ time.
worth _____ all the _____ while.
End solo

It's

some - thing un - pre - dict - a - ble, _____ but

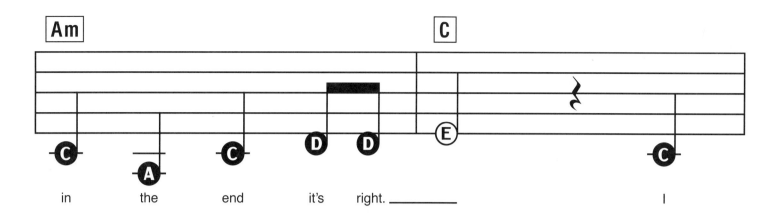

in the the end it's right. _____ I

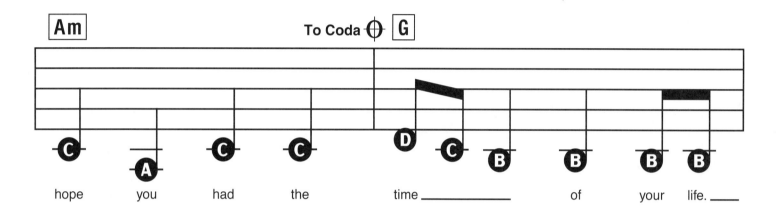

hope you had the time _____ of your life. ____

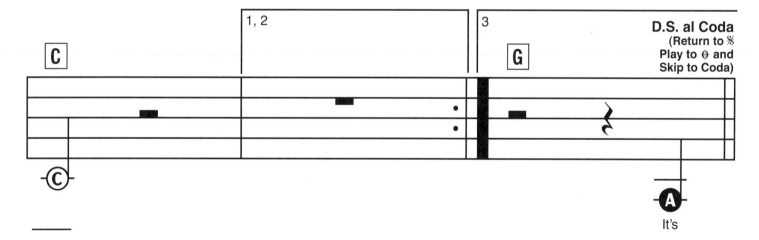

_____ It's

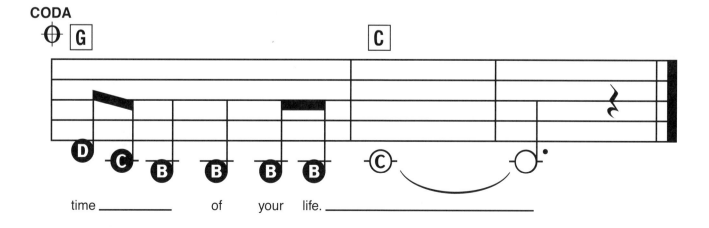

time _____ of your life. _____

Hello

Registration 8
Rhythm: Ballad

Words and Music by Adele Adkins
and Greg Kurstin

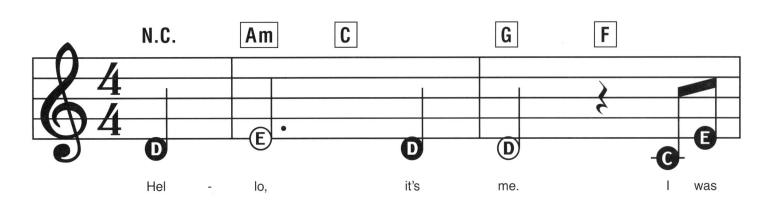

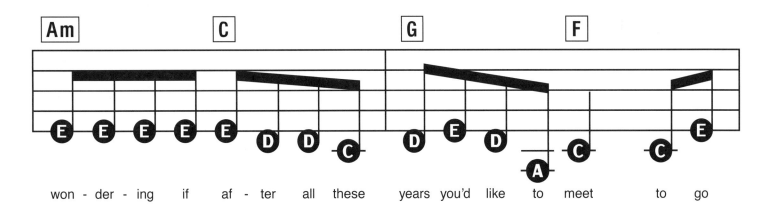

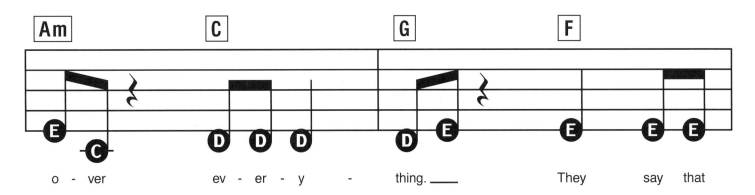

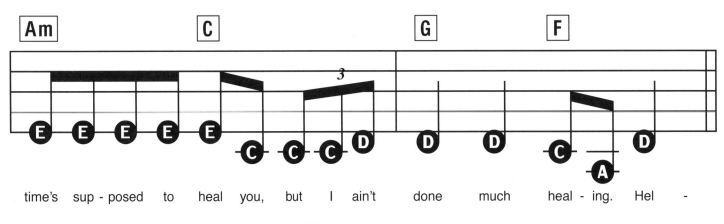

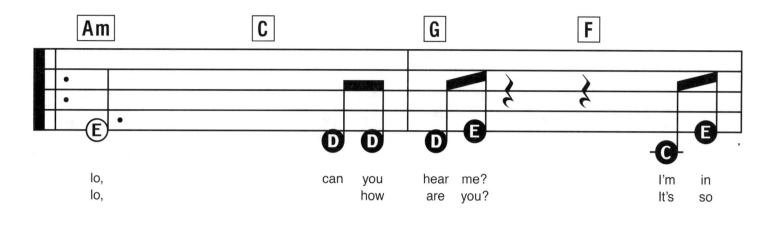

lo,
lo,

can you hear me? I'm in
how are you? It's so

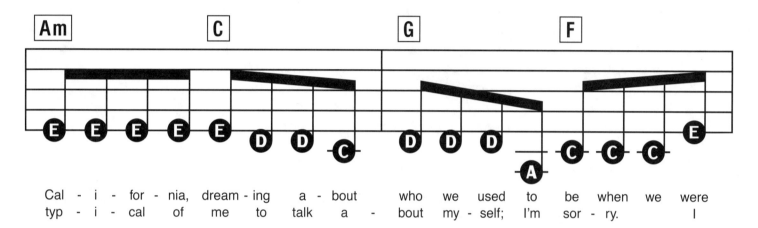

Cal - i - for - nia, dream - ing a - bout who we used to be when we were
typ - i - cal of me to talk a - bout my - self; I'm sor - ry. I

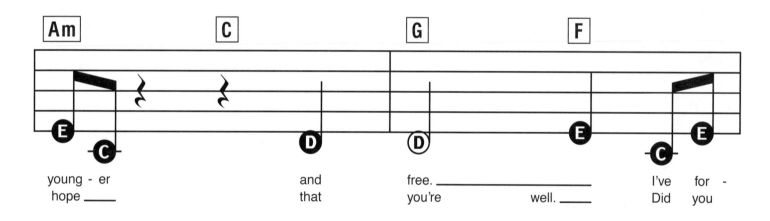

young - er and free. _____ I've for -
hope ____ that you're well. ____ Did you

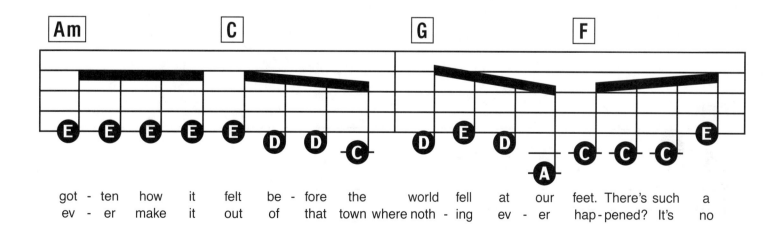

got - ten how it felt be - fore the world fell at our feet. There's such a
ev - er make it out of that town where noth - ing ev - er hap - pened? It's no

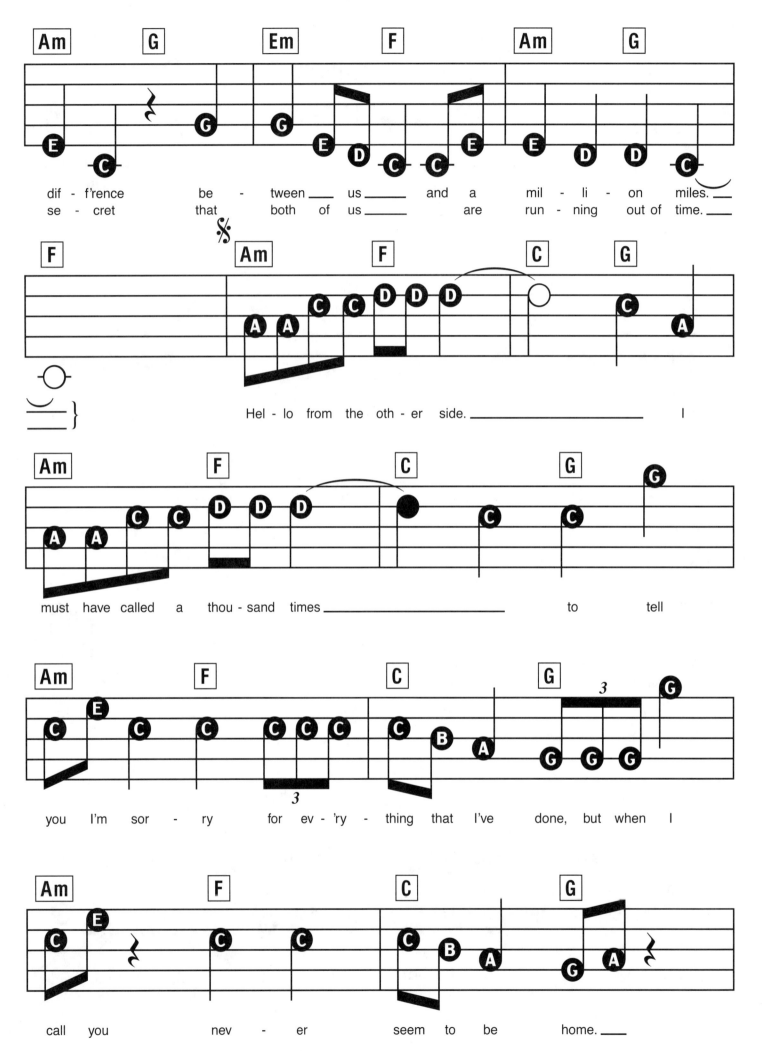

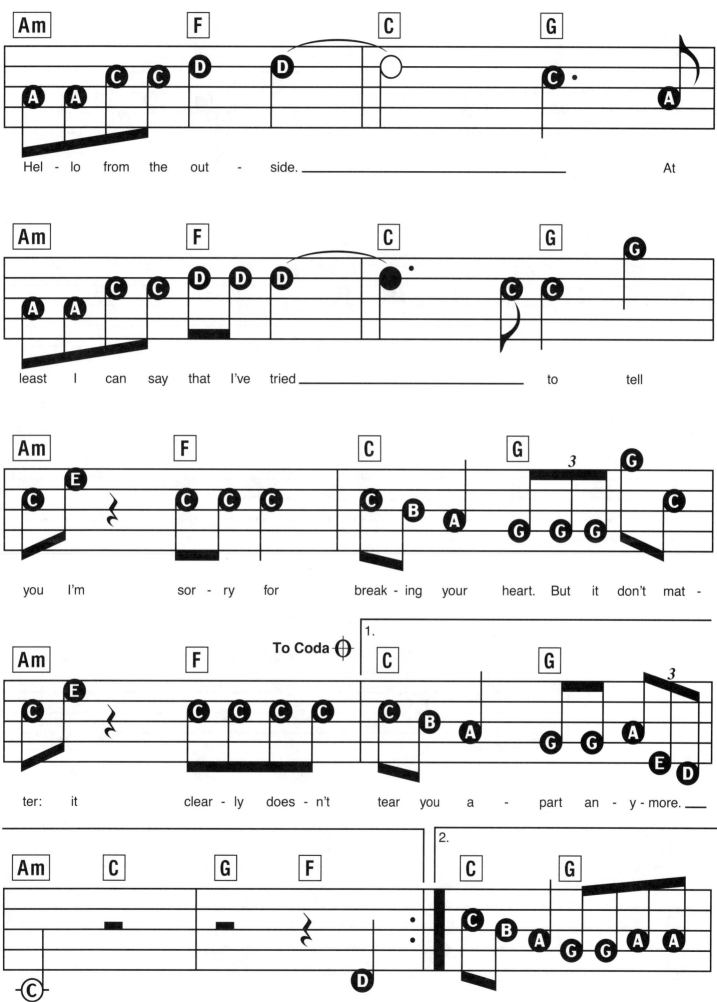

60

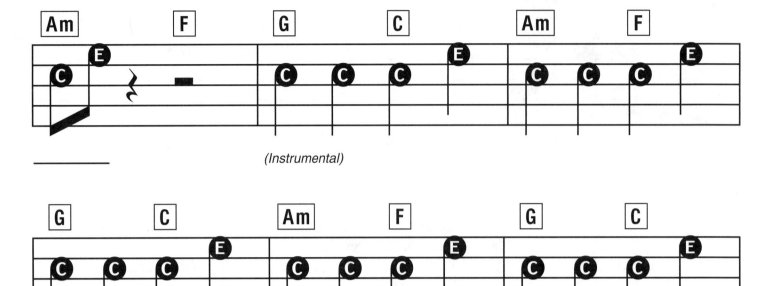

(Instrumental)

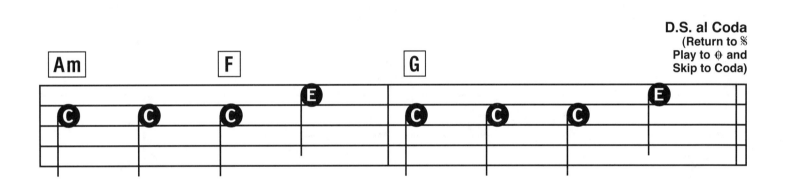

D.S. al Coda
(Return to 𝄋
Play to ⊕ and
Skip to Coda)

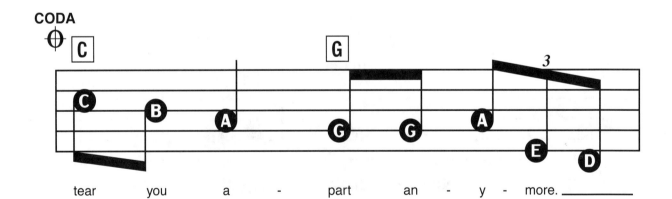

tear   you   a - part   an - y - more. _____

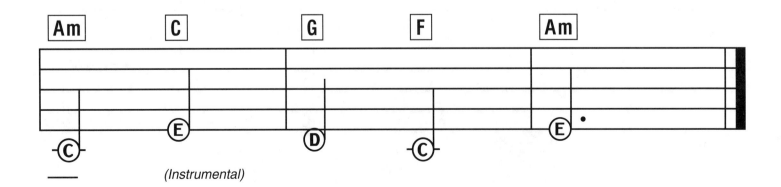

(Instrumental)

Ho Hey

Registration 4
Rhythm: Folk

Words and Music by Jeremy Fraites
and Wesley Schultz

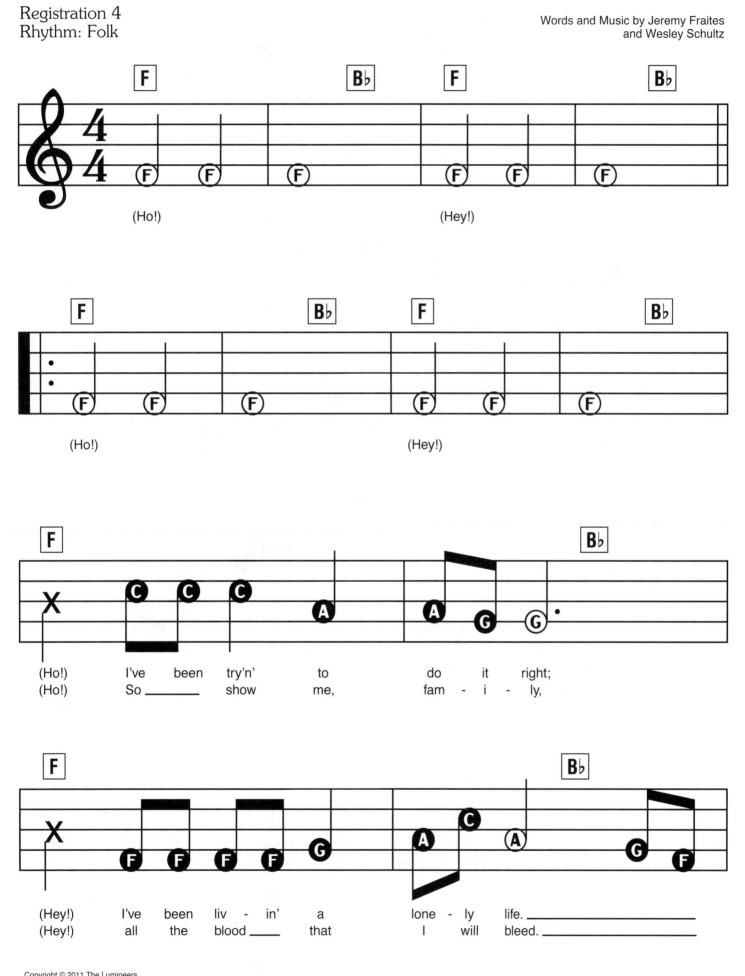

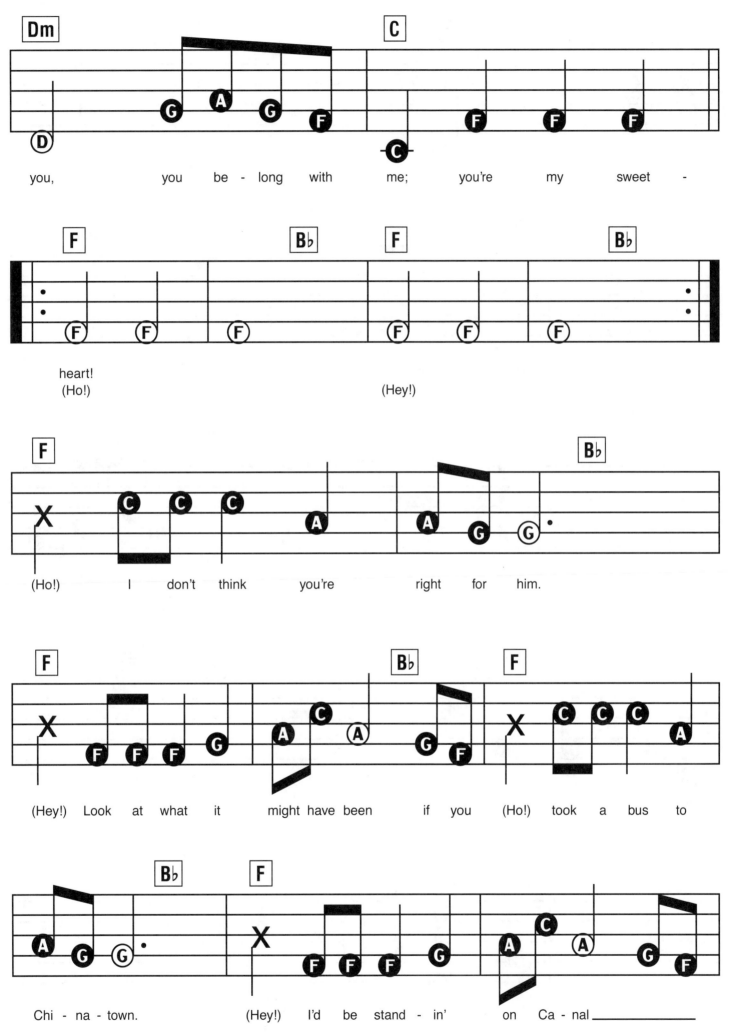

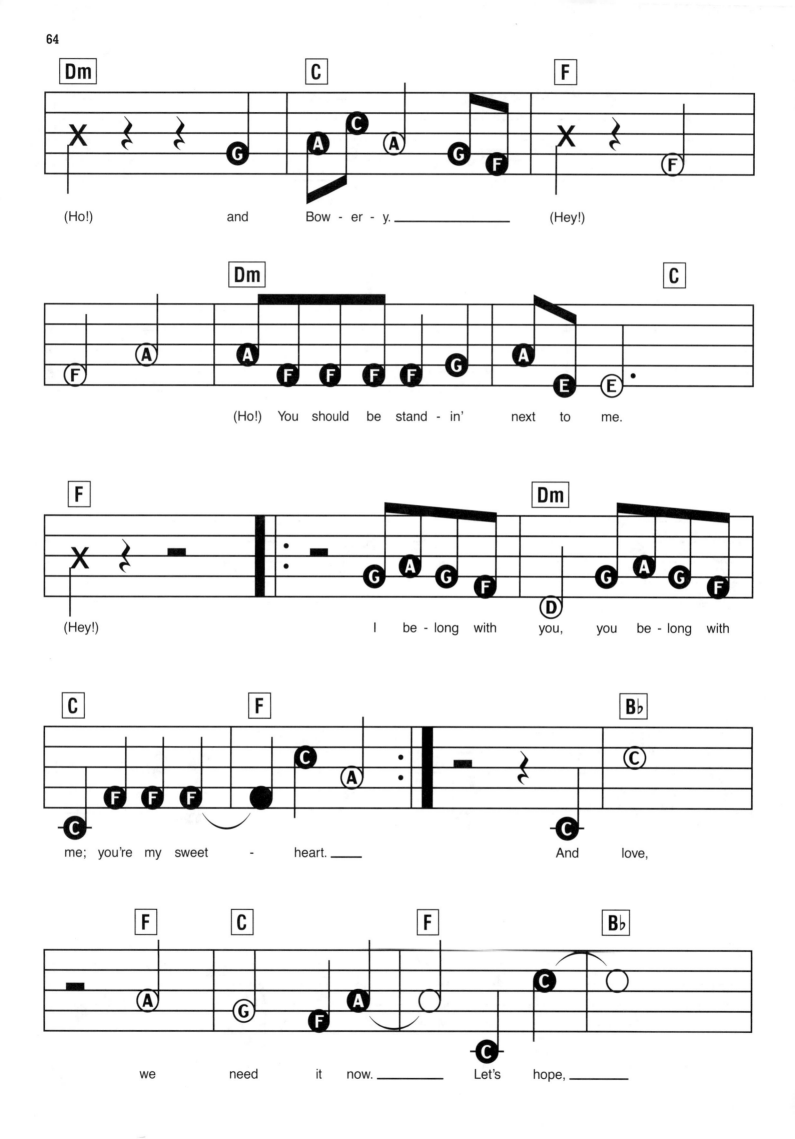

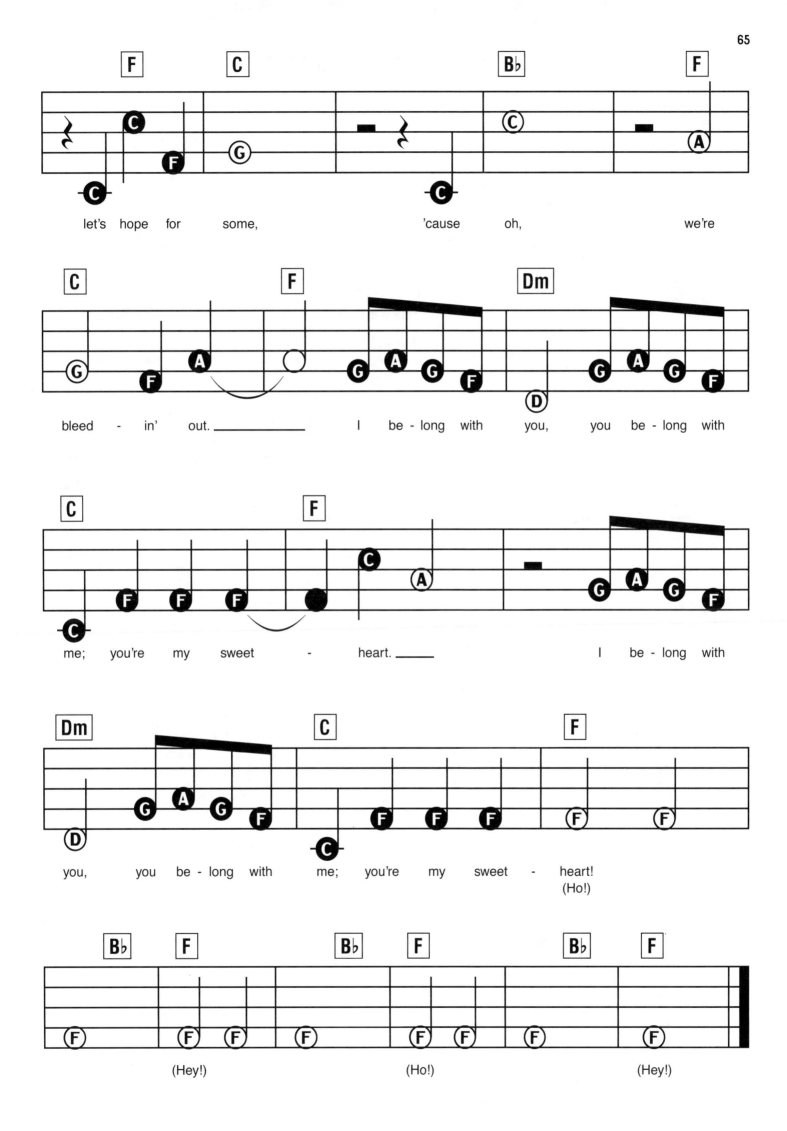

Hey, Soul Sister

Registration 4
Rhythm: Country Rock

Words and Music by Pat Monahan,
Espen Lind and Amund Bjorklund

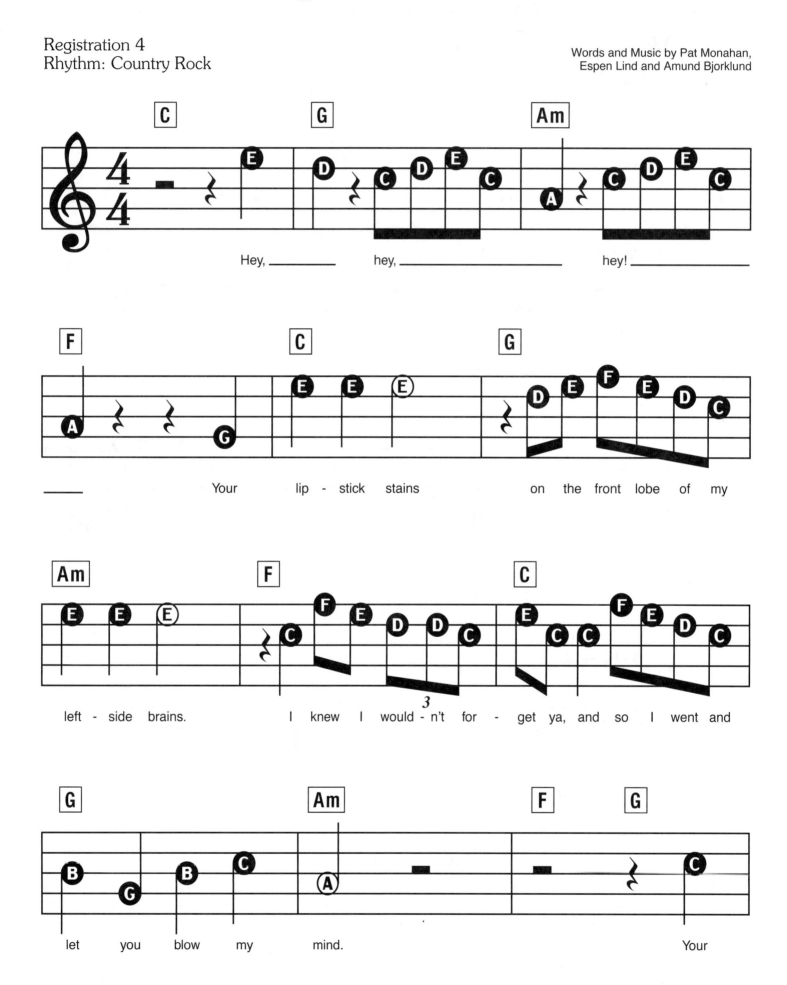

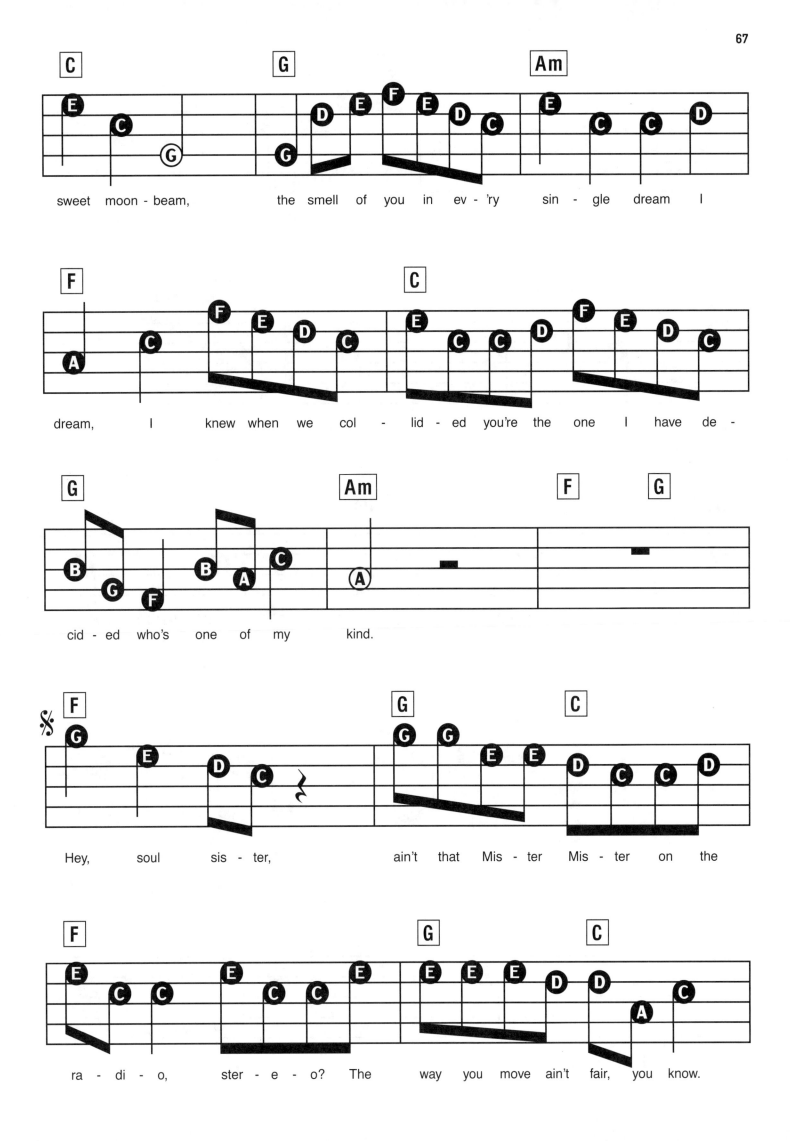

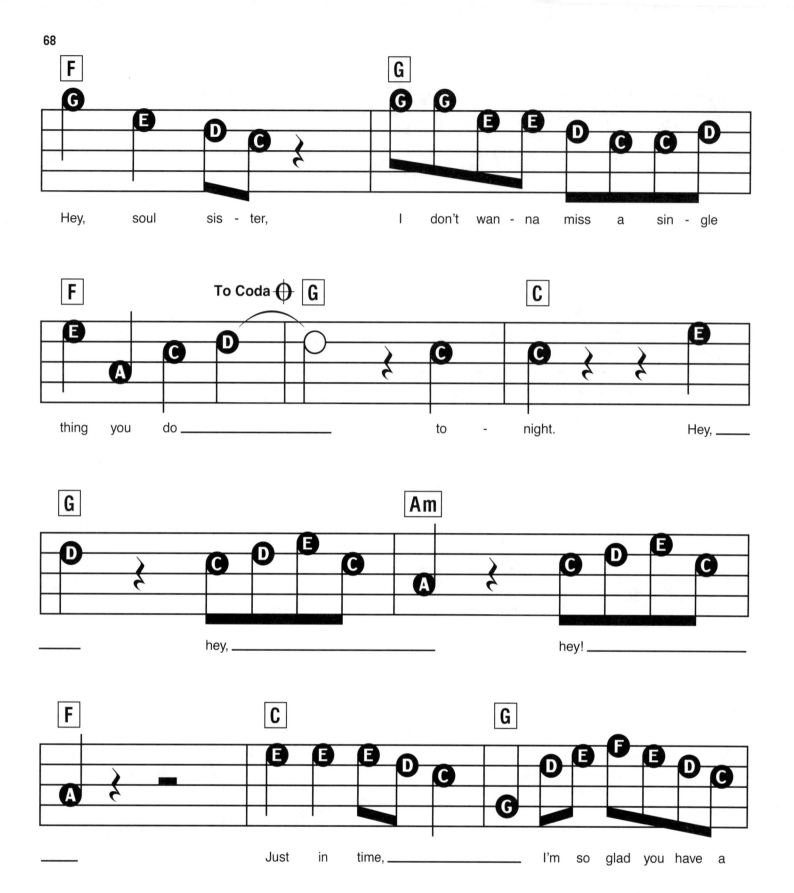

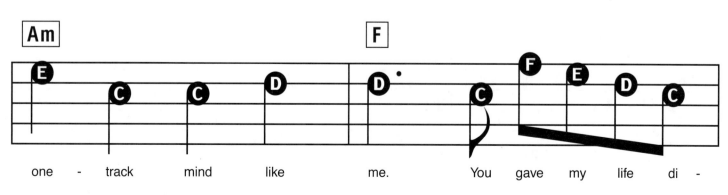

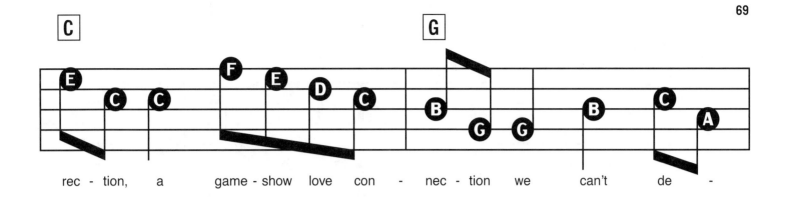

rec - tion, a game-show love con - nec - tion we can't de -

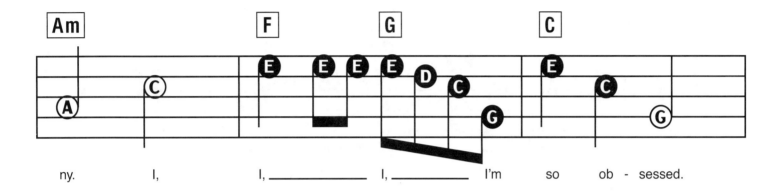

ny. I, I, _____ I, _____ I'm so ob - sessed.

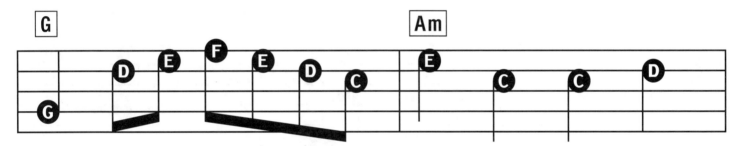
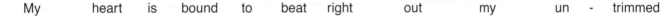

My heart is bound to beat right out my un - trimmed

chest. I be - lieve in you. Like a vir - gin, you're Ma -

D.S. al Coda
(Return to 𝄋
Play to ⊕ and
Skip to Coda)

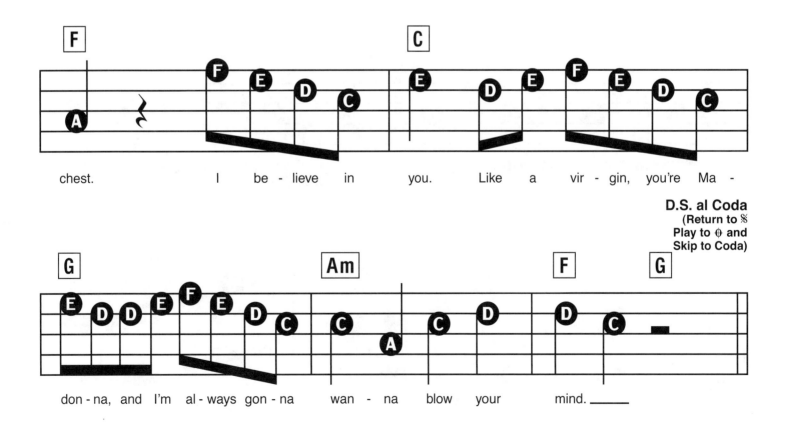

don - na, and I'm al - ways gon - na wan - na blow your mind. _____

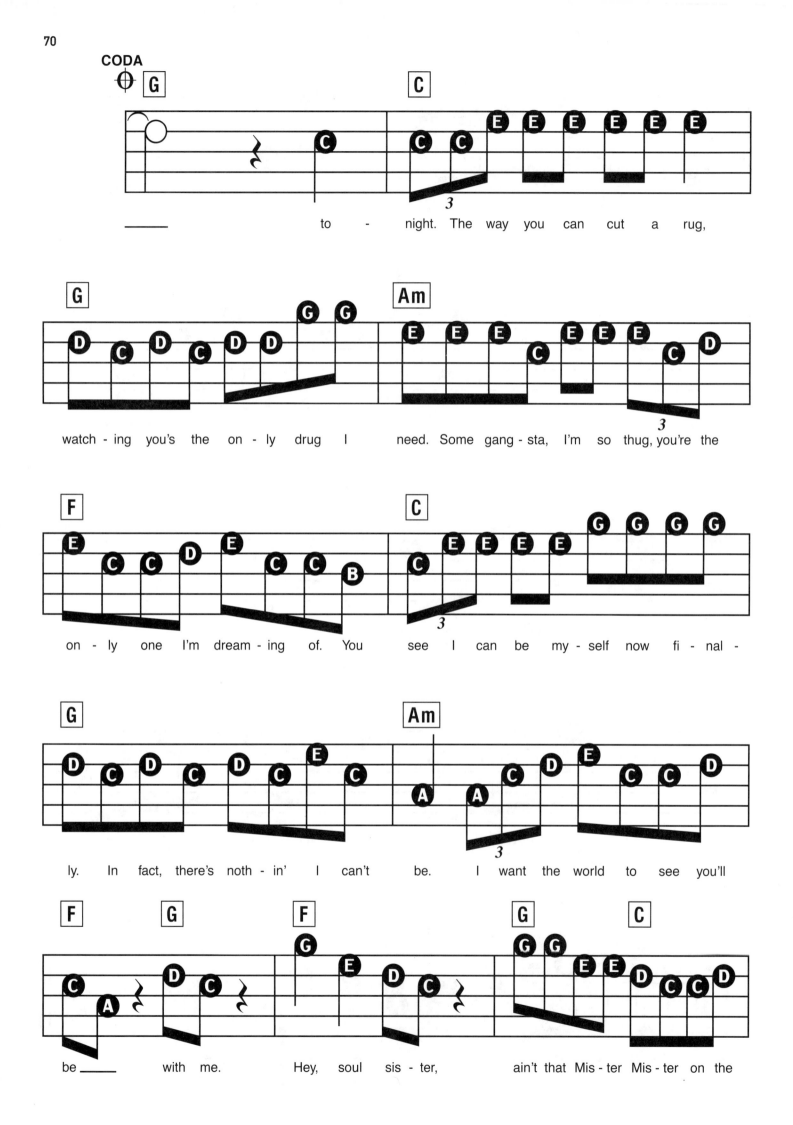

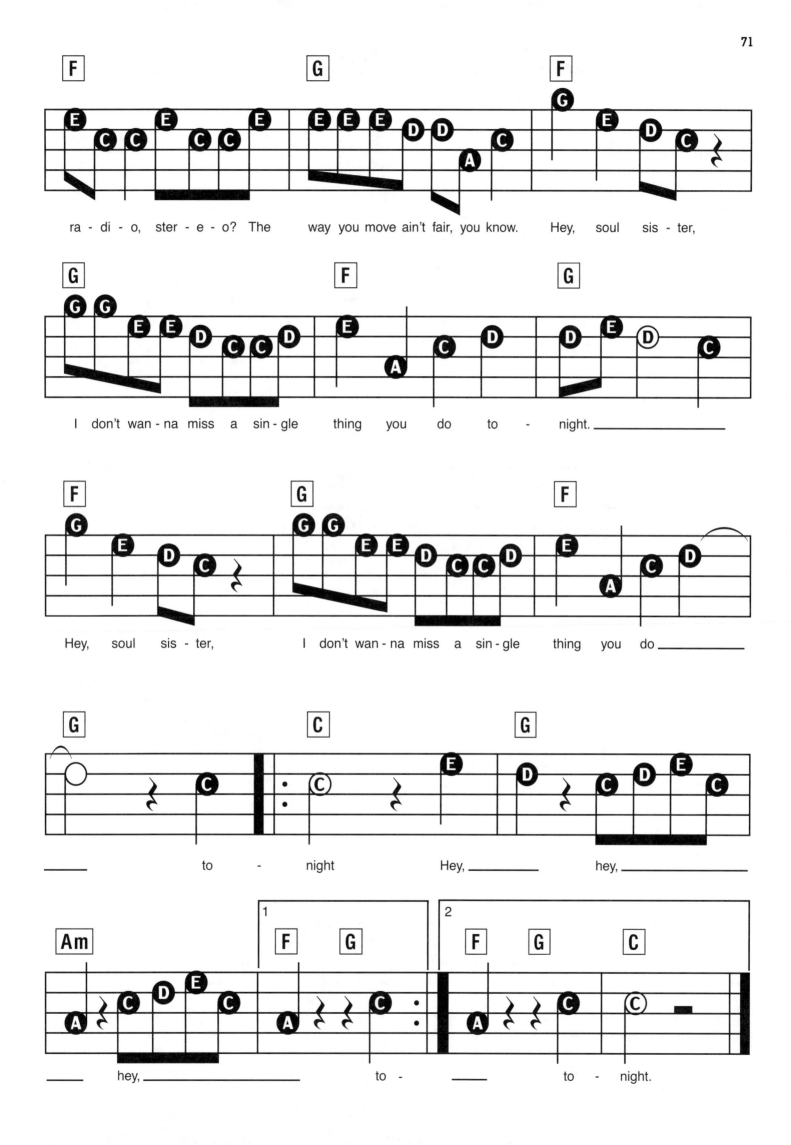

I Just Called to Say I Love You

Registration 8
Rhythm: Rock

Words and Music by
Stevie Wonder

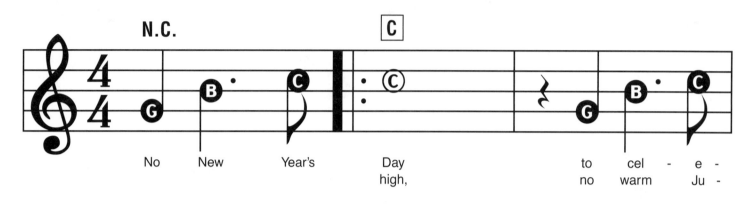

No   New   Year's   Day   to   cel   e -
high,   no   warm   Ju -

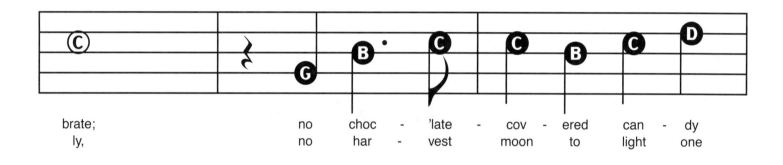

brate;   no   choc - 'late - cov - ered   can - dy
ly,   no   har - vest moon to   light one

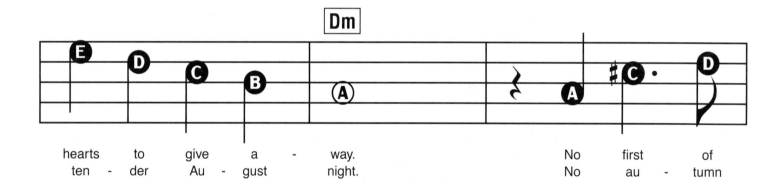

hearts to   give   a - way.   No   first   of
ten - der Au - gust night.   No   au - tumn

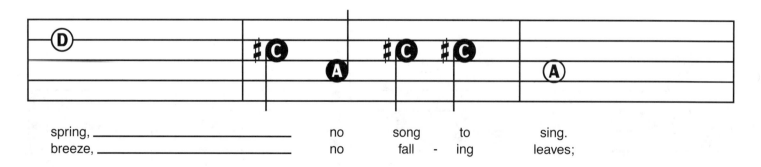

spring, _____   no   song   to   sing.
breeze, _____   no   fall - ing   leaves;

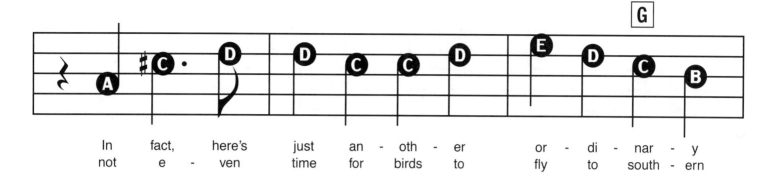

In fact, here's just an - oth - er or - di - nar - y
not e - ven just time for birds to fly to south - ern

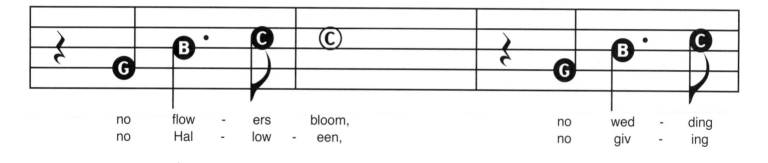

day. No A - pril rain,
skies. No Li - bra sun,

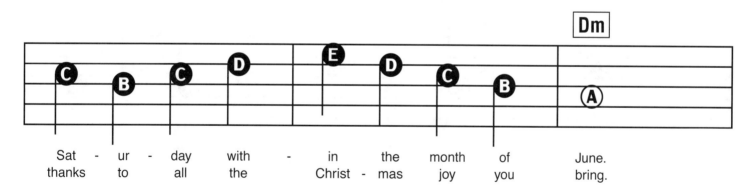

no flow - ers bloom, no wed - ding
no Hal - low - een, no giv - ing

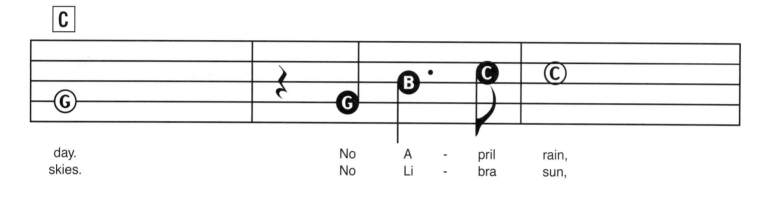

Sat - ur - day with - in the month of June.
thanks to all with the Christ - mas joy of you bring.

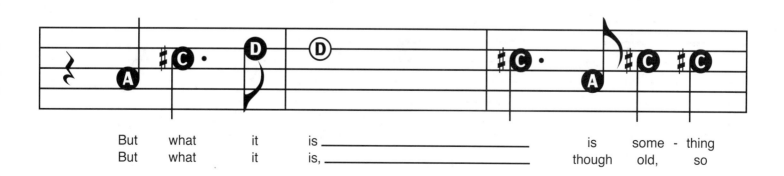

But what it is _____ is some - thing
But what it is, _____ though old, so

74

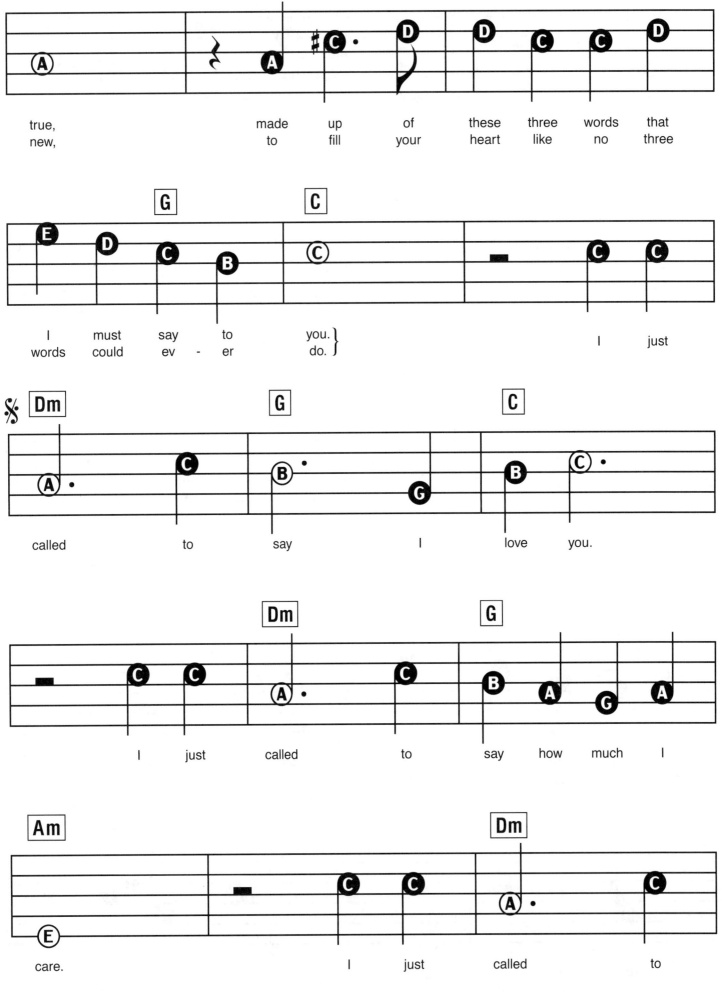

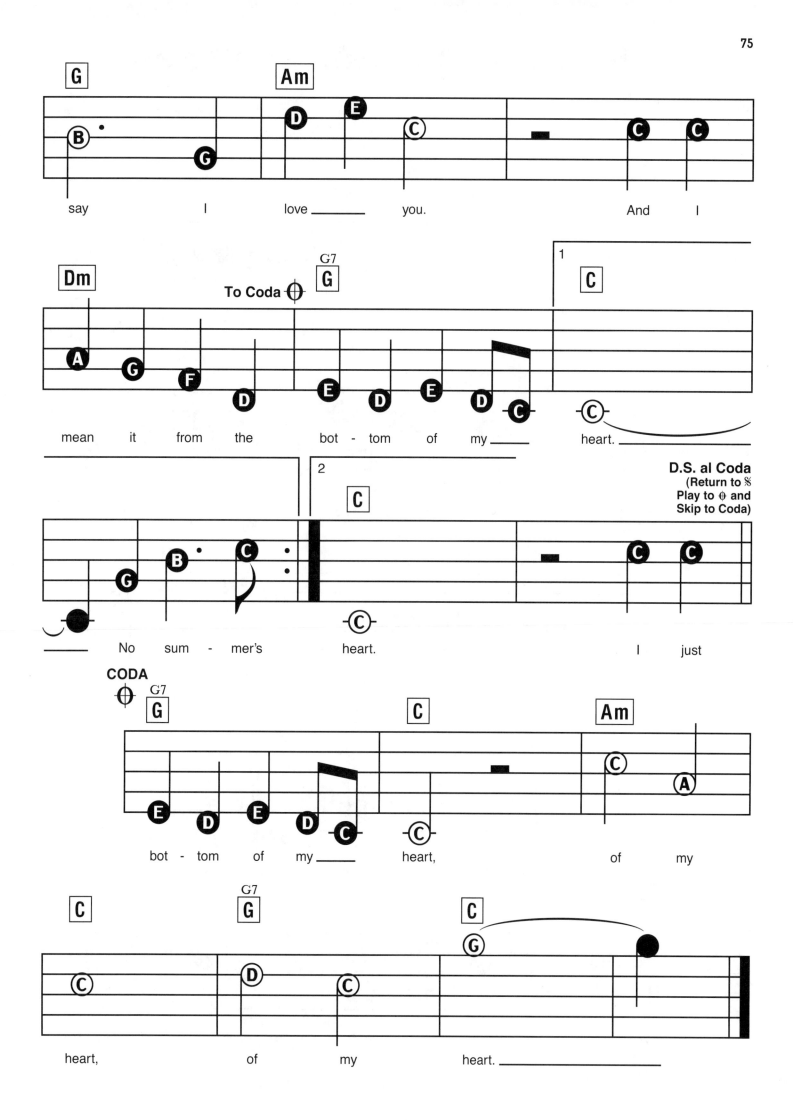

I Saw Her Standing There

Registration 2
Rhythm: Rock

Words and Music by John Lennon
and Paul McCartney

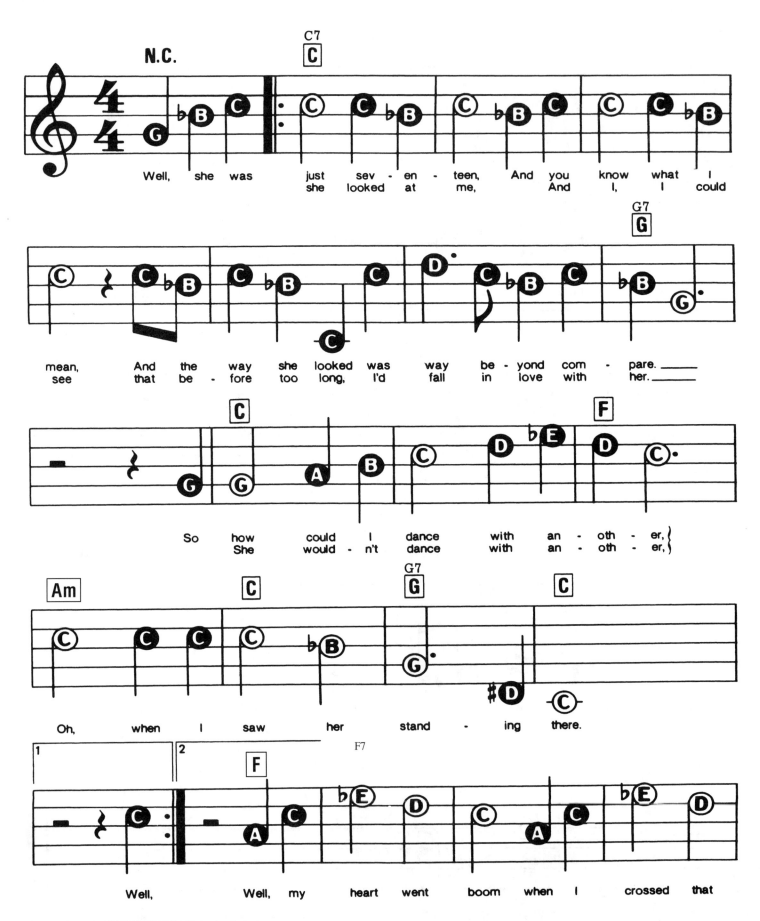

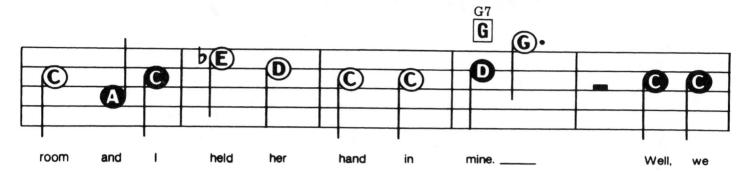

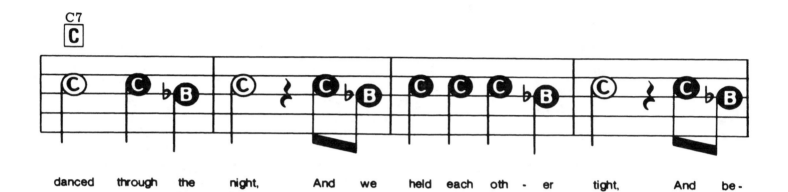

room and I held her hand in mine. _____ Well, we

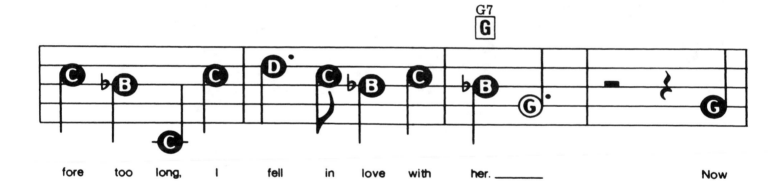

danced through the night, And we held each oth - er tight, And be -

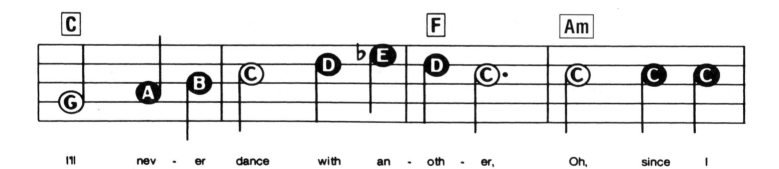

fore too long, I fell in love with her. _____ Now

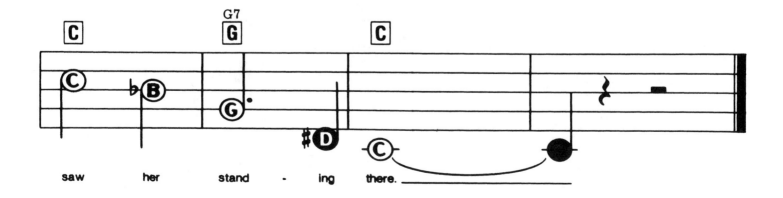

I'll nev - er dance with an - oth - er, Oh, since I

saw her stand - ing there. _____

I Shot the Sheriff

Registration 10
Rhythm: Reggae or Rock

Words and Music by
Bob Marley

Gm | **Cm**

1. I shot the sher - iff, but I did not shoot the

2-4. *(See additional lyrics)*

Gm

dep - u - ty. I shot the sher - iff,

Cm | **Gm** | **E♭** | **Dm**

but I did - n't shoot the dep - u - ty. All a - round in my

Gm | **E♭** | **Dm** | **Gm**

home town, they're try - ing to track me down. They

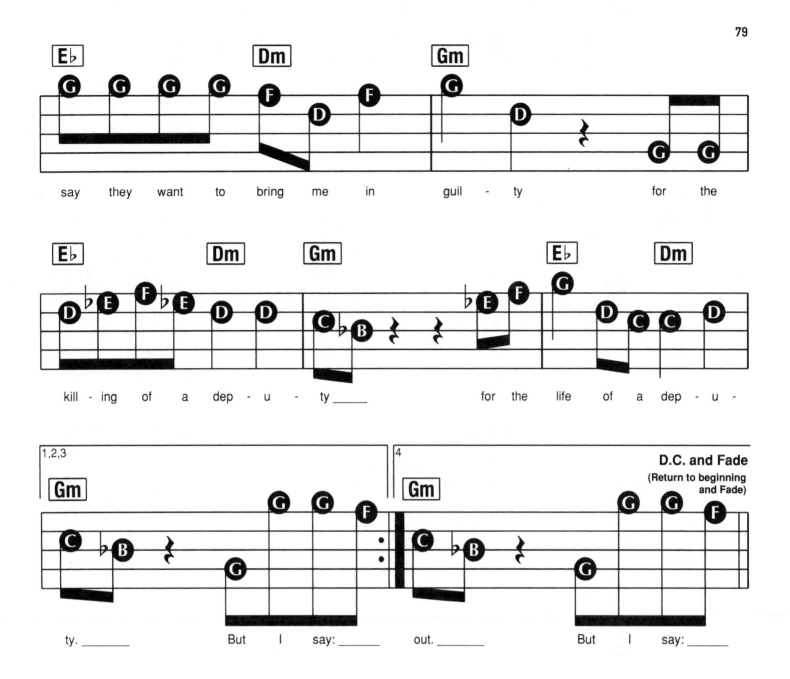

Additional Lyrics

2. I shot the sheriff, but I swear it was in self-defense.
    I shot the sheriff, and they say it is a capital offense.
    Sheriff John Brown always hated me; for what, I don't know.
    Every time that I plant a seed, he said, "Kill it before it grows."
    He said, "Kill it before it grows." But I say:

3. I shot the sheriff, but I swear it was in self-defense.
    I shot the sheriff, but I swear it was in self-defense.
    Freedom came my way one day, and I started out of town.
    All of a sudden, I see sheriff John Brown aiming to shoot me down.
    So I shot, I shot him down. But I say:

4. I shot the sheriff, but I did not shoot the deputy.
    I shot the sheriff, but I didn't shoot the deputy.
    Reflexes got the better of me, and what is to be must be.
    Every day, the bucket goes to the well, but one day the bottom will drop out.
    Yes, one day the bottom will drop out. But I say:

I Will Always Love You

Registration 3
Rhythm: Pops or 8-Beat

Words and Music by
Dolly Parton

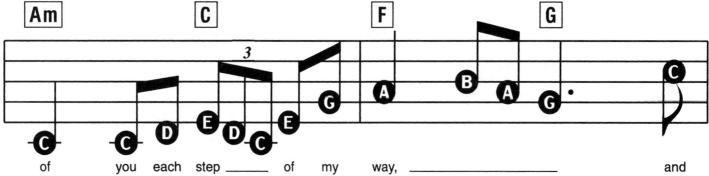

Chorus

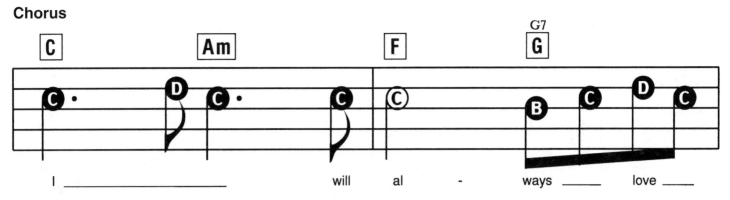

I _____ will al - ways _____ love _____

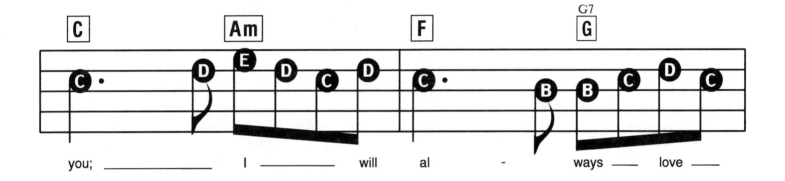

you; _____ I _____ will al - ways _____ love _____

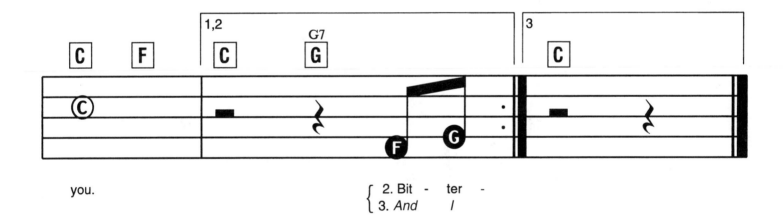

you.

2. Bit - ter -
3. And I

Additional Lyrics

2. Bittersweet memories, that's all I have and all I'm taking with me.
   Good-bye, oh please don't cry, 'cause we both know that I'm not what you need. But…
   Chorus

   (Spoken:)
3. *And I hope life will treat you kind, and I hope that you have all that you ever dreamed of.*
   Oh, I do wish you joy, and I wish you happiness, but above all this, I wish you love. And…
   Chorus

I'll Be

Registration 4
Rhythm: Waltz

Words and Music by
Edwin McCain

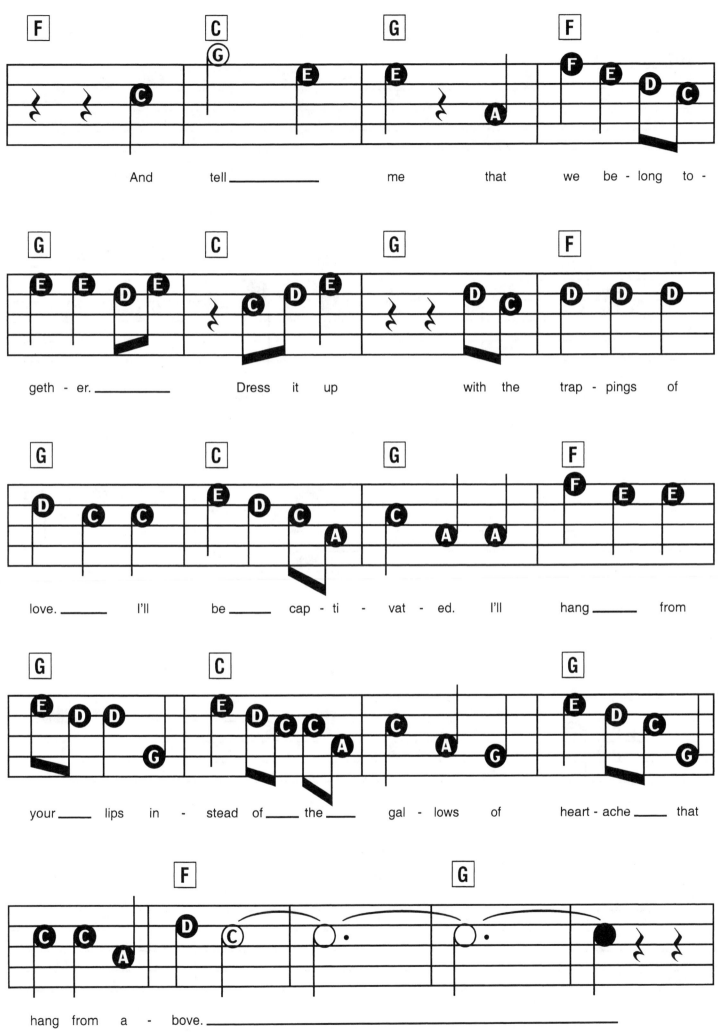

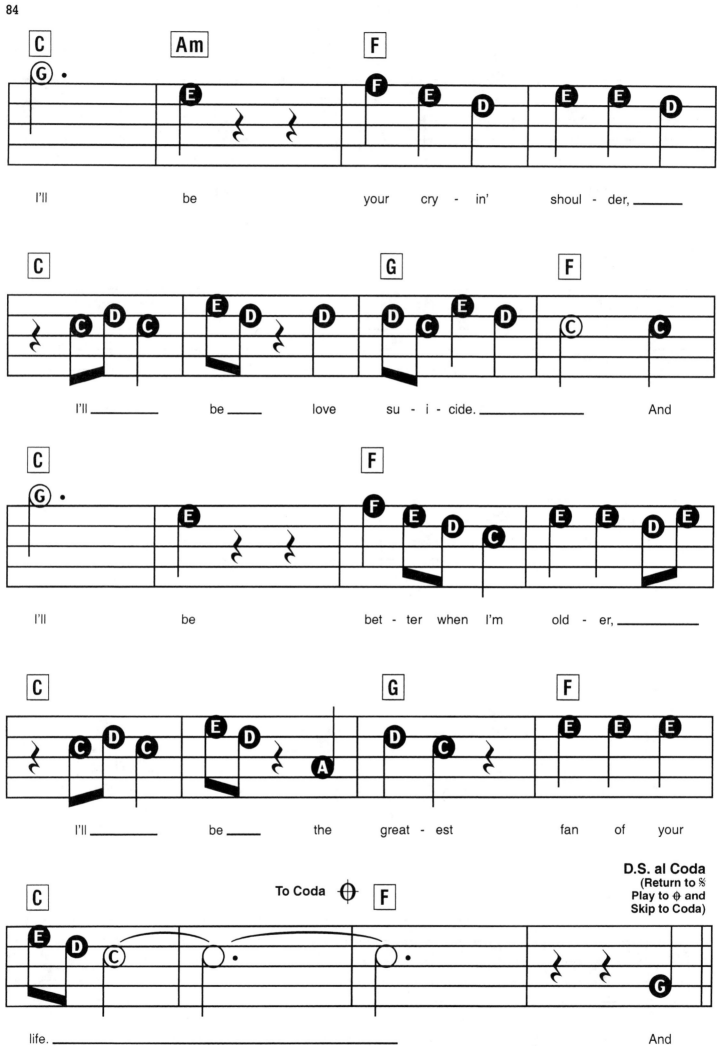

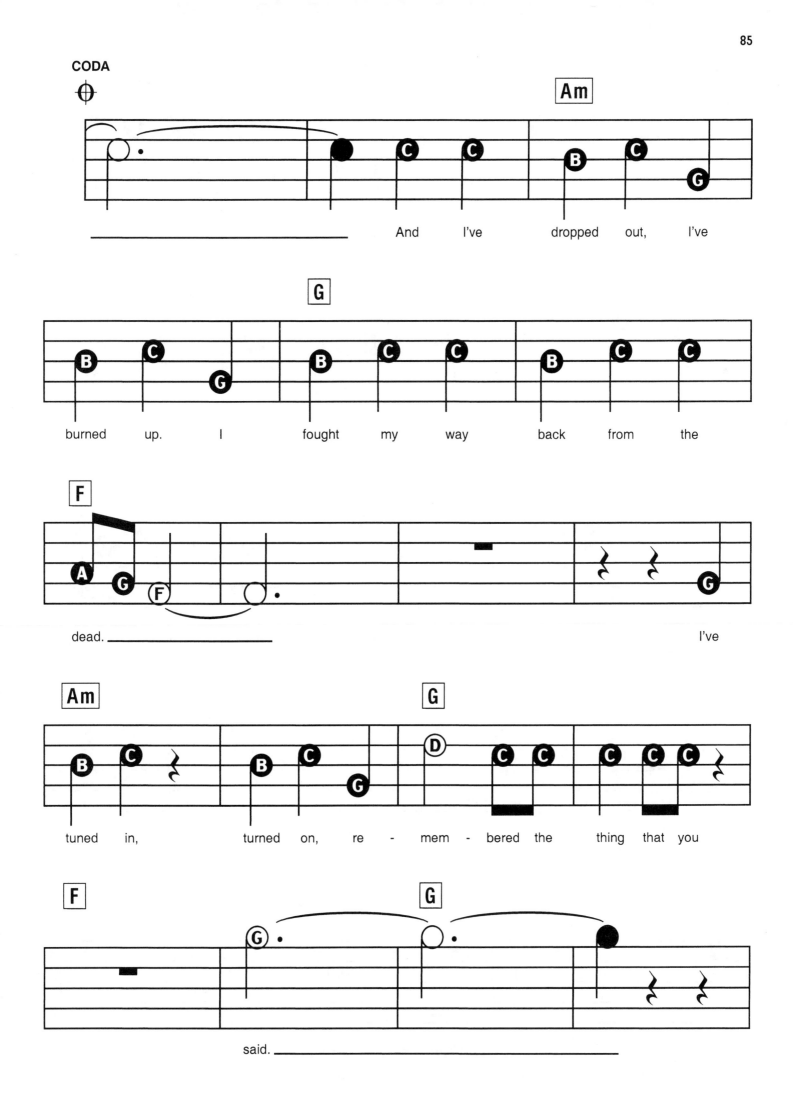

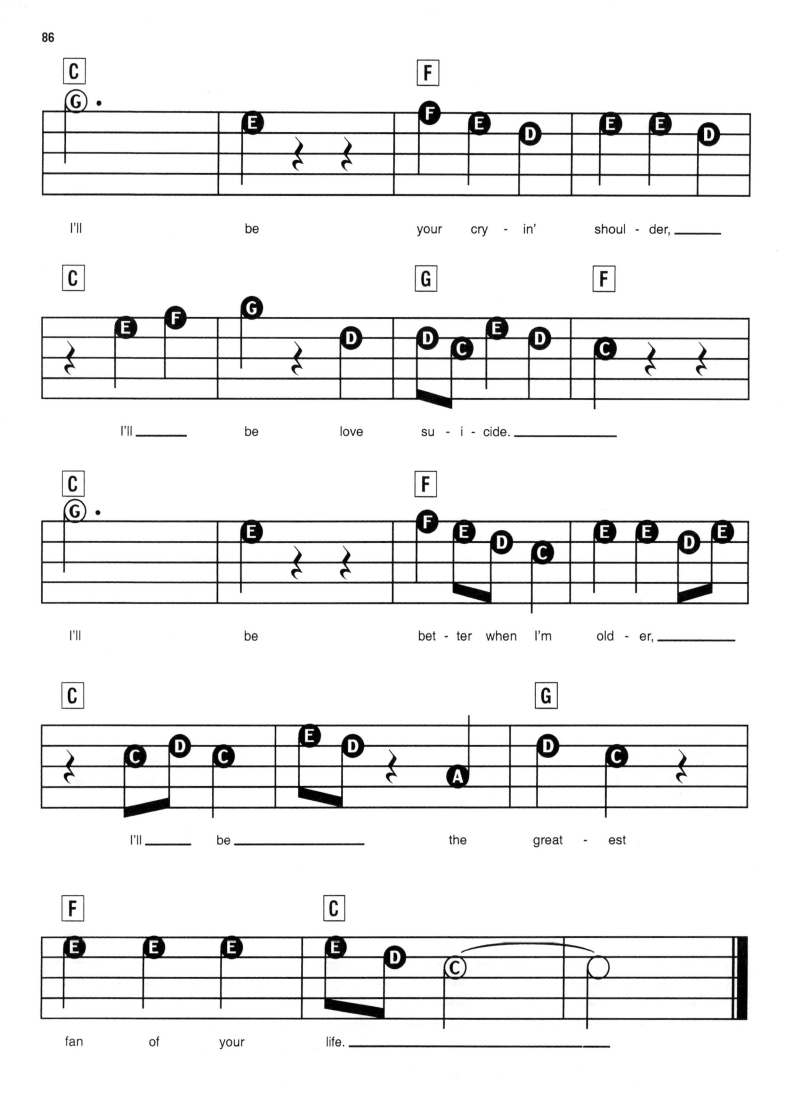

I'm Yours

Registration 4
Rhythm: Calypso or Folk

Words and Music by
Jason Mraz

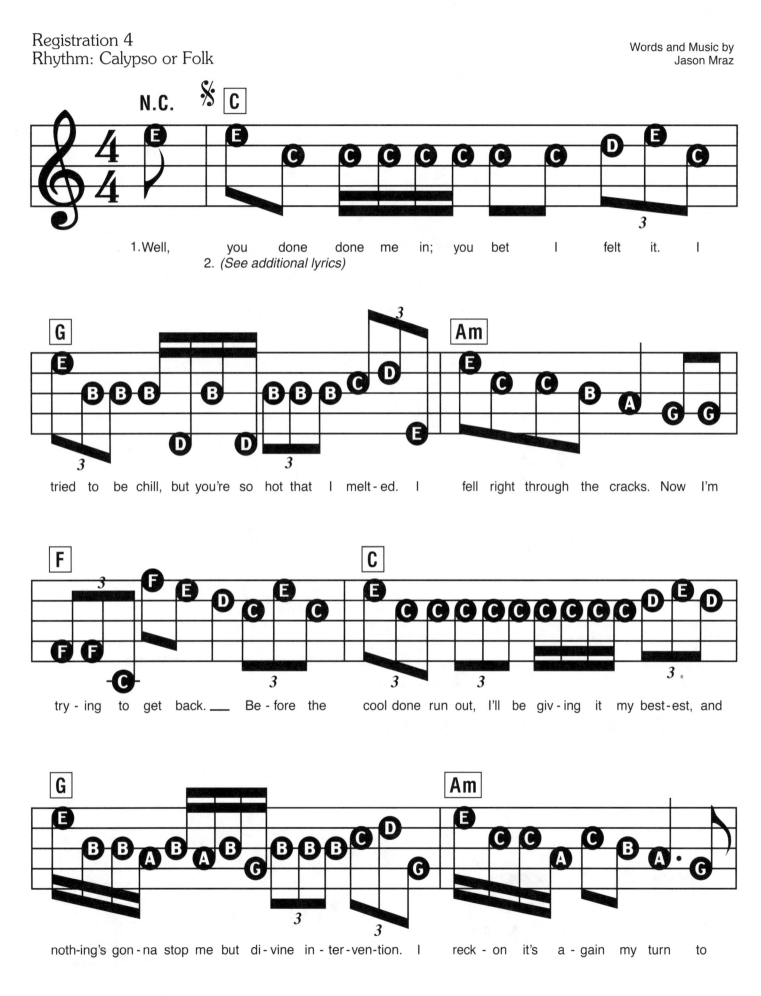

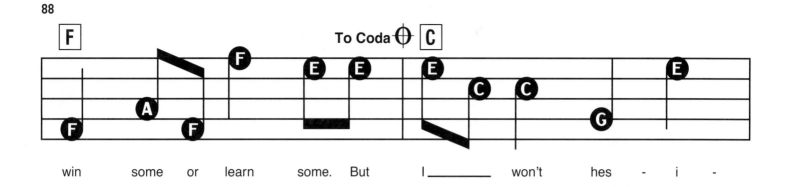

win   some   or   learn   some.   But   I _____ won't   hes - i -

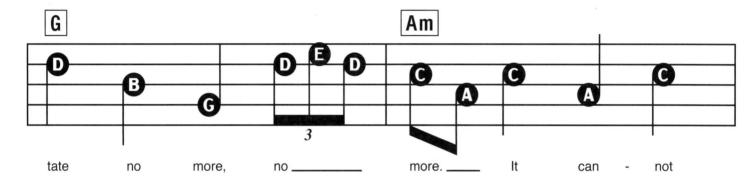

tate   no   more,   no _____ more. ____ It   can - not

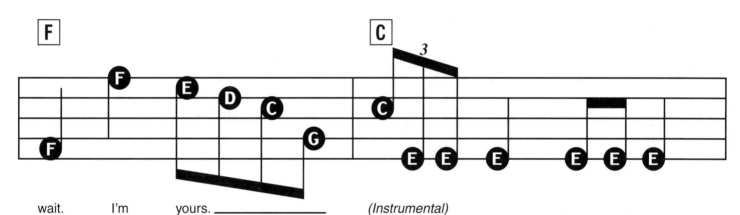

wait.   I'm   yours. _____   (Instrumental)

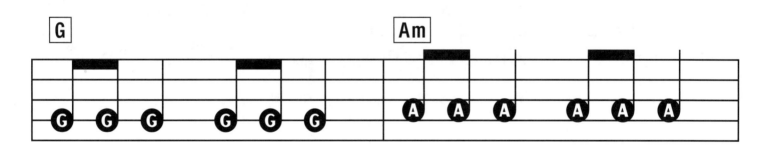

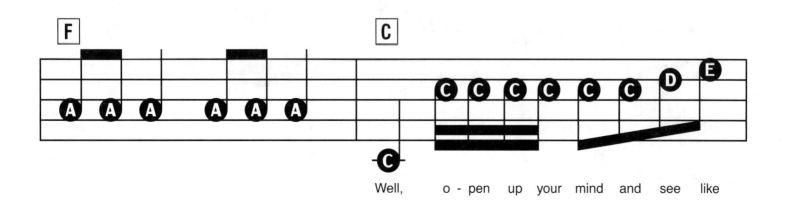

Well,   o - pen   up   your   mind   and   see   like

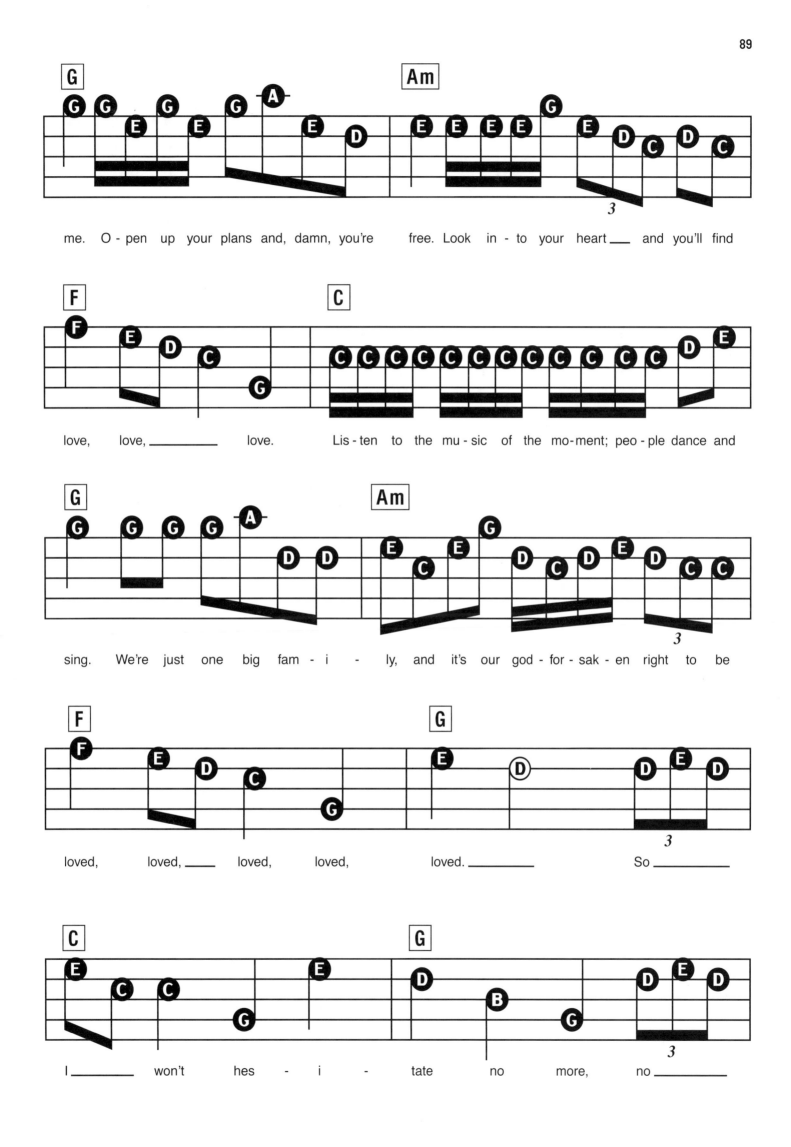

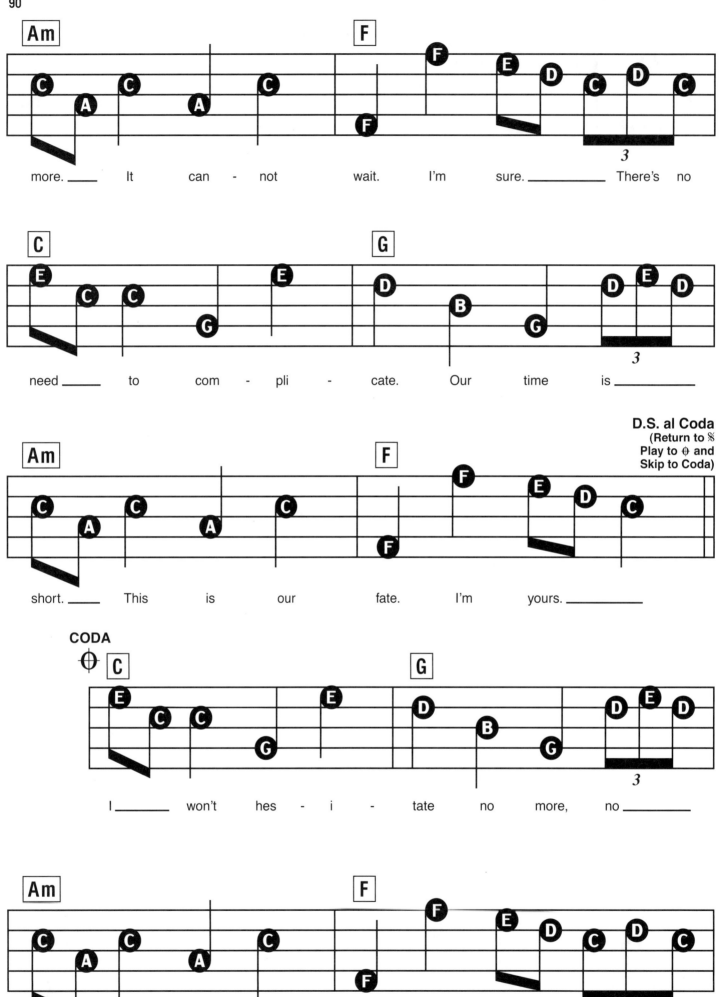

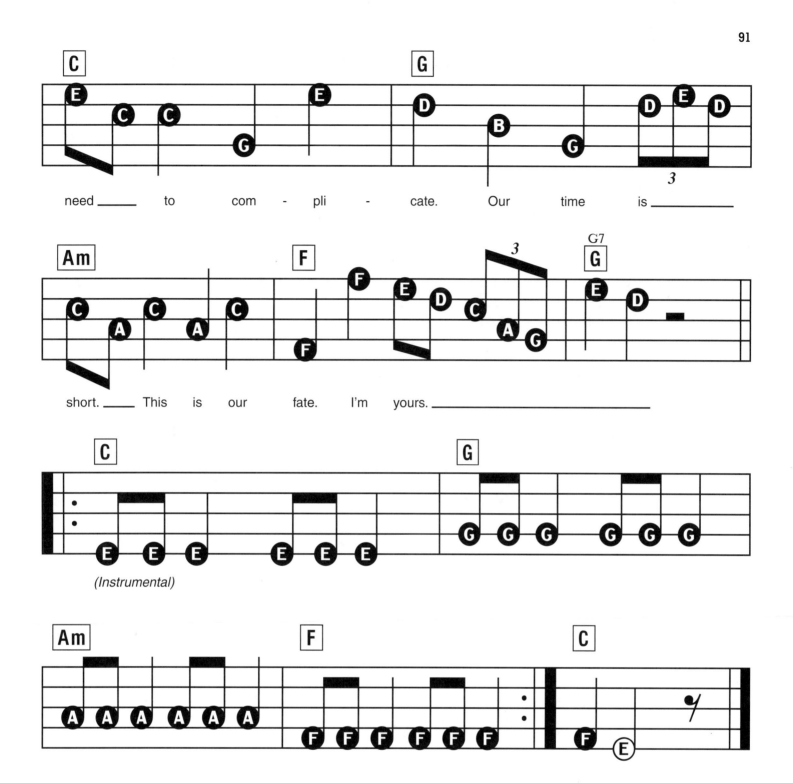

Additional Lyrics

2. I've been spending way too long
   Checking my tongue in the mirror
   And bending over backwards
   Just to try to see it clearer.
   But my breath fogged up the glass,
   And so I drew a new face and I laughed.
   I guess what I'll be saying
   Is there ain't no better reason
   To rid yourself of vanities
   And just go with the seasons.
   It's what we aim to do.
   Our name is our virtue.

   But I won't hesitate no more…

Knockin' on Heaven's Door

Registration 4
Rhythm: 8-Beat or Rock

Words and Music by
Bob Dylan

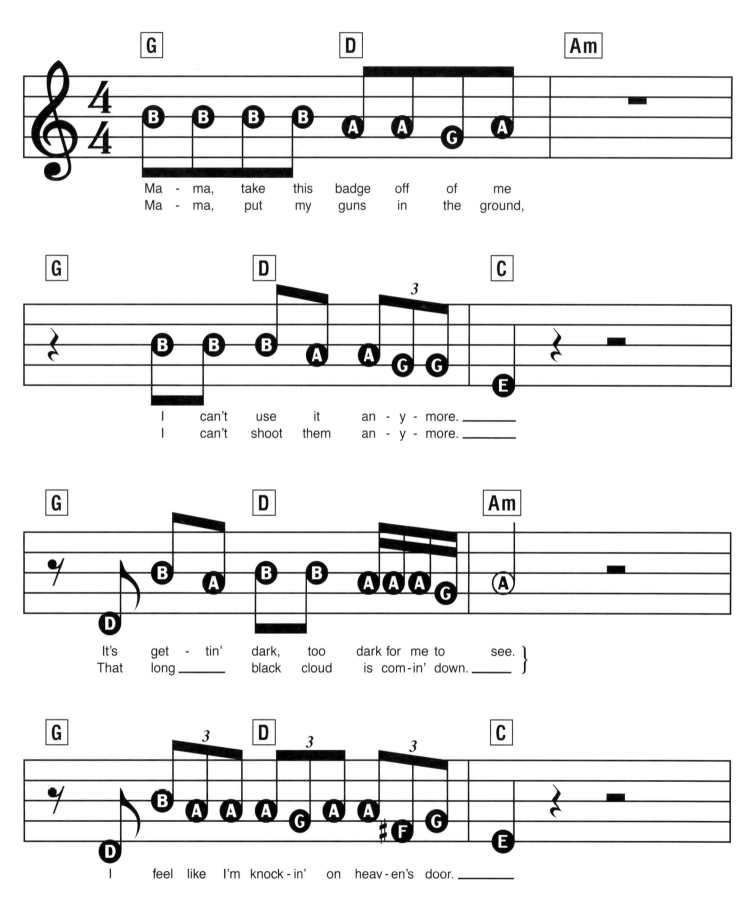

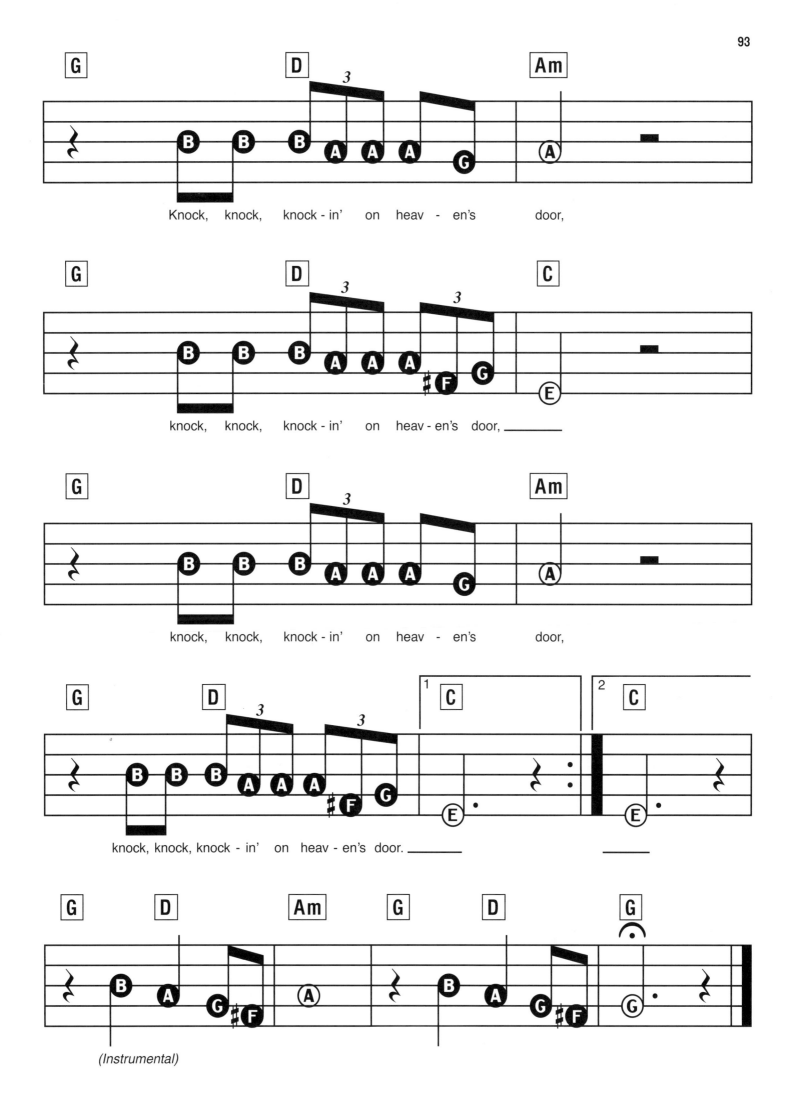

Let It Be

Registration 3
Rhythm: Rock

Words and Music by John Lennon
and Paul McCartney

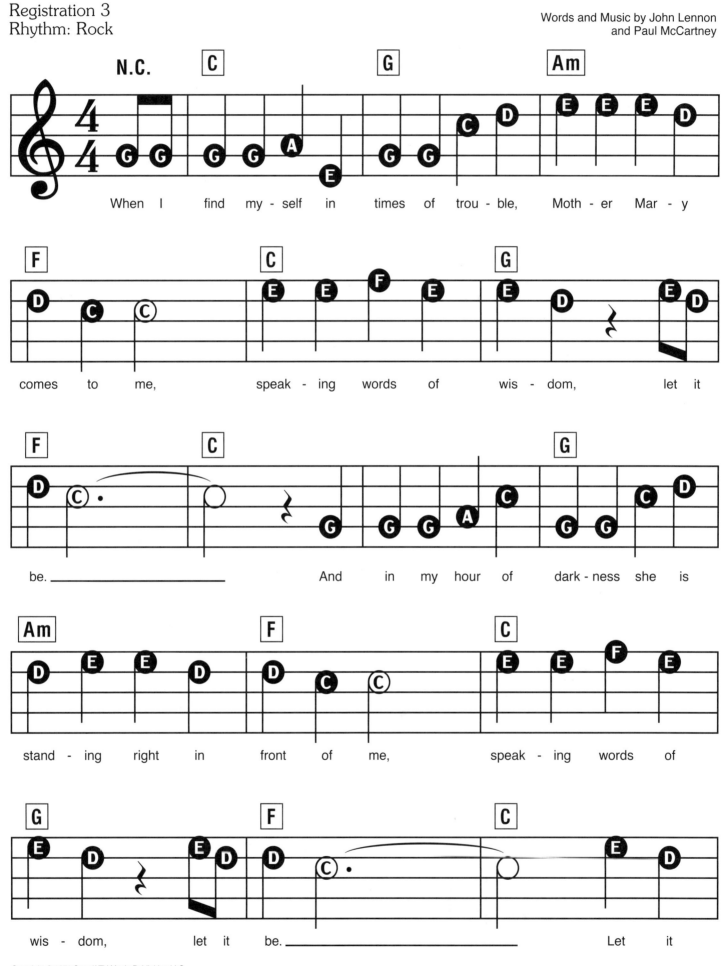

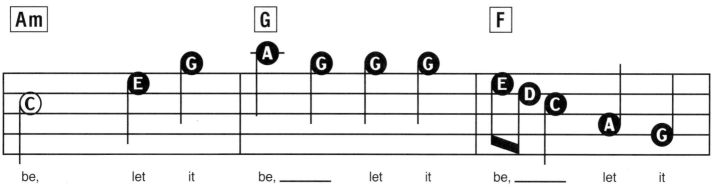

be,   let   it   be, _____ let it   be, _____ let it

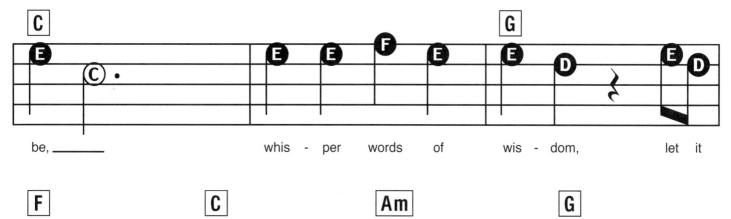

be, _____   whis - per words of   wis - dom,   let it

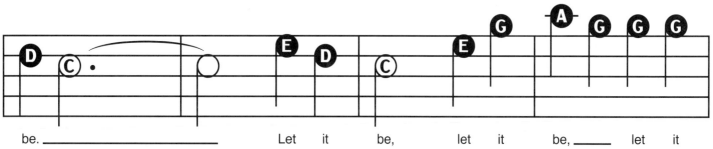

be. _____   Let   it   be,   let it   be, ____ let it

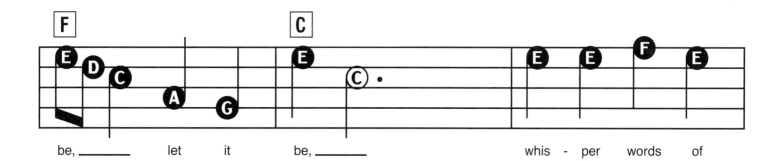

be, _____ let it   be, _____   whis - per words   of

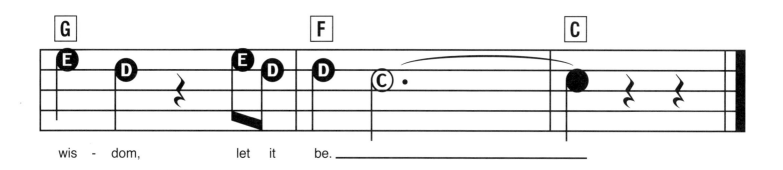

wis - dom,   let it   be. _____

Let the Sunshine In
from the Broadway Musical Production HAIR

Registration 4
Rhythm: Rock

Words by James Rado and Gerome Ragni
Music by Galt MacDermot

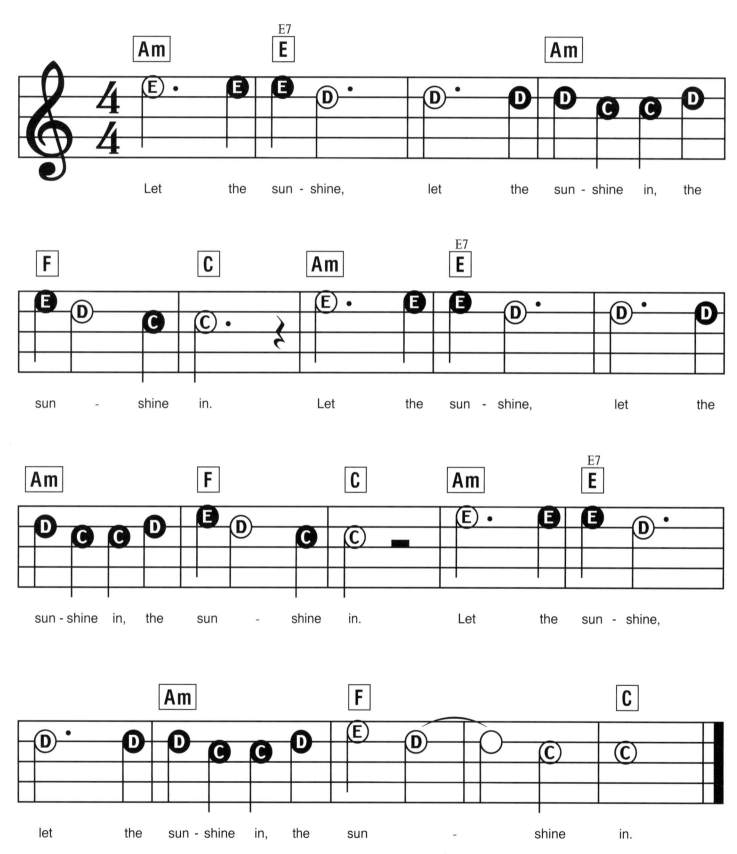

People Get Ready

Registration 1
Rhythm: 4/4 Ballad or 8-Beat

Words and Music by
Curtis Mayfield

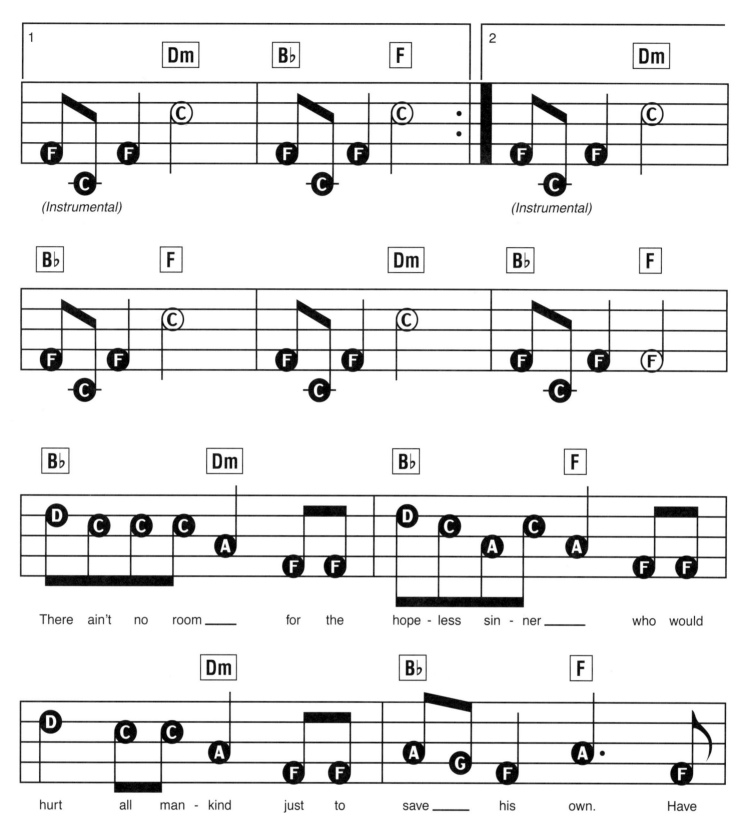

(Instrumental)   (Instrumental)

There ain't no room ____ for the hope - less sin - ner ____ who would

hurt all man - kind just to save ____ his own. Have

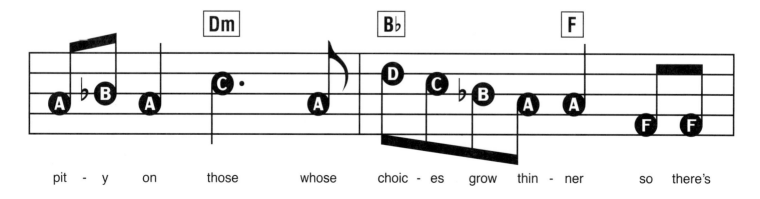

pit - y on those whose choic - es grow thin - ner so there's

D.C. al Coda
(Return to beginning
Play to ⊕ and
Skip to Coda)

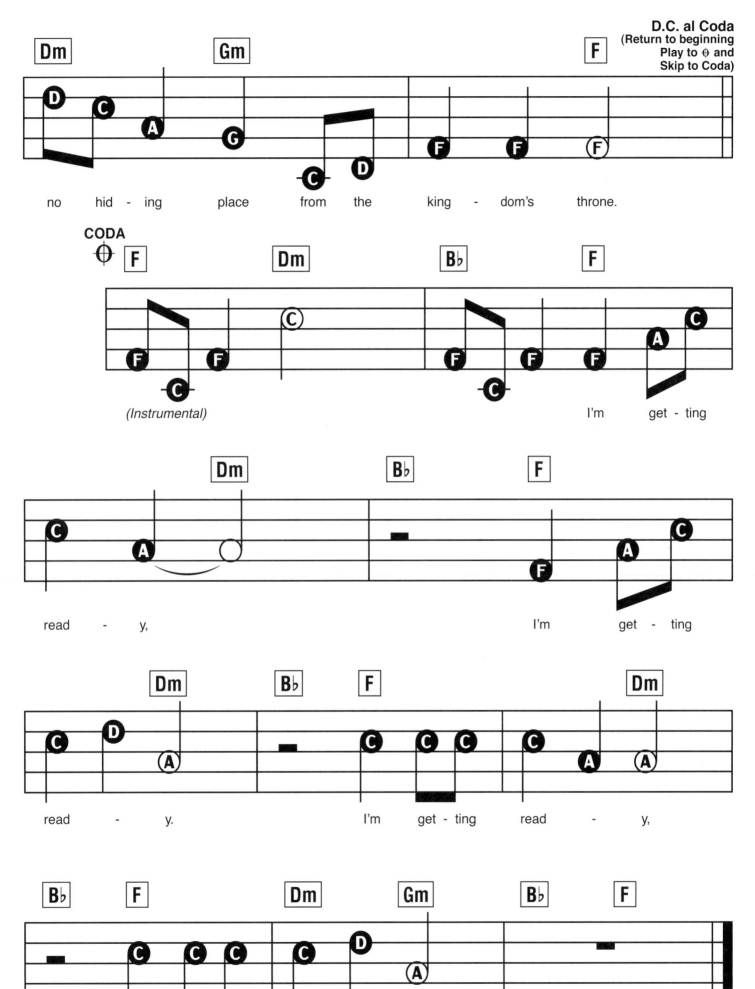

Mack the Knife
from THE THREEPENNY OPERA

English Words by Marc Blitzstein
Original German Words by Bert Brecht
Music by Kurt Weill

Registration 8
Rhythm: Swing

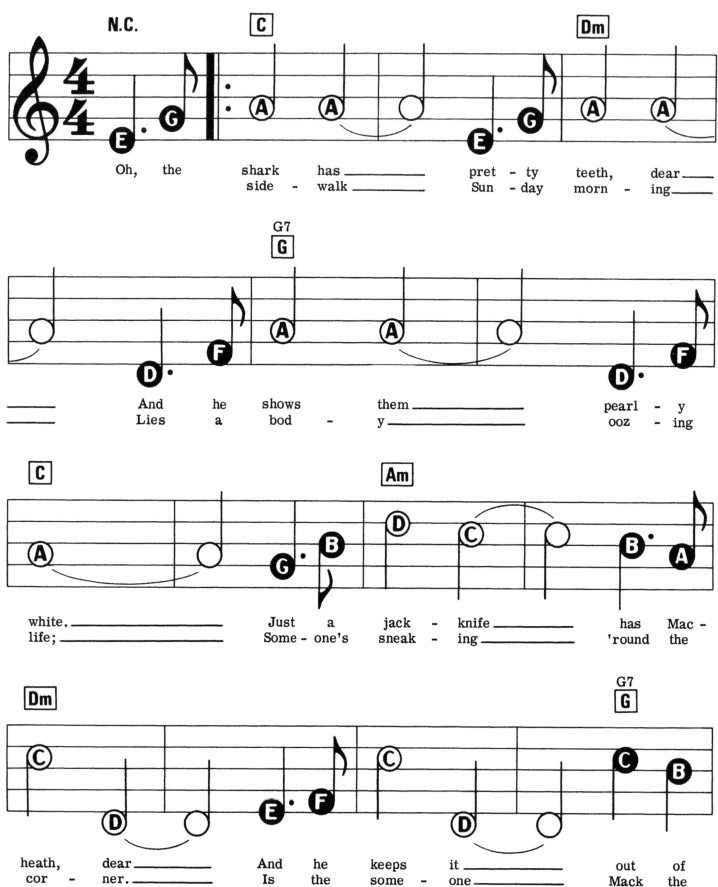

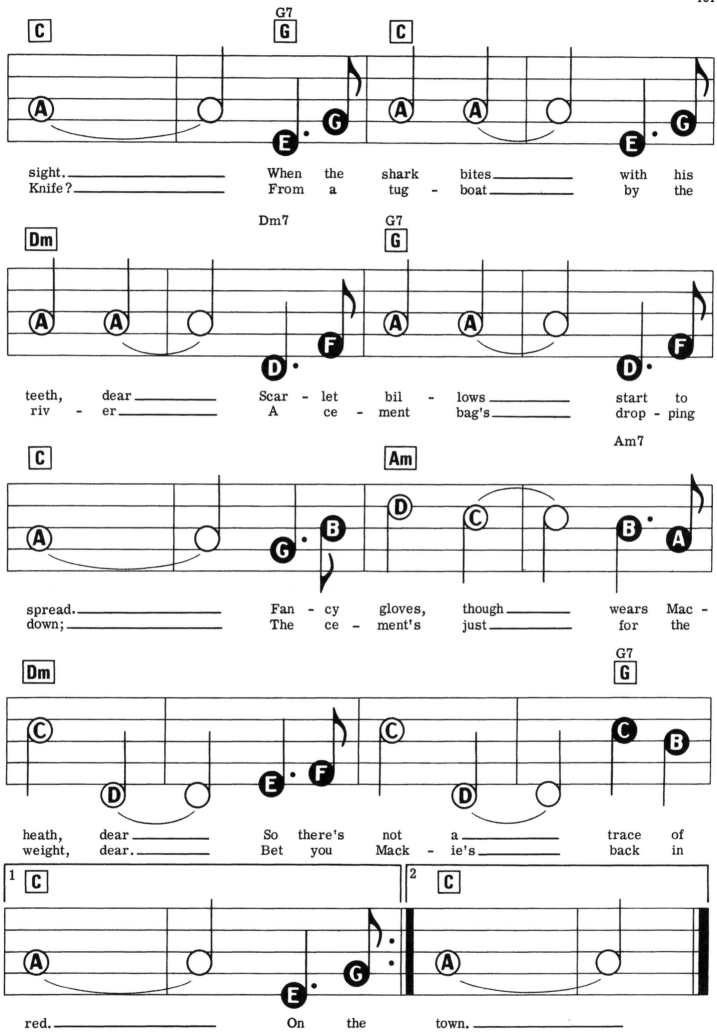

Mean

Registration 4
Rhythm: Bluegrass or Fox Trot

Words and Music by
Taylor Swift

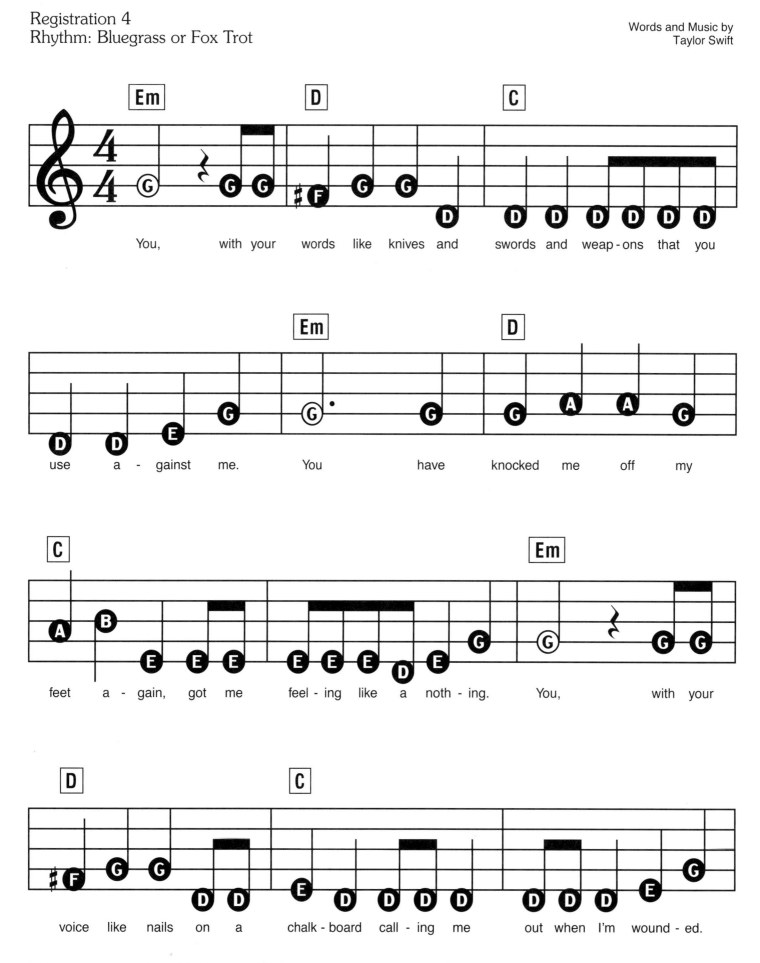

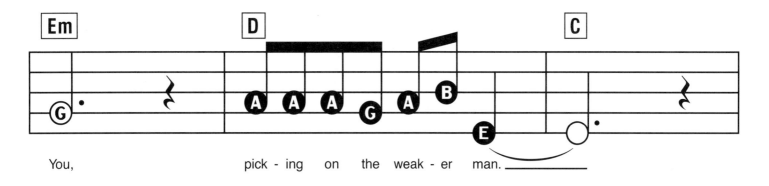

You, pick - ing on the weak - er man. _____

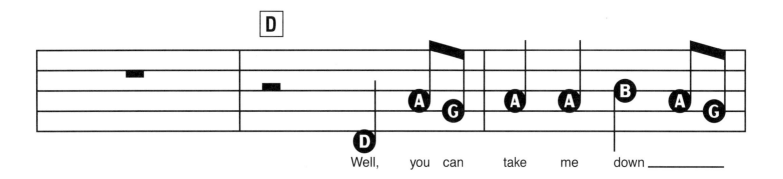

Well, you can take me down _____

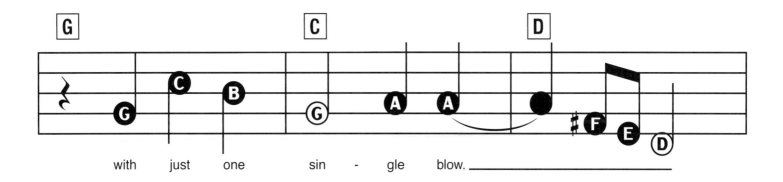

with just one sin - gle blow. _____

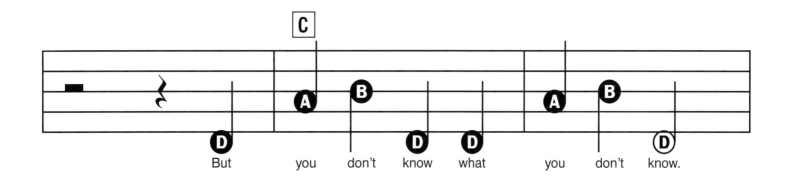

But you don't know what you don't know.

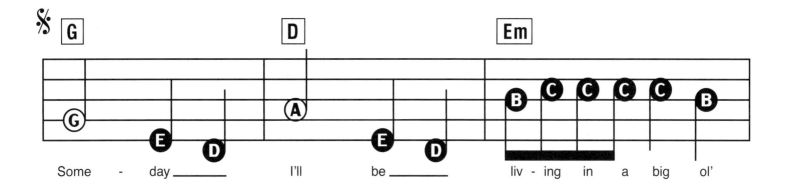

Some - day _____ I'll be _____ liv - ing in a big ol'

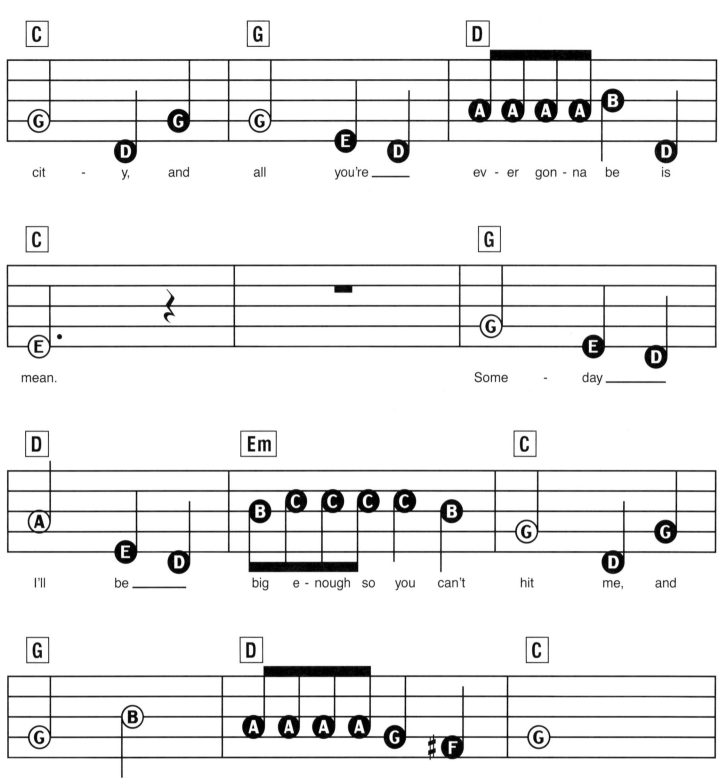

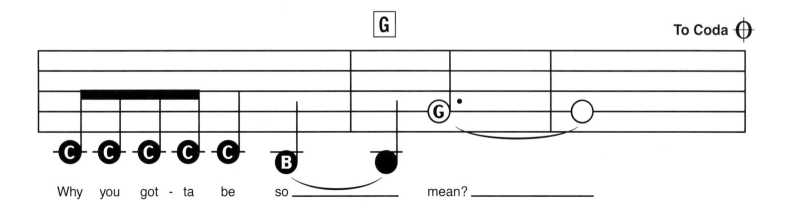

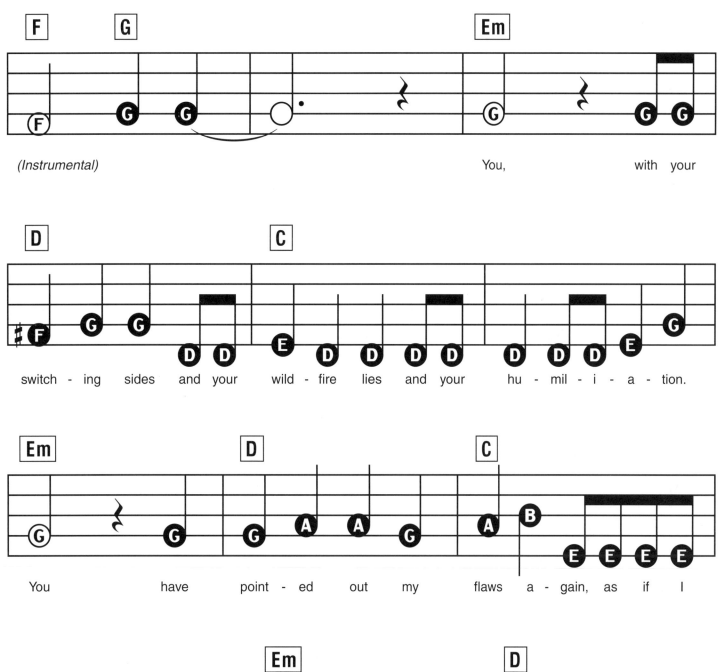

(Instrumental) You, with your

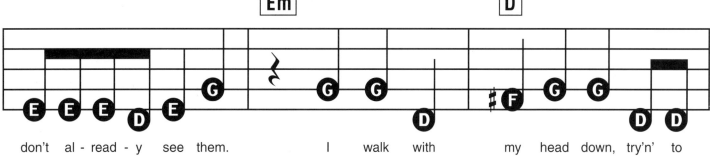

switch - ing sides and your wild - fire lies and your hu - mil - i - a - tion.

You have point - ed out my flaws a - gain, as if I

don't al - read - y see them. I walk with my head down, try'n' to

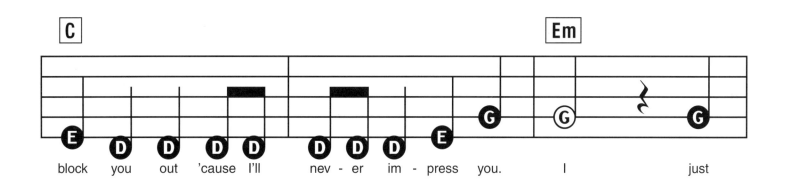

block you out 'cause I'll nev - er im - press you. I just

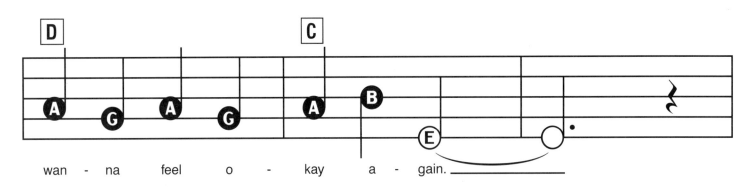

wan - na feel o - kay a - gain. _____

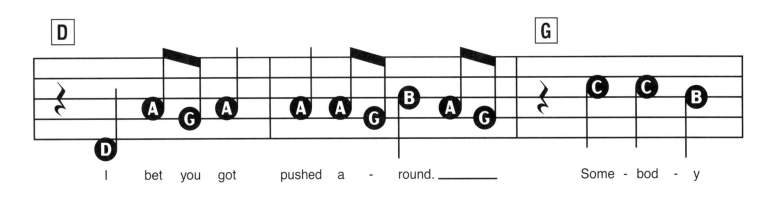

I bet you got pushed a - round. _____ Some - bod - y

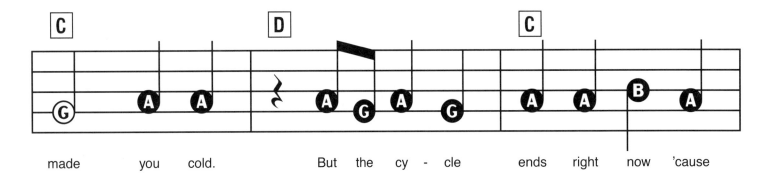

made you cold. But the cy - cle ends right now 'cause

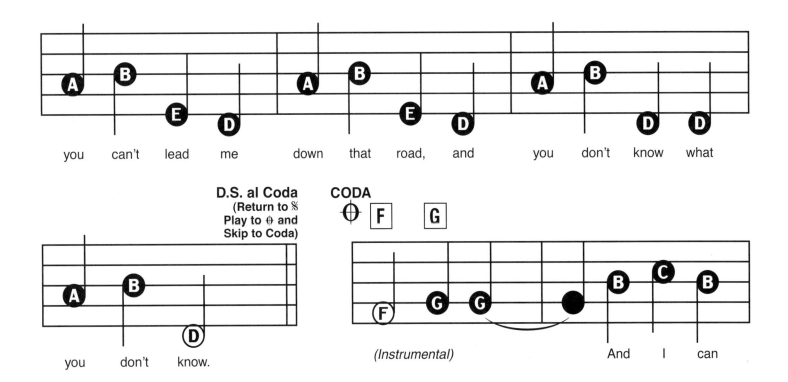

you can't lead me down that road, and you don't know what

D.S. al Coda
(Return to 𝄋
Play to ⊕ and
Skip to Coda)

you don't know.

CODA

(Instrumental) And I can

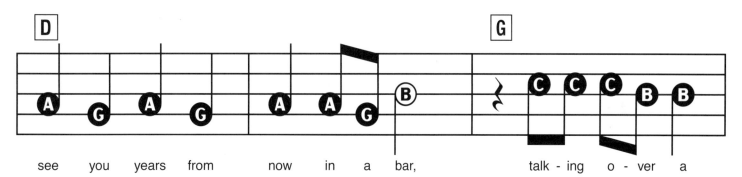

see you years from now in a bar, talk - ing o - ver a

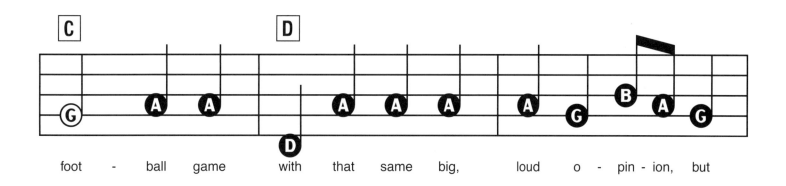

foot - ball game with that same big, loud o - pin - ion, but

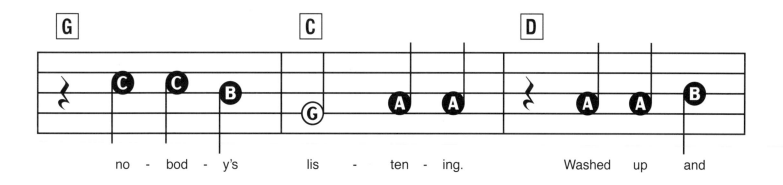

no - bod - y's lis - ten - ing. Washed up and

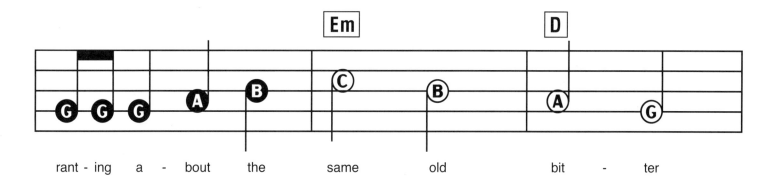

rant - ing a - bout the same old bit - ter

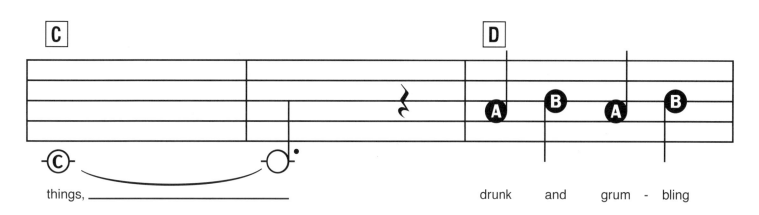

things, _____ drunk and grum - bling

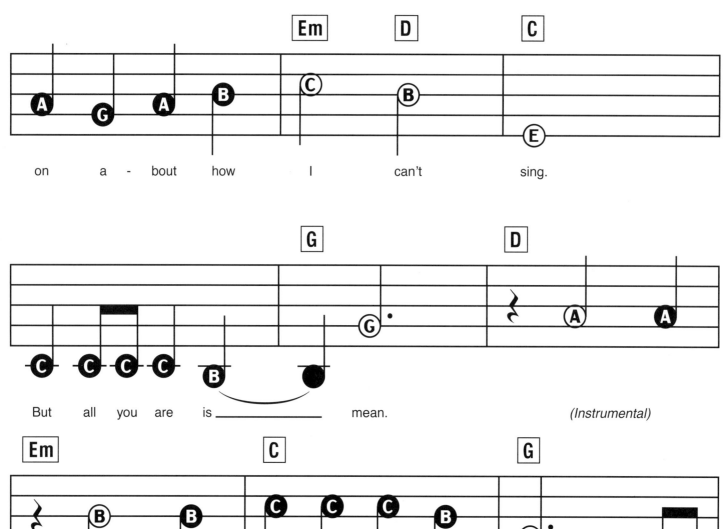

on a - bout how I can't sing.

But all you are is _____ mean. *(Instrumental)*

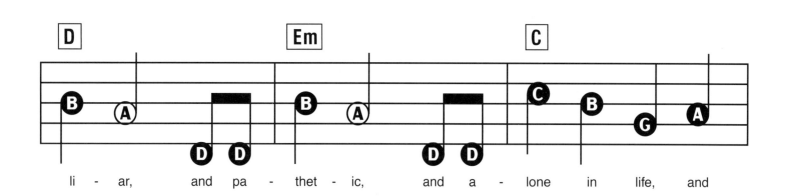

All you are is mean, and a

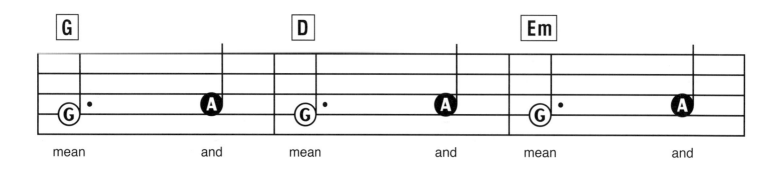

li - ar, and pa - thet - ic, and a - lone in life, and

mean and mean and mean and

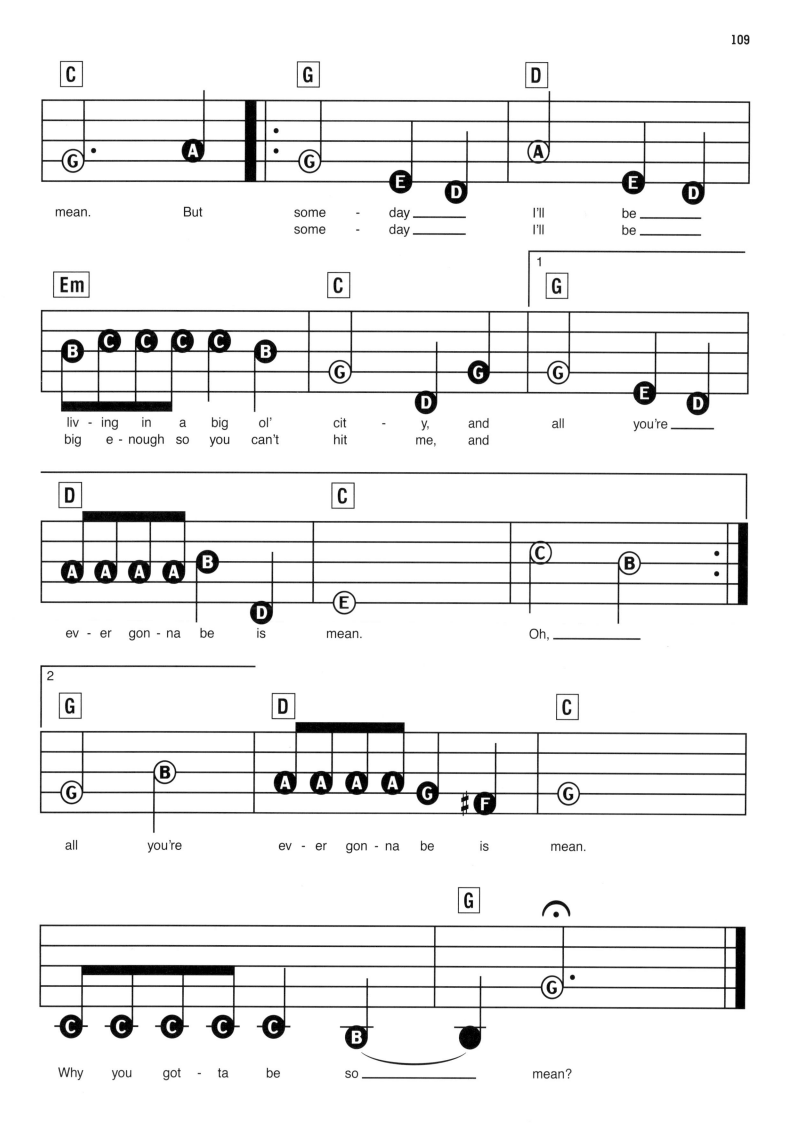

Peace Train

Registration 4
Rhythm: Country Rock or Rock

Words and Music by
Cat Stevens

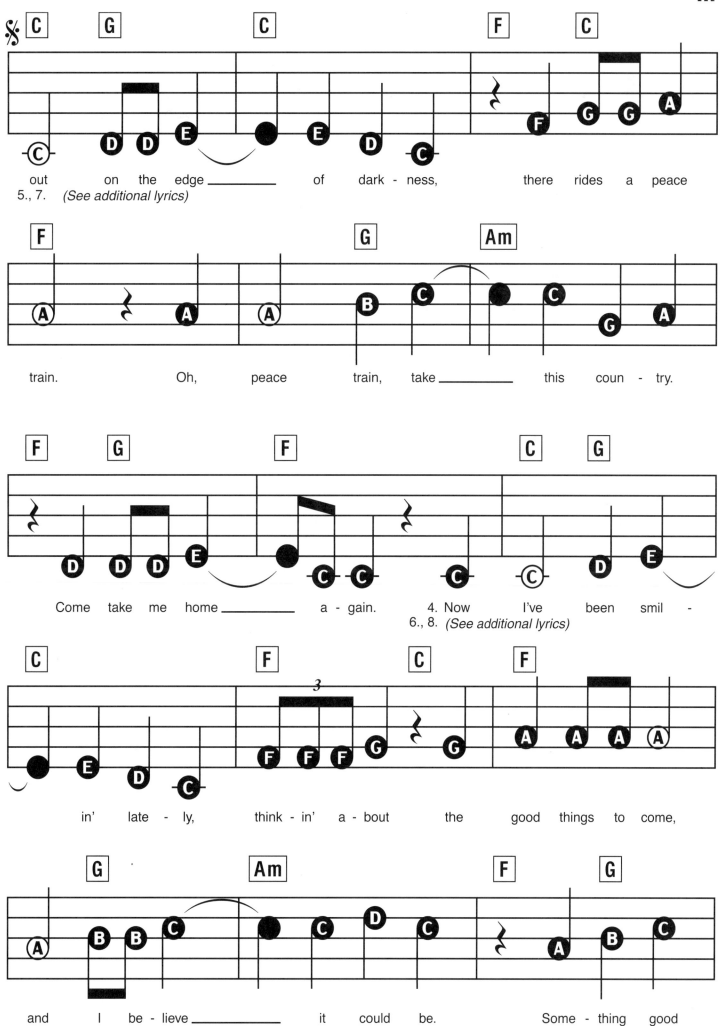

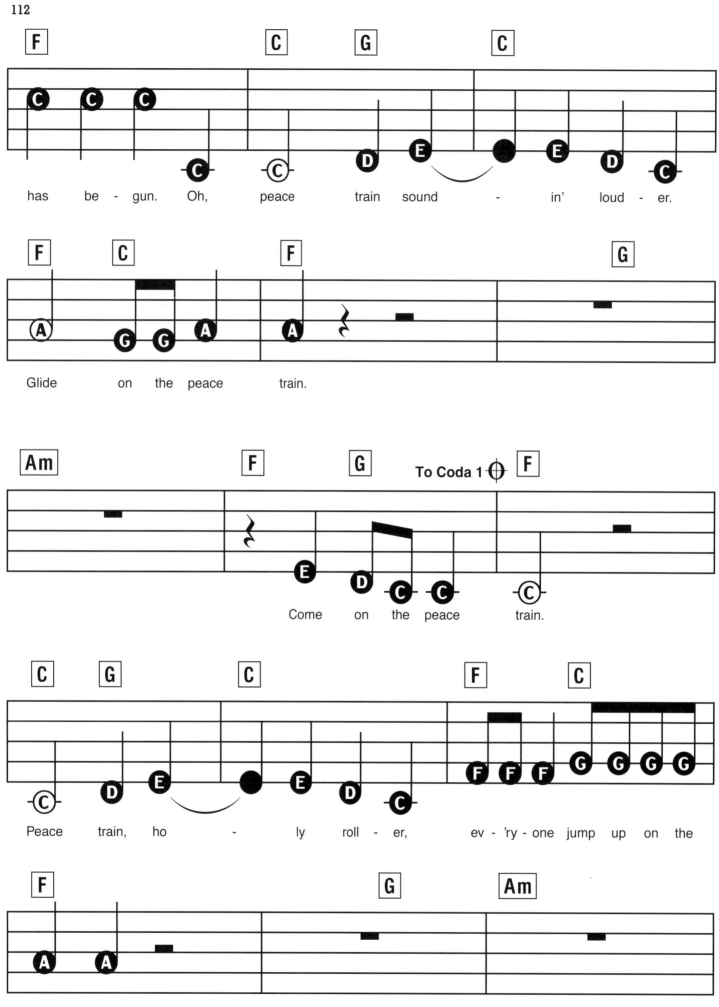

peace   train.

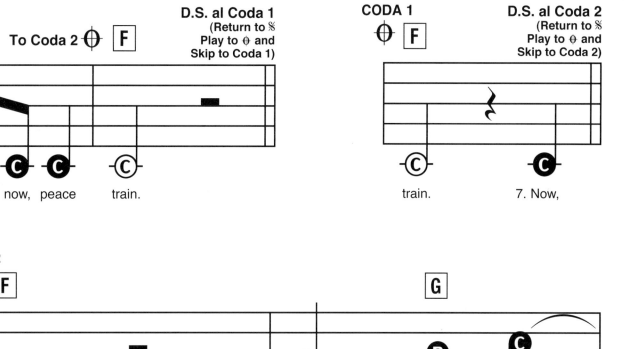

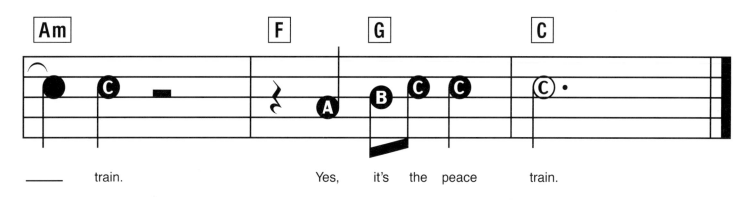

Additional Lyrics

5. Get your bags together.
   Go bring your good friends, too,
   Because it's gettin' nearer.
   It soon will be with you.

6. Oh, come and join the living;
   It's not so far from you,
   And it's gettin' nearer.
   Soon it will all be true.

7. Now, I've been cryin' lately,
   Thinkin' about the world as it is.
   Why must we go on hating?
   Why can't we live in bliss?

8. 'Cause out on the edge of darkness,
   There rides a peace train.
   Oh, peace train take this country.
   Come take me home again.

Peaceful Easy Feeling

Registration 4
Rhythm: Soft Rock

Words and Music by
Jack Tempchin

F	B♭	F

I like the way your spark - lin' ear - rings _____
I found out a long time a -

B♭	F	B♭

lay _____ a - gainst your skin _____ so
go _____ what a wom - an can do to your

C	F

brown. _____ And I wan - na
soul. _____ Ah, but she

B♭	F	B♭

sleep with you in the des - ert _____ to - night,
can't _____ take you _____ an - y way _____

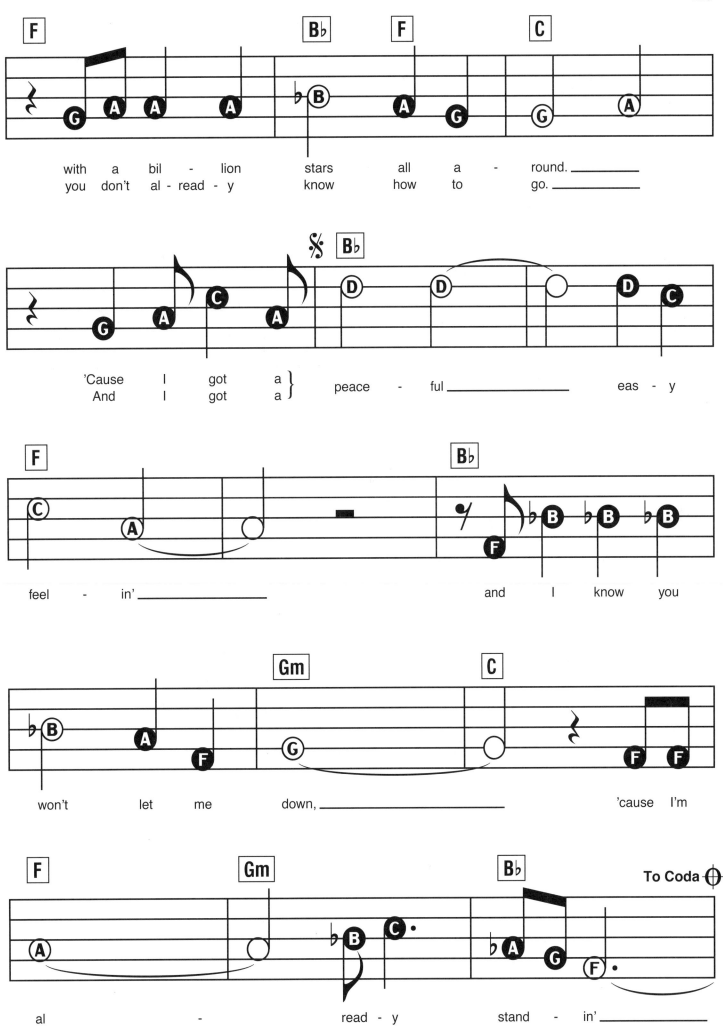

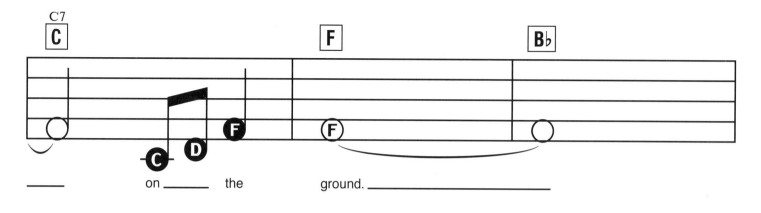

on _____ the ground. _____

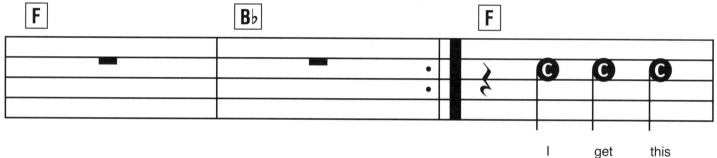

I get this

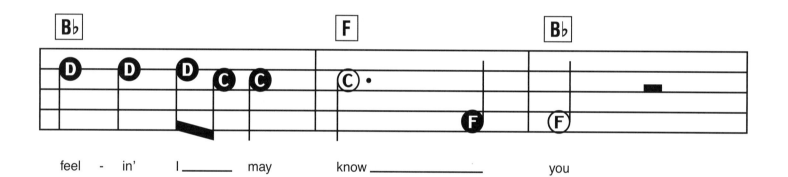

feel - in' I _____ may know _____ you

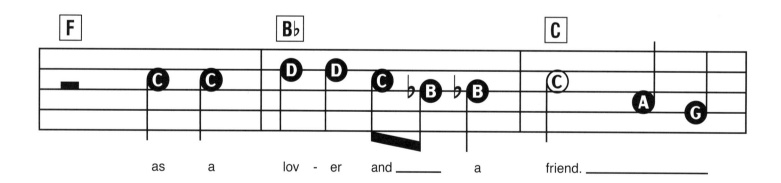

as a lov - er and _____ a friend. _____

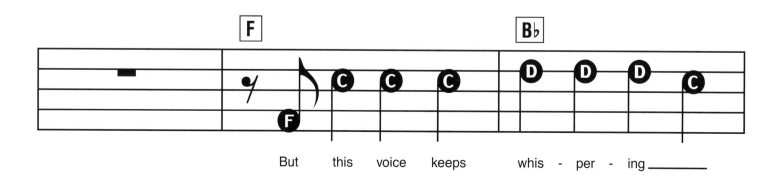

But this voice keeps whis - per - ing _____

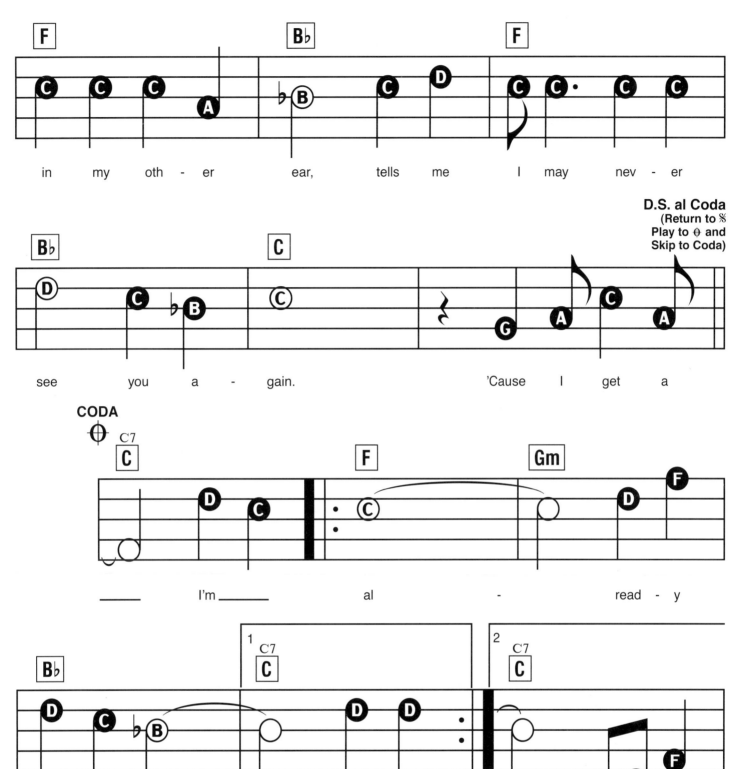

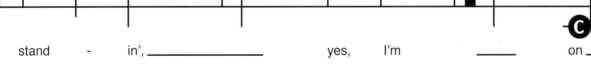

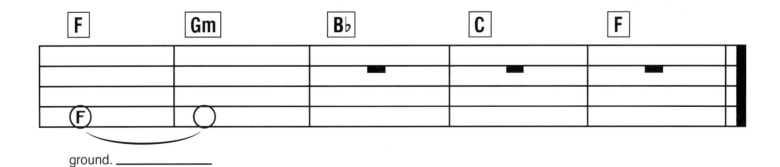

Poker Face

Registration 4
Rhythm: Rock or Dance

Words and Music by Stefani Germanotta
and RedOne

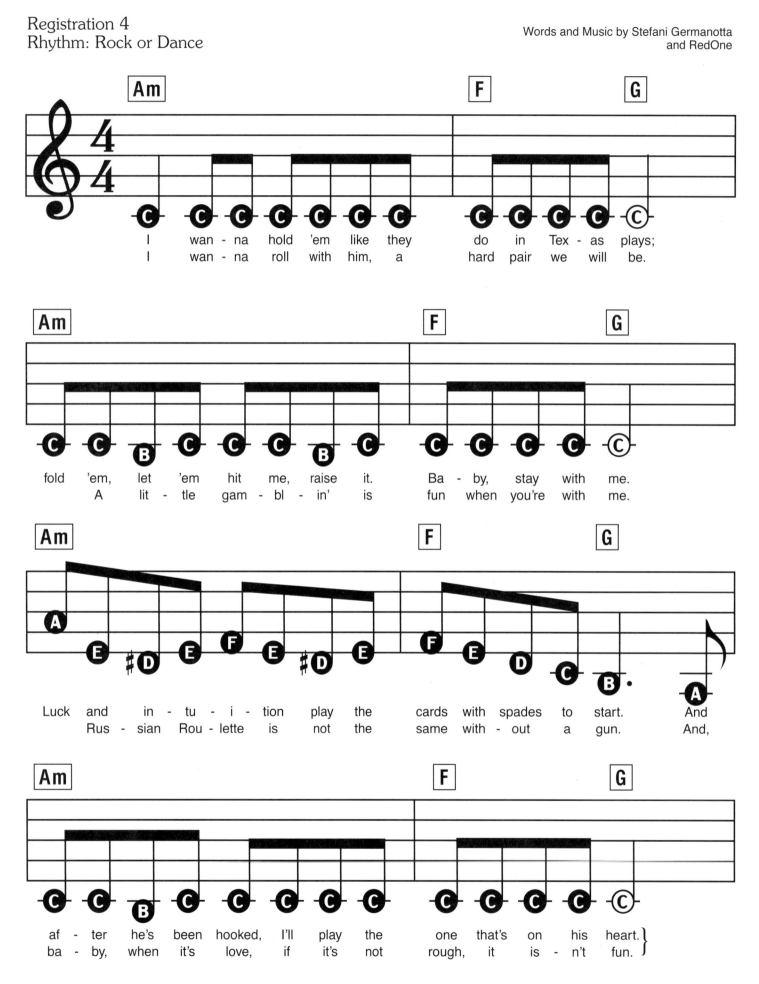

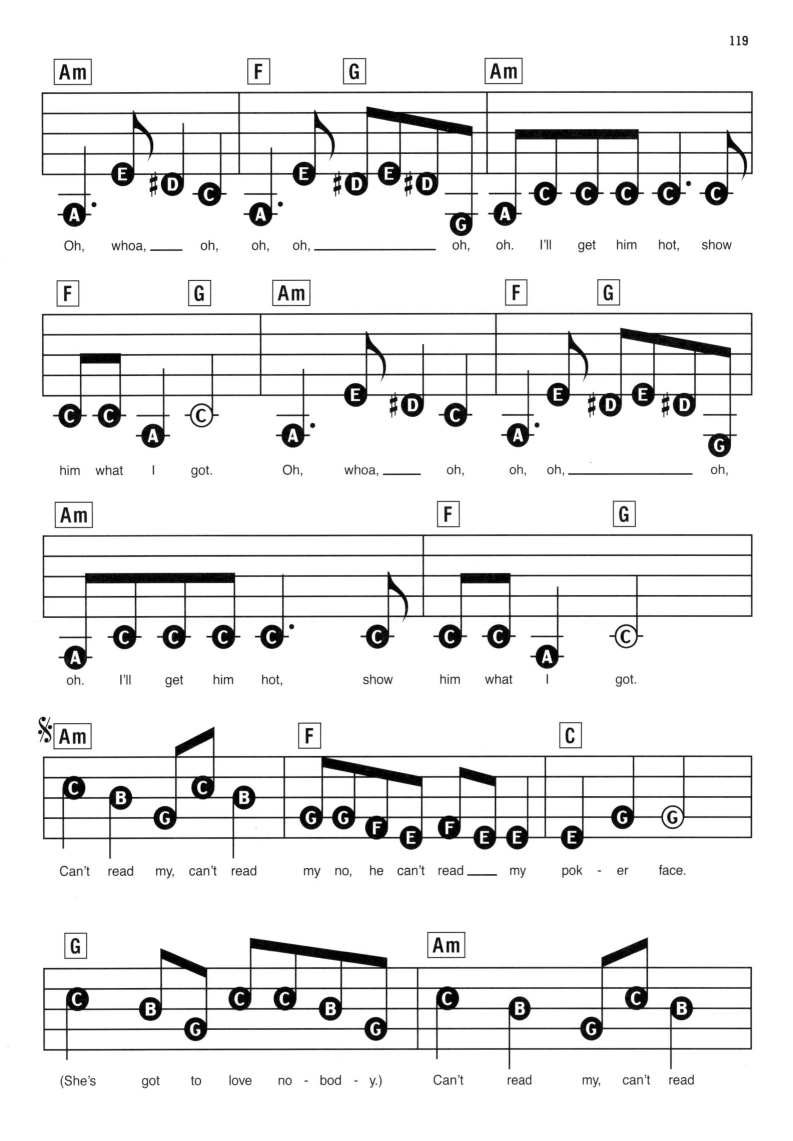

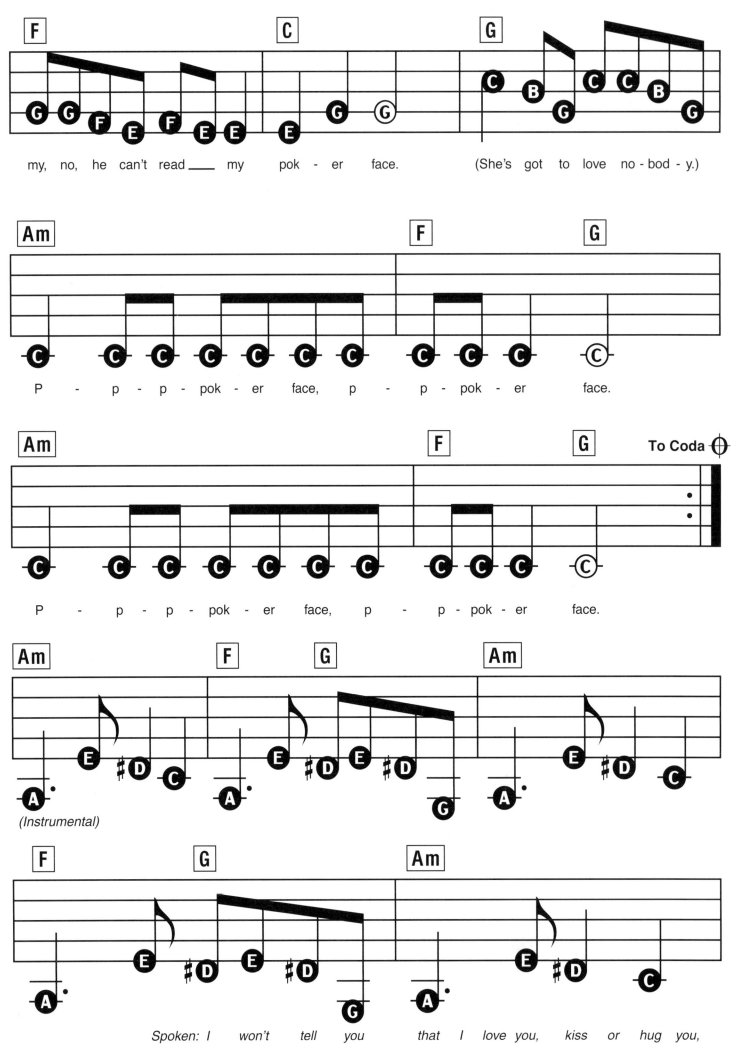

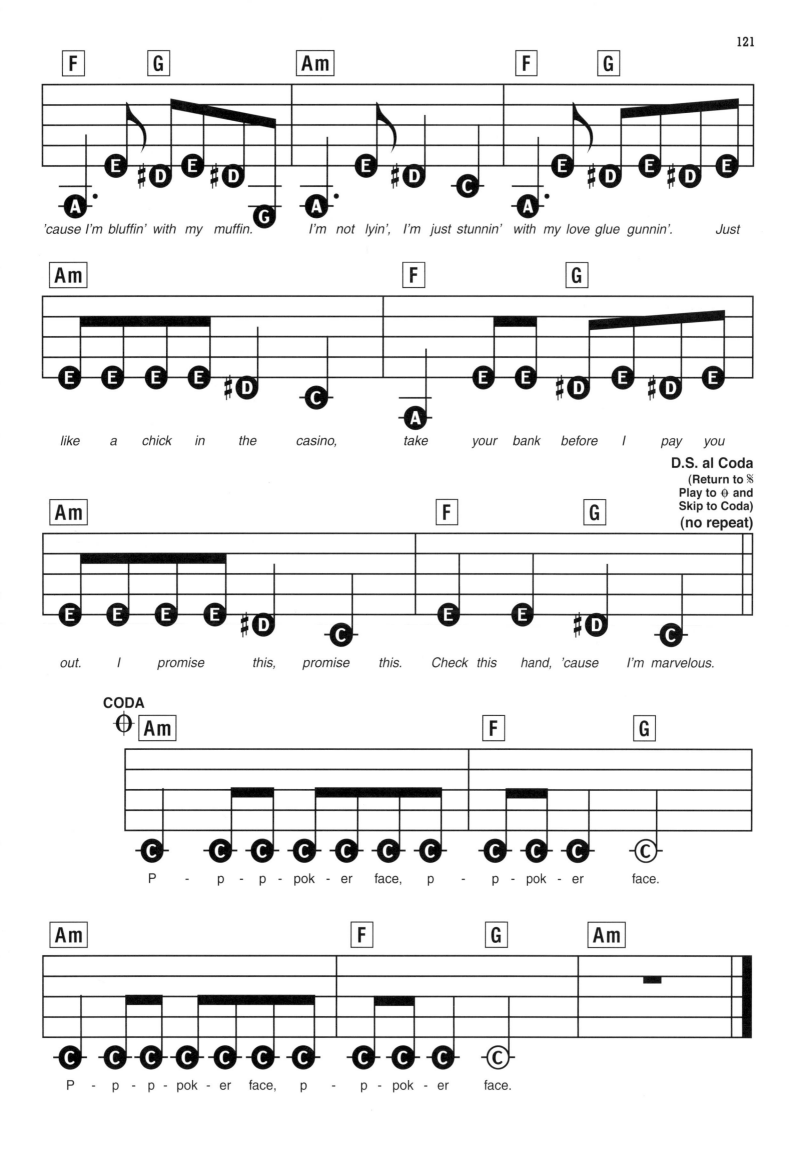

Red, Red Wine

Registration 2
Rhythm: Country

Words and Music by
Neil Diamond

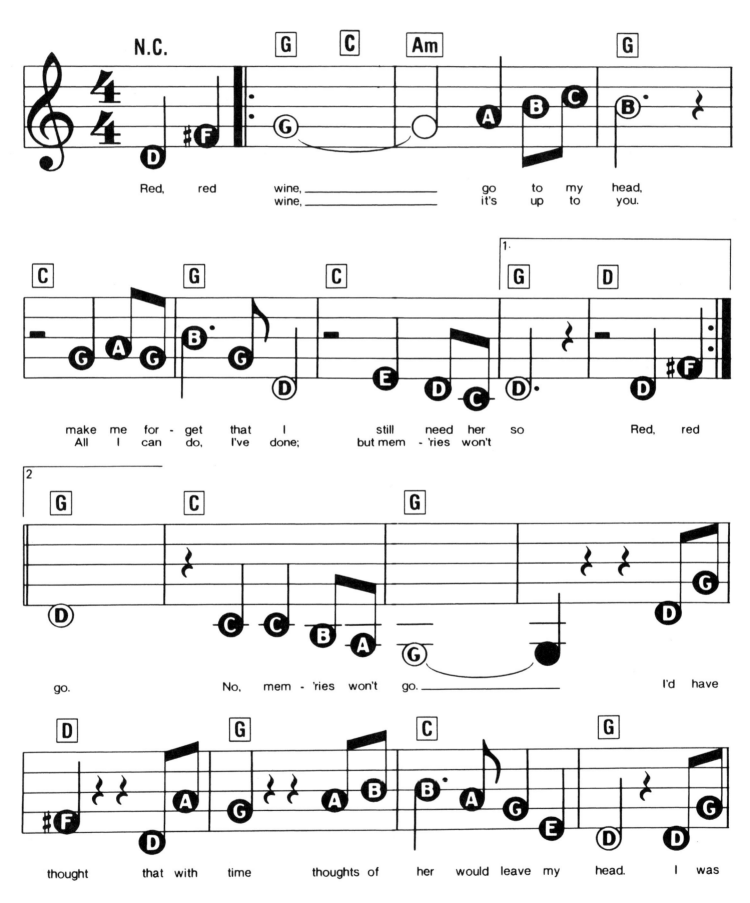

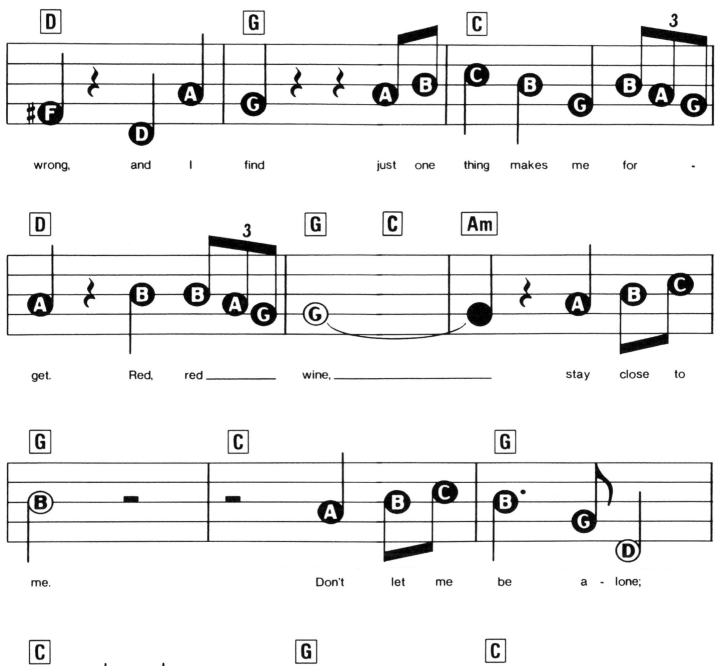

wrong,   and   I   find   just   one   thing   makes   me   for -

get.   Red,   red _____ wine, _____   stay   close   to

me.   Don't   let   me   be   a - lone;

it's   tear - ing   a - part   my   blue,   blue

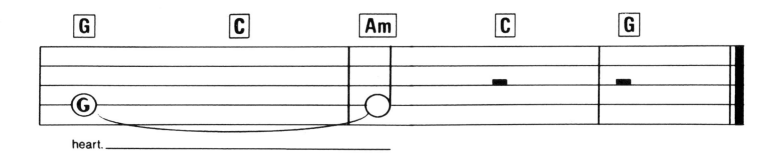

heart. _____

Roar

Registration 1
Rhythm: 8-Beat or Rock

Words and Music by Katy Perry,
Max Martin, Dr. Luke,
Bonnie McKee and Henry Walter

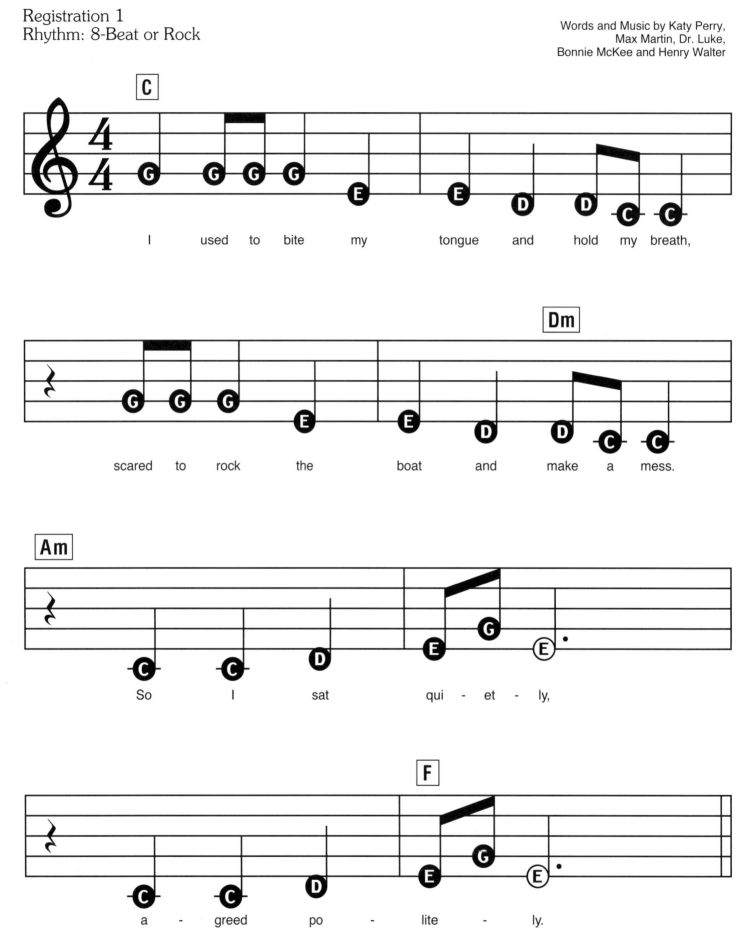

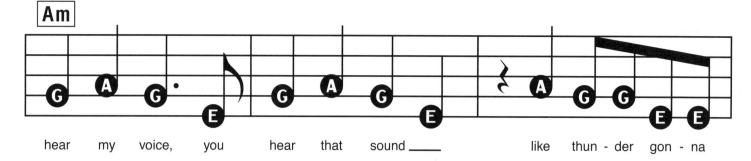

hear my voice, you hear that sound ___ like thun-der gon-na

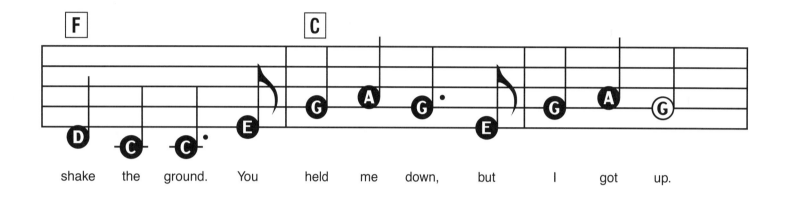

shake the ground. You held me down, but I got up.

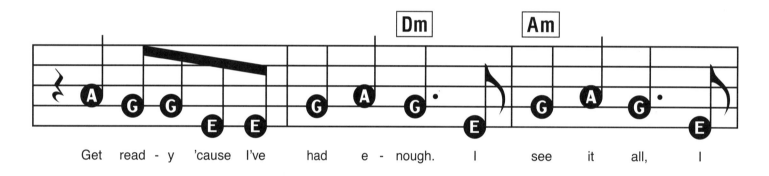

Get read-y 'cause I've had e-nough. I see it all, I

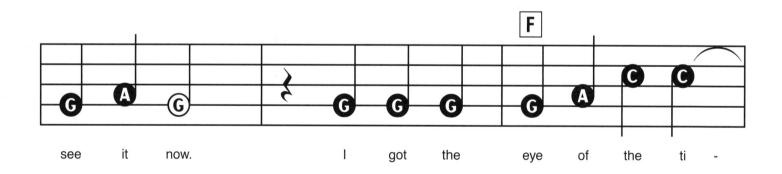

see it now. I got the eye of the ti-

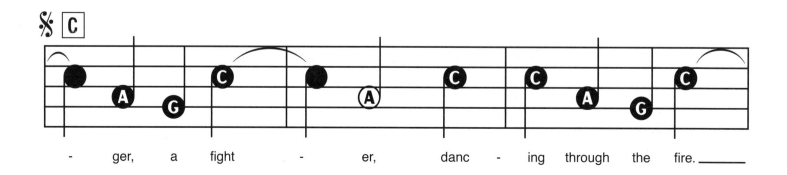

-ger, a fight - er, danc-ing through the fire.___

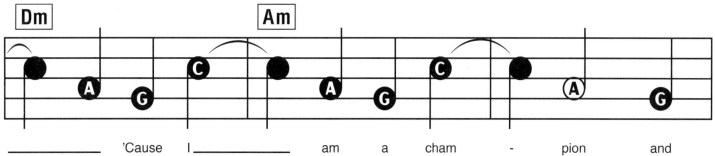

127

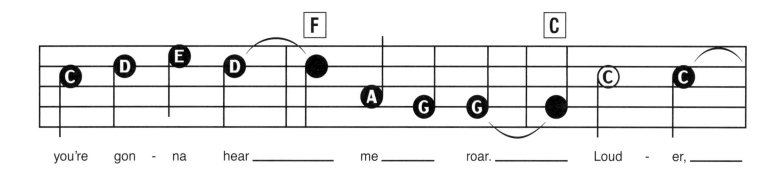

'Cause I _____ am a cham - pion and

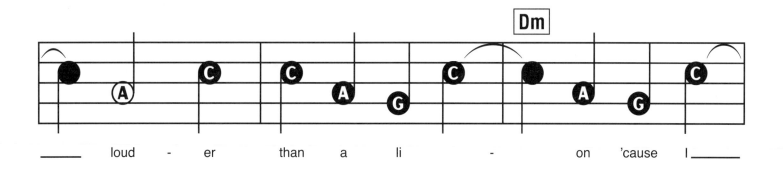

you're gon - na hear _____ me _____ roar. _____ Loud - er, _____

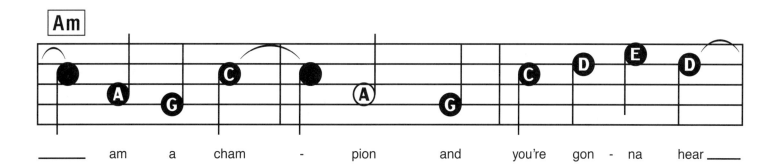

_____ loud - er than a li - on 'cause I _____

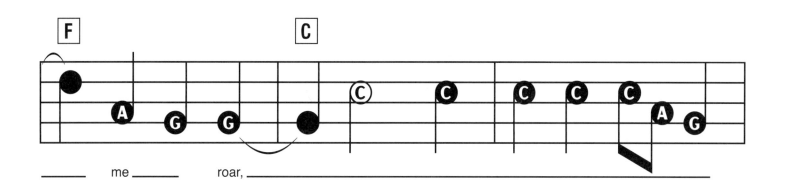

_____ am a cham - pion and you're gon - na hear_____

_____ me _____ roar, _____

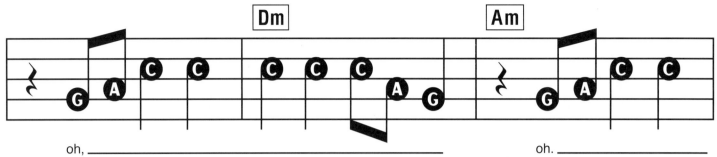

oh, _____ oh. _____

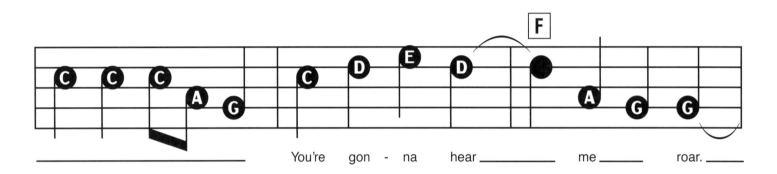

_____ You're gon - na hear _____ me _____ roar. _____

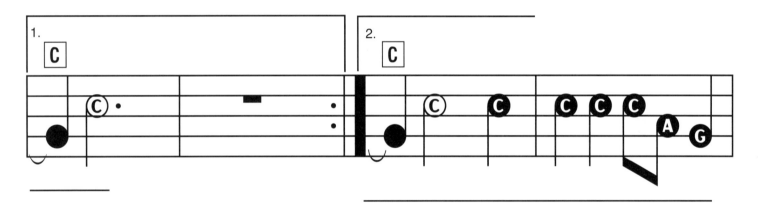

_____ _____

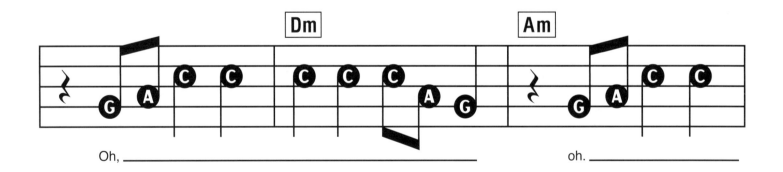

Oh, _____ oh. _____

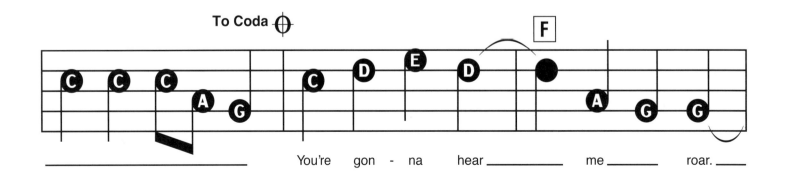

To Coda ⊕

_____ You're gon - na hear _____ me _____ roar. _____

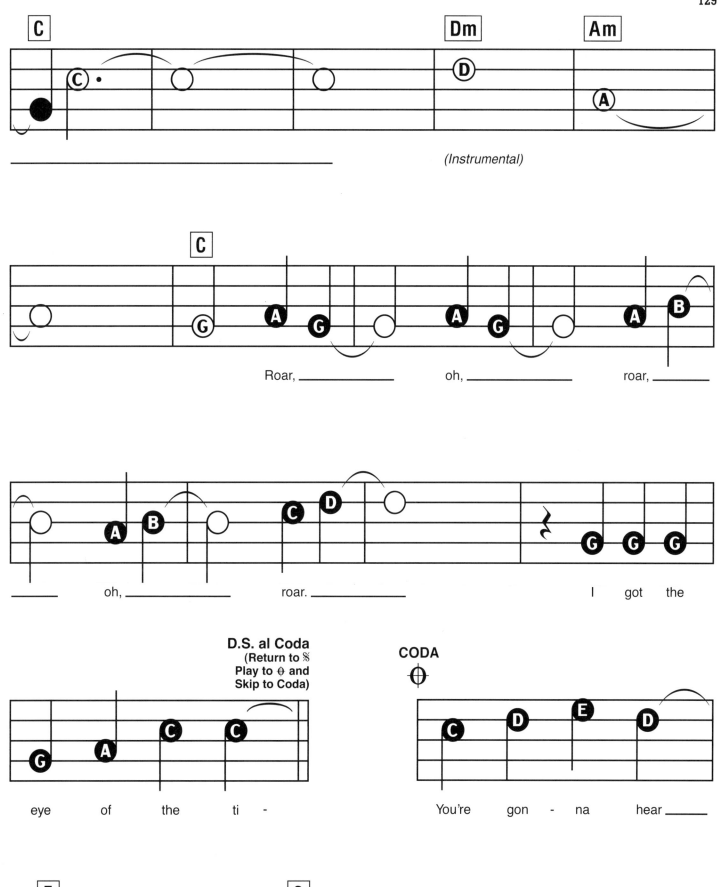

(Instrumental)

Roar, _____ oh, _____ roar, _____

_____ oh, _____ roar. _____ I got the

D.S. al Coda
(Return to 𝄋
Play to ⊕ and
Skip to Coda)

CODA
⊕

eye of the ti -   You're gon - na hear _____

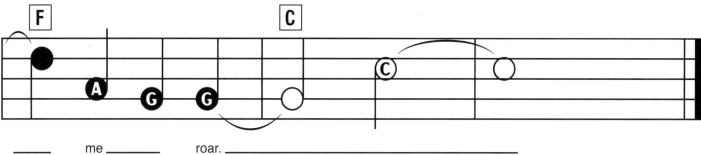

____ me _____ roar. _____

7 Years

Registration 2
Rhythm: Rock or 8-Beat

Words and Music by Lukas Forchhammer,
Morten Ristorp, Stefan Forrest,
David Labrel, Christopher Brown
and Morten Pilegaard

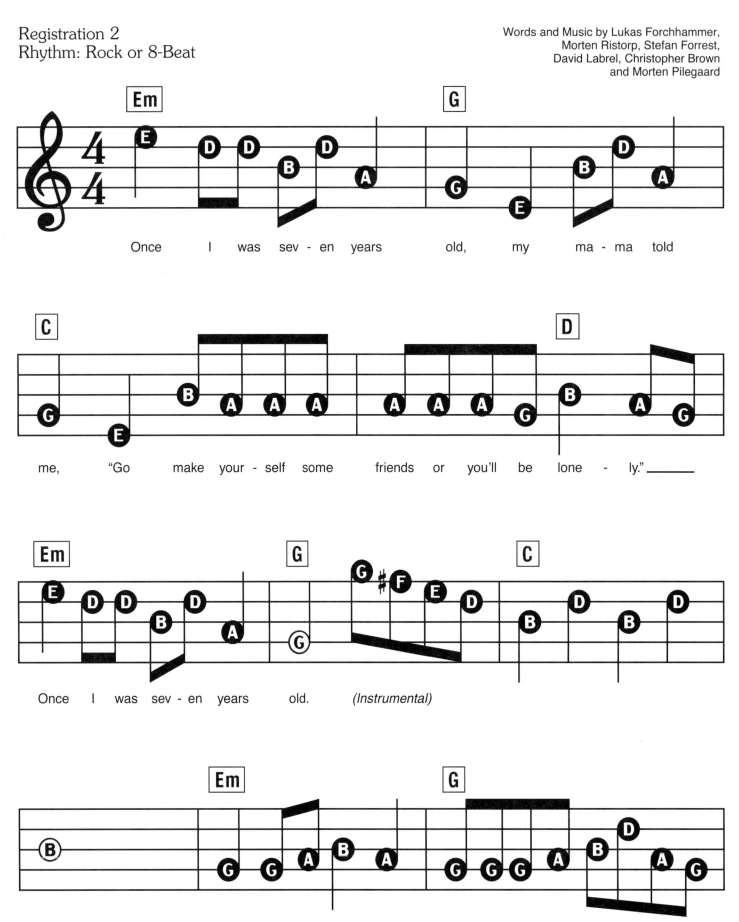

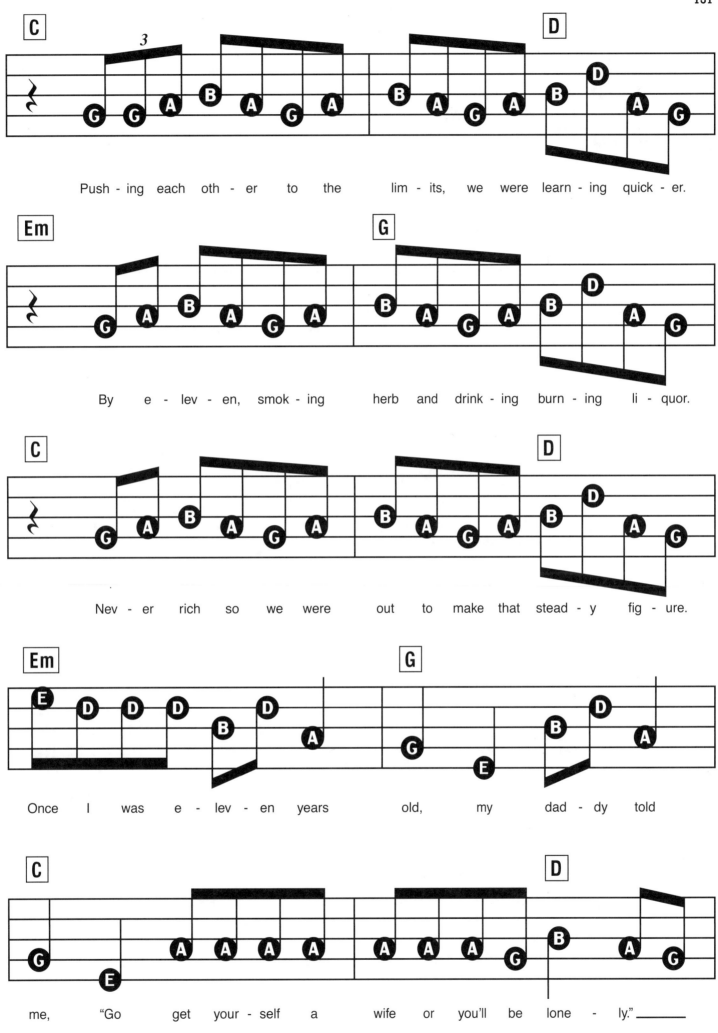

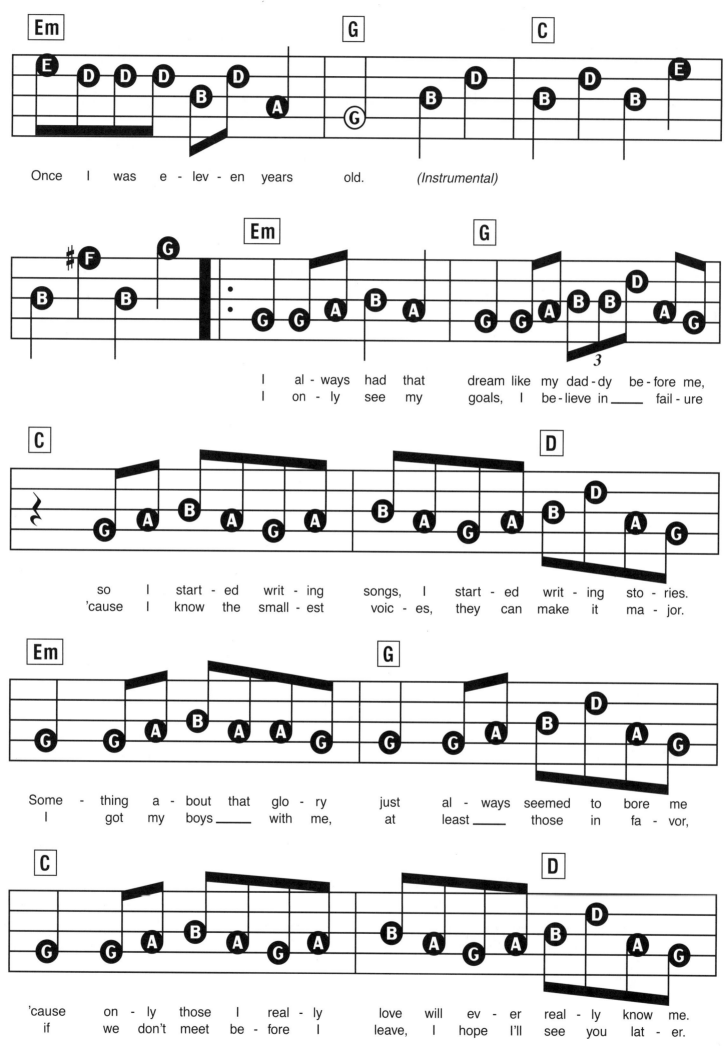

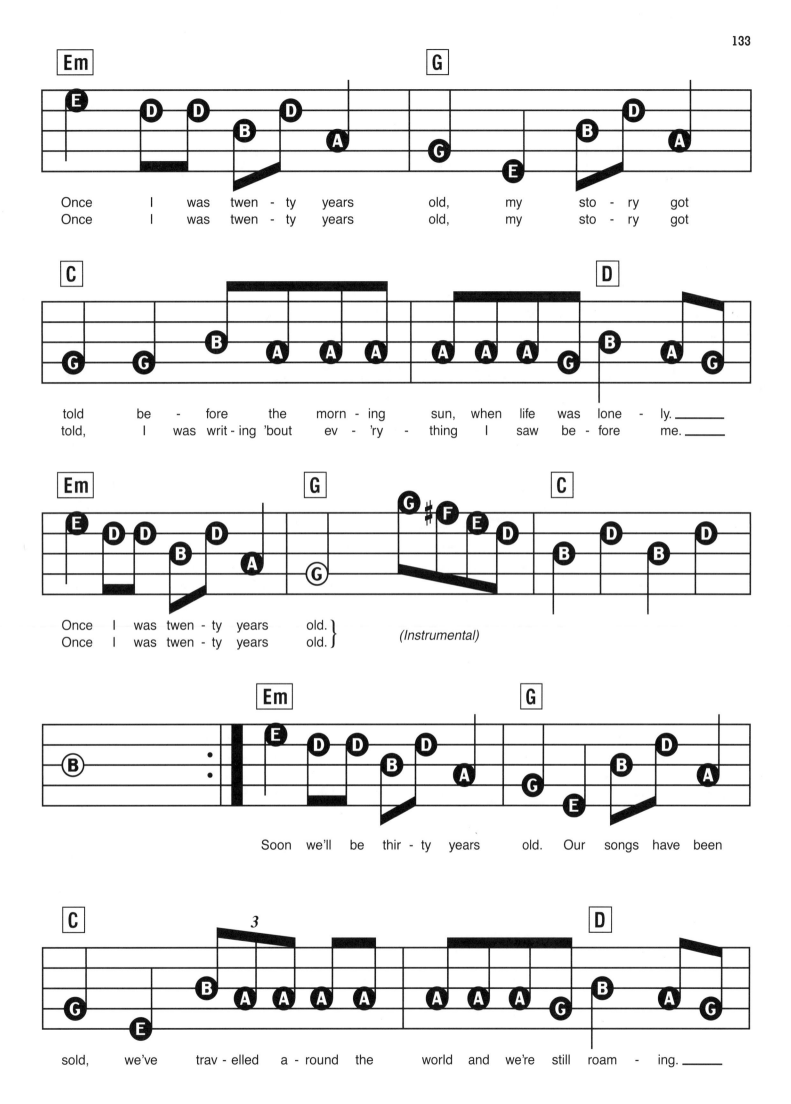

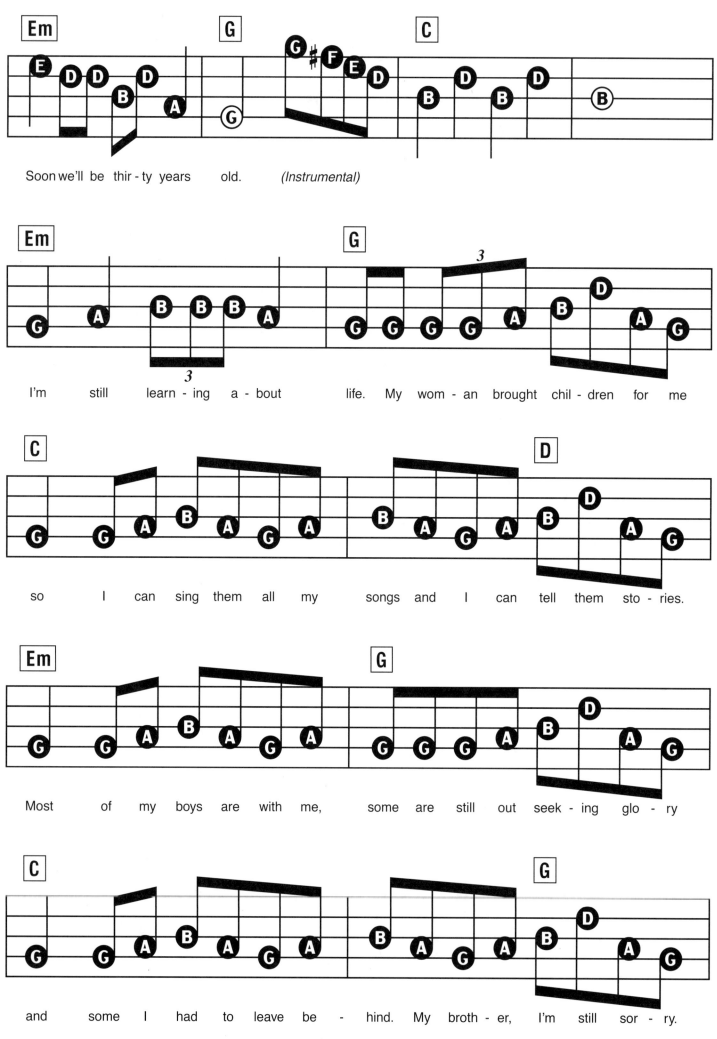

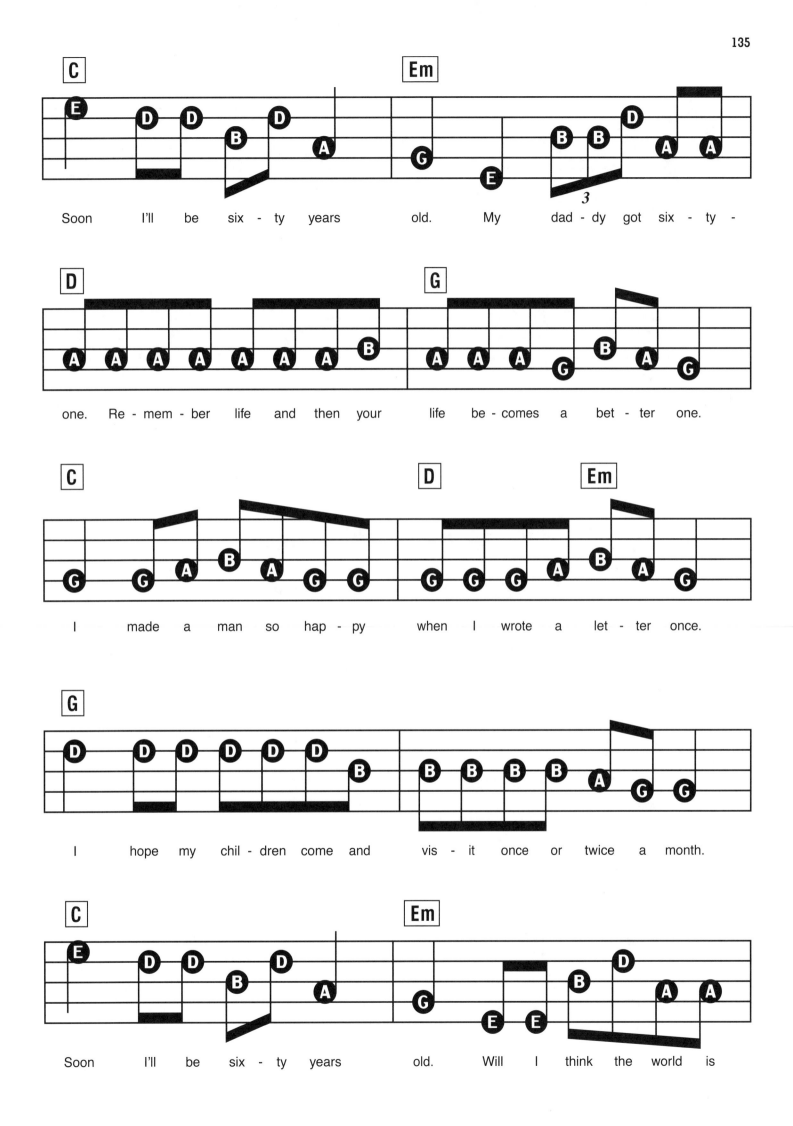

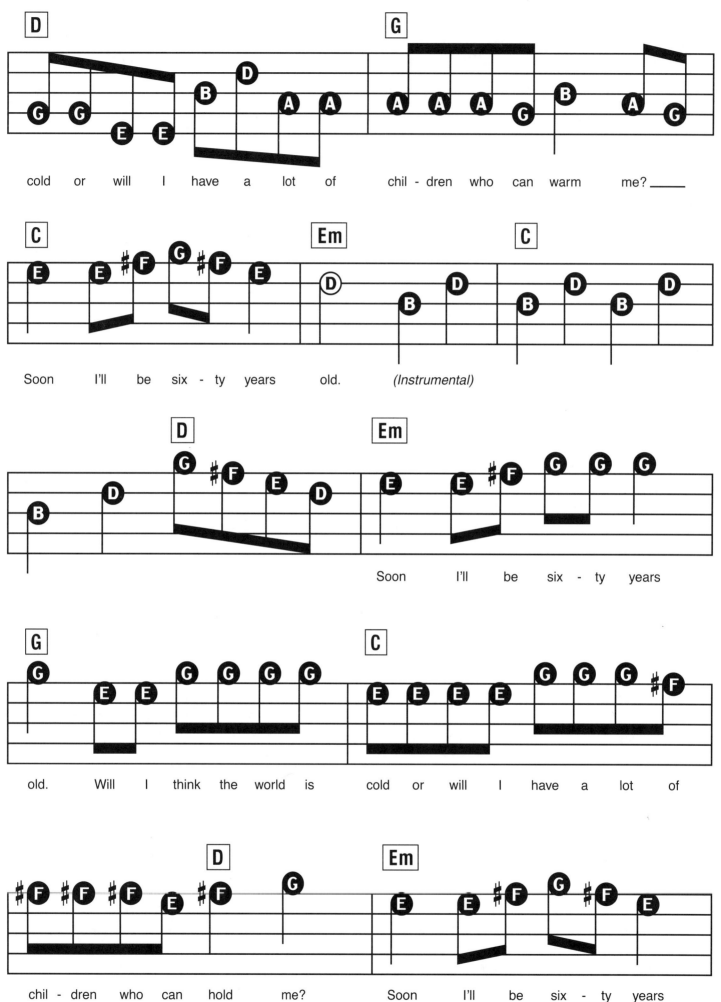

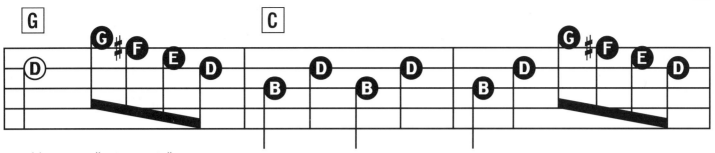

old.   *(Instrumental)*

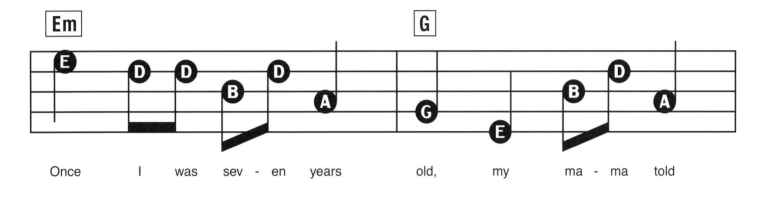

Once   I   was   sev - en   years   old,   my   ma - ma   told

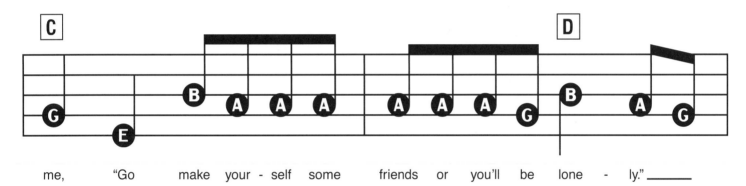

me,   "Go   make   your - self   some   friends   or   you'll   be   lone - ly." _____

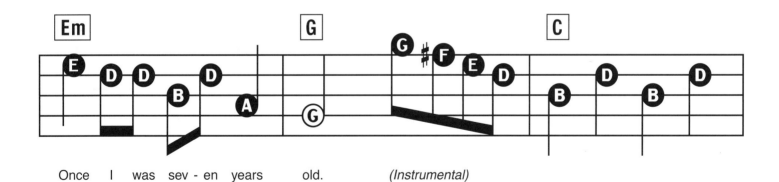

Once   I   was   sev - en   years   old.   *(Instrumental)*

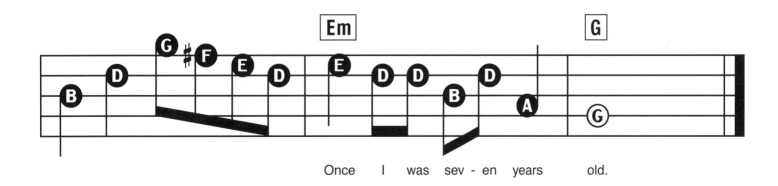

Once   I   was   sev - en   years   old.

Sky Full of Stars

Registration 8
Rhythm: Dance or Rock

Words and Music by Guy Berryman,
Jon Buckland, Will Champion,
Chris Martin and Tim Bergling

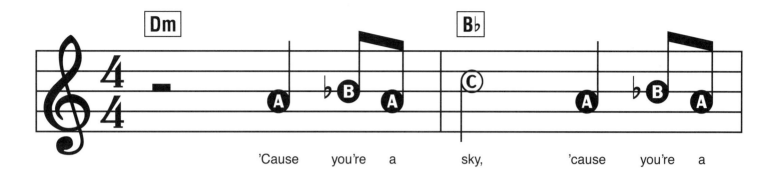

'Cause you're a sky, 'cause you're a

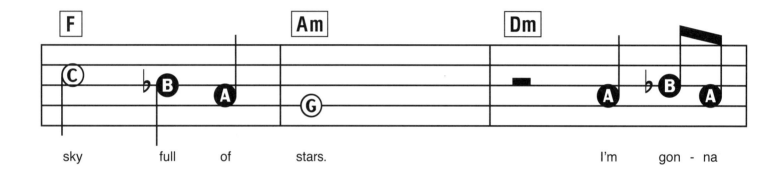

sky full of stars. I'm gon - na

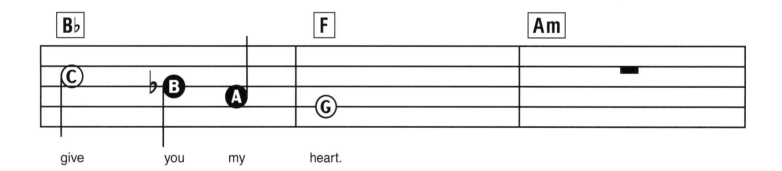

give you my heart.

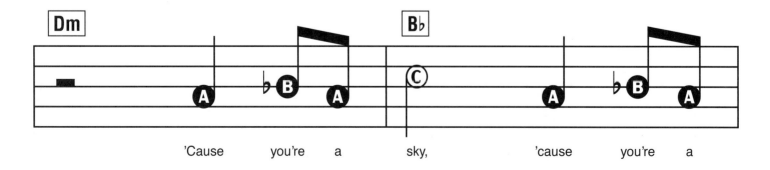

'Cause you're a sky, 'cause you're a

139

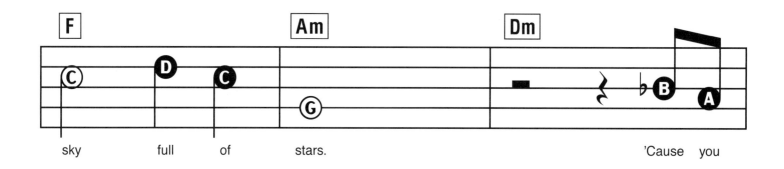

sky   full   of   stars.   'Cause   you

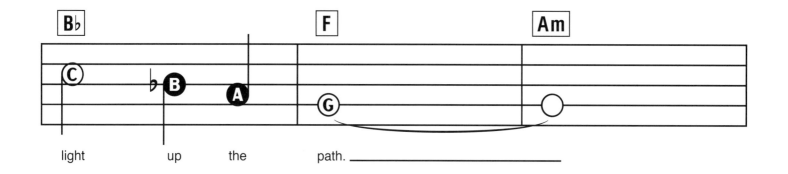

light   up   the   path. _____

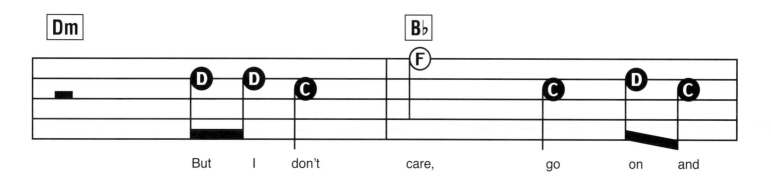

But   I   don't   care,   go   on   and

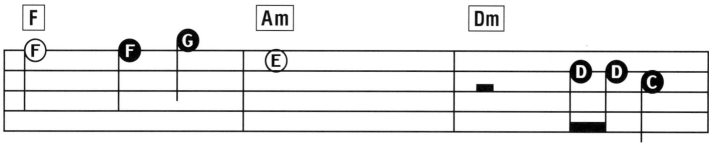

tear   me   a - part.   But   I   don't

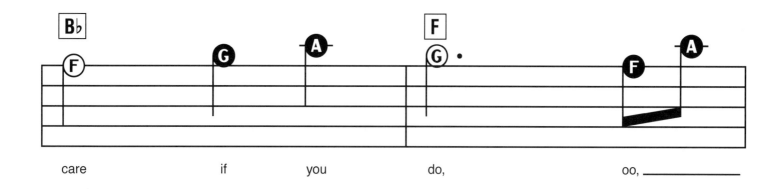

care   if   you   do,   oo, _____

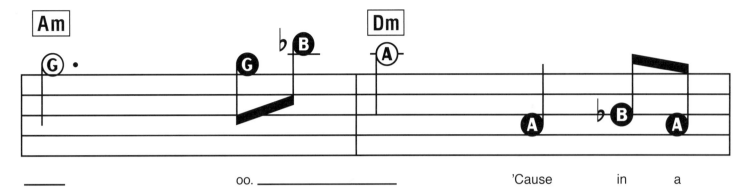

_____ oo. _____ 'Cause in a

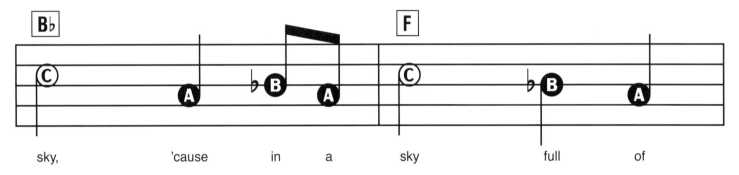

sky, 'cause in a sky full of

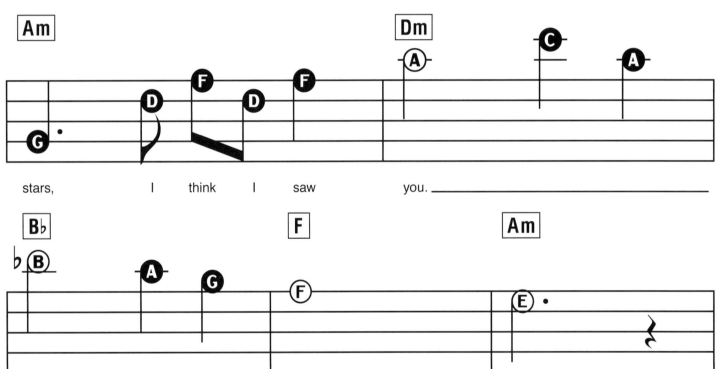

stars, I think I saw you. _____

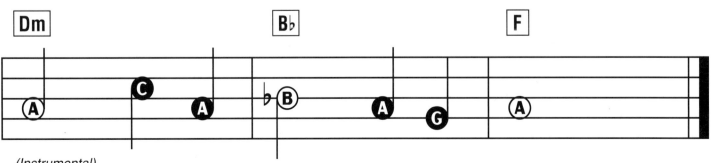

(Instrumental)

Some Nights

Registration 2
Rhythm: March

Words and Music by Jeff Bhasker,
Andrew Dost, Jack Antonoff
and Nate Ruess

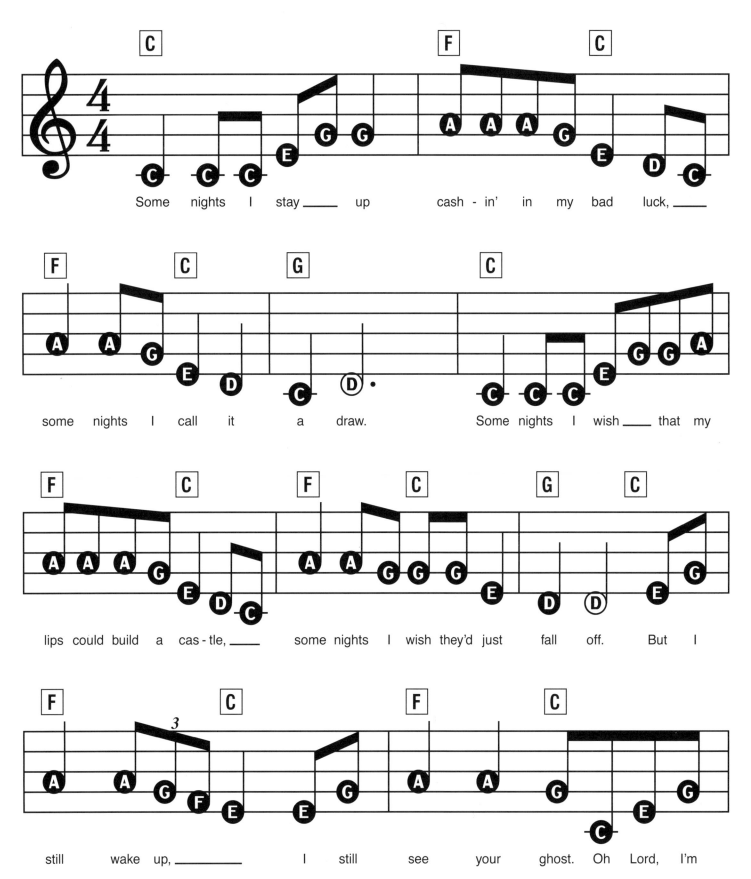

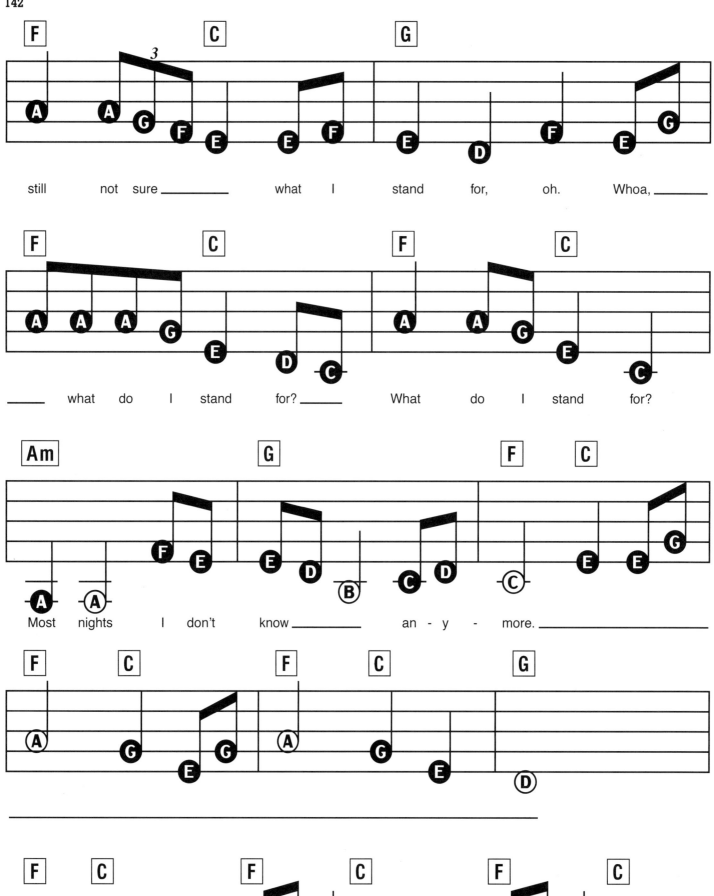

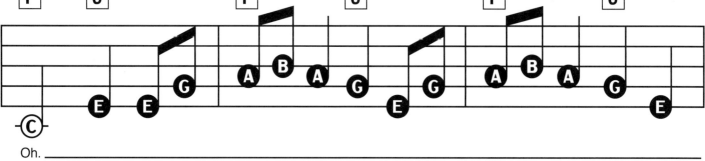

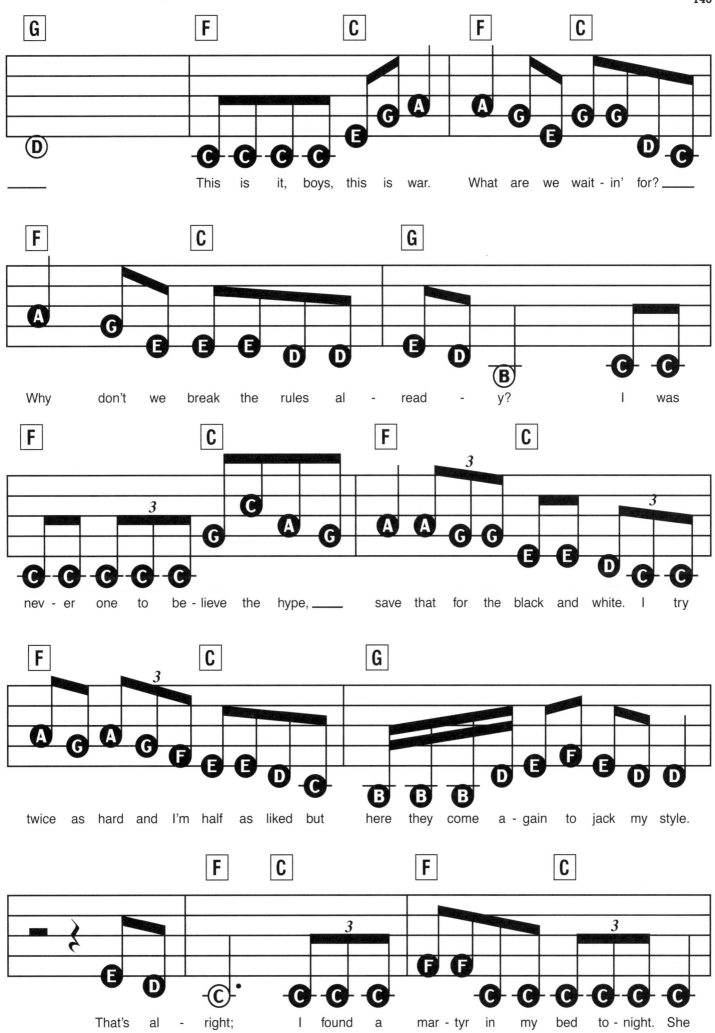

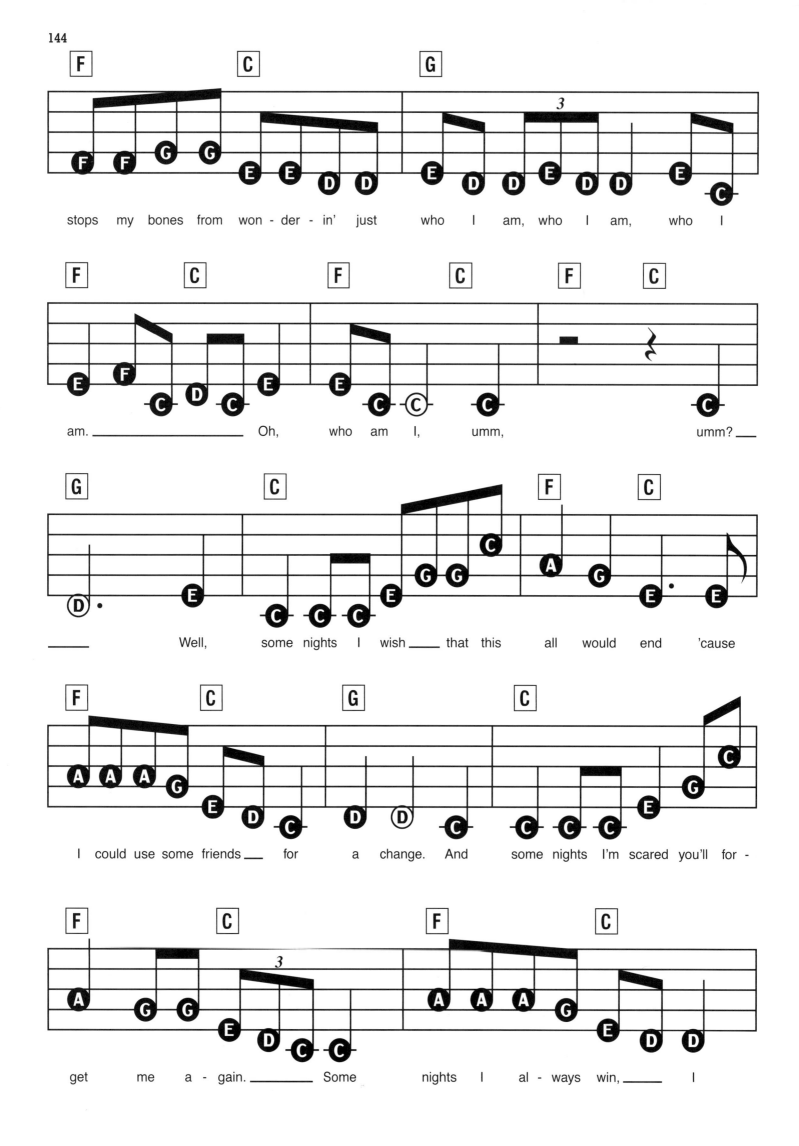

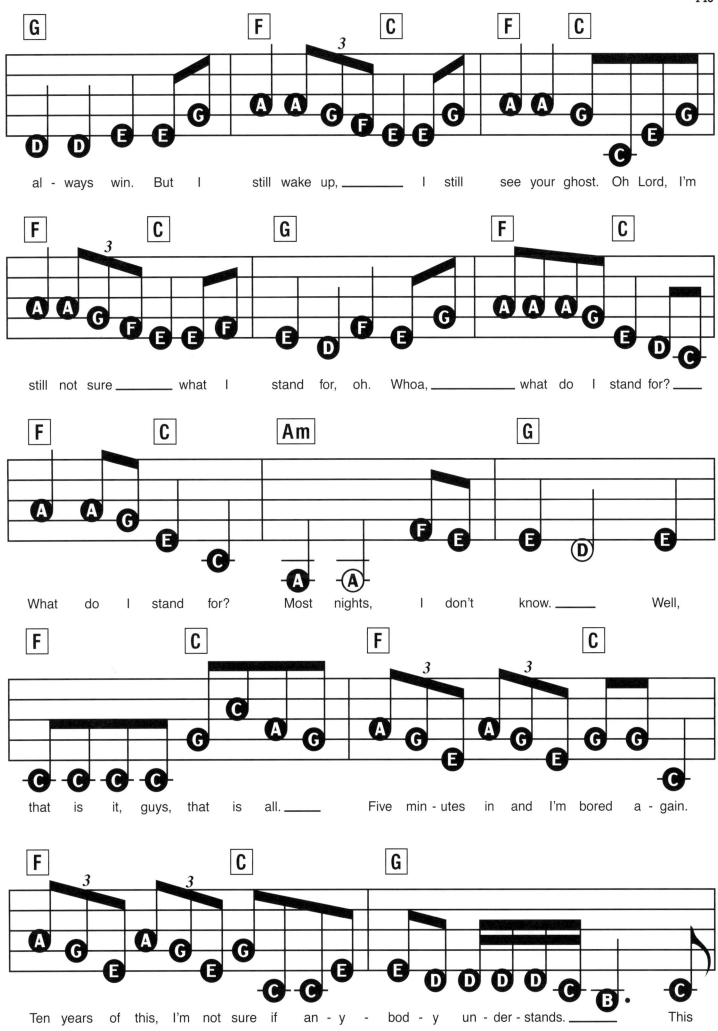

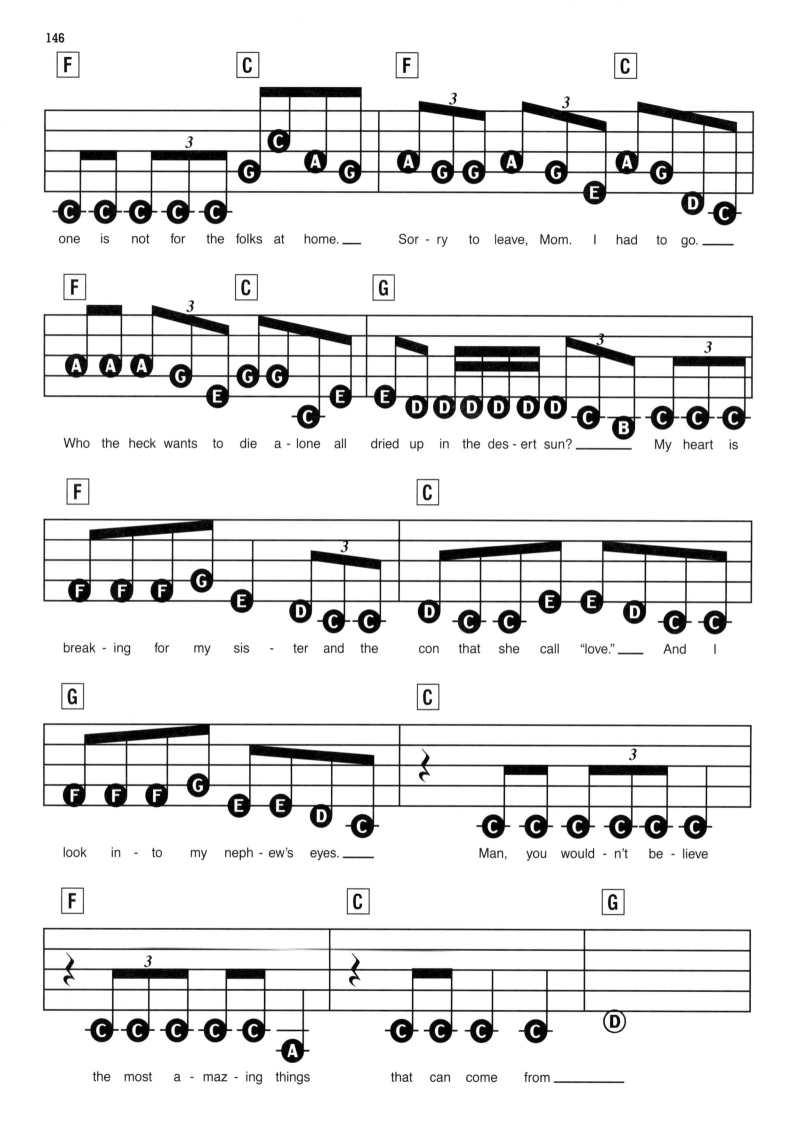

147

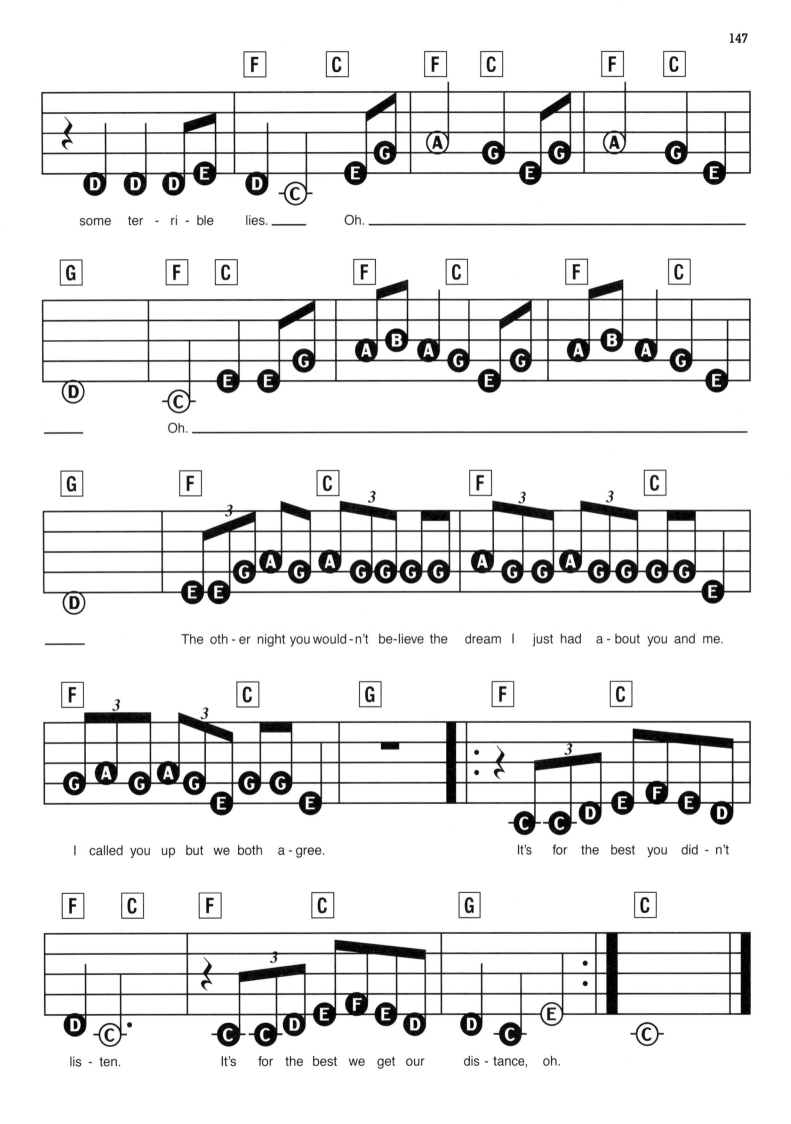

Southern Cross

Registration 1
Rhythm: Rock or Slow Rock

Words and Music by Stephen Stills,
Richard Curtis and Michael Curtis

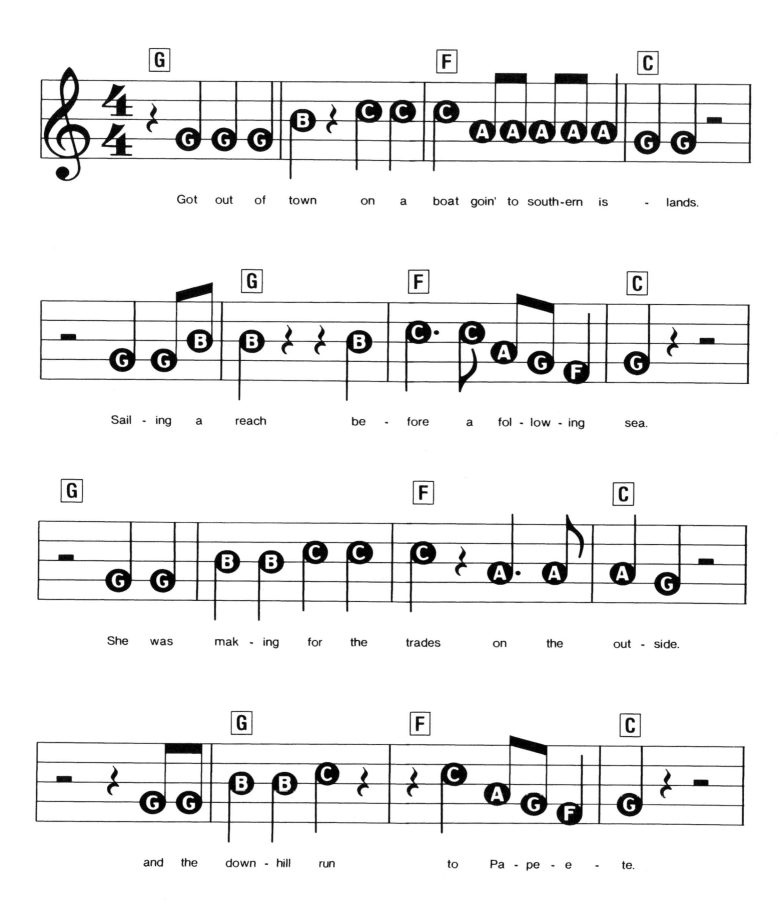

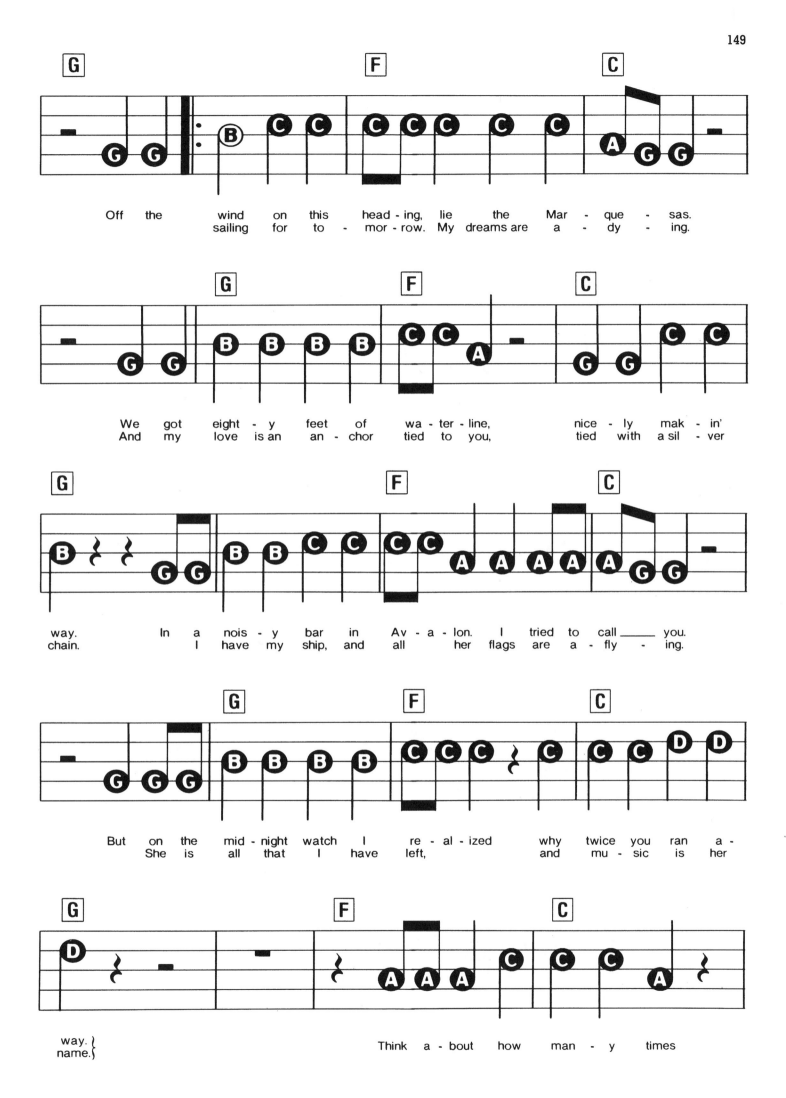

Off the wind on this head - ing, lie the Mar - que - sas.
sailing for to - mor - row. My dreams are a - dy - ing.

We got eight - y feet of wa - ter - line, nice - ly mak - in'
And my love is an an - chor tied to you, tied with a sil - ver

way. In a nois - y bar in Av - a - lon. I tried to call _____ you.
chain. I have my ship, and all her flags are a - fly - ing.

But on the mid - night watch I re - al - ized why twice you ran a -
She is all that I have left, and mu - sic is her

way. }
name. }

Think a - bout how man - y times

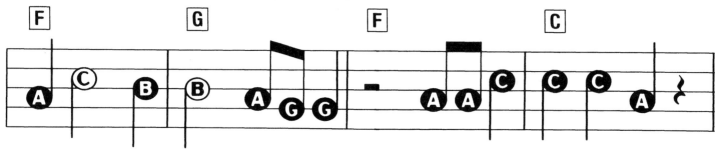

I have fall - en. Spir - its are us - in' me;

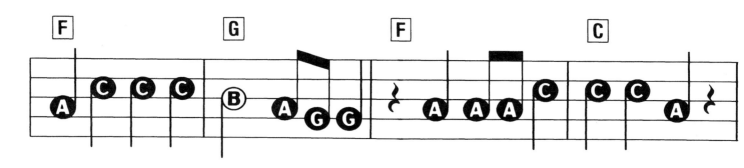

larg - er voic - es call - in'. What heav - en brought you and me

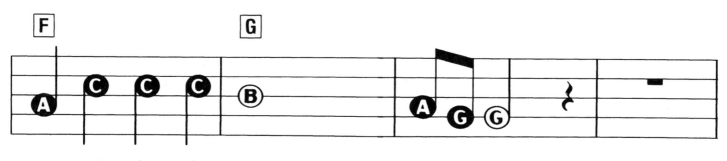

can - not be for - got - ten.

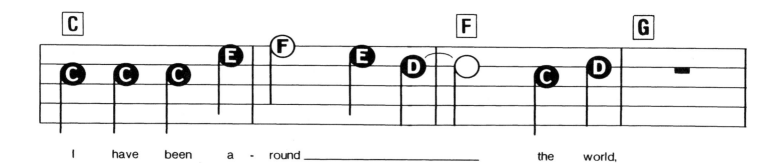
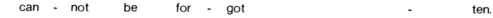

I have been a - round _____ the world,

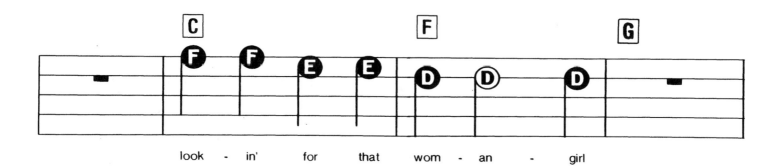

look - in' for that wom - an - girl

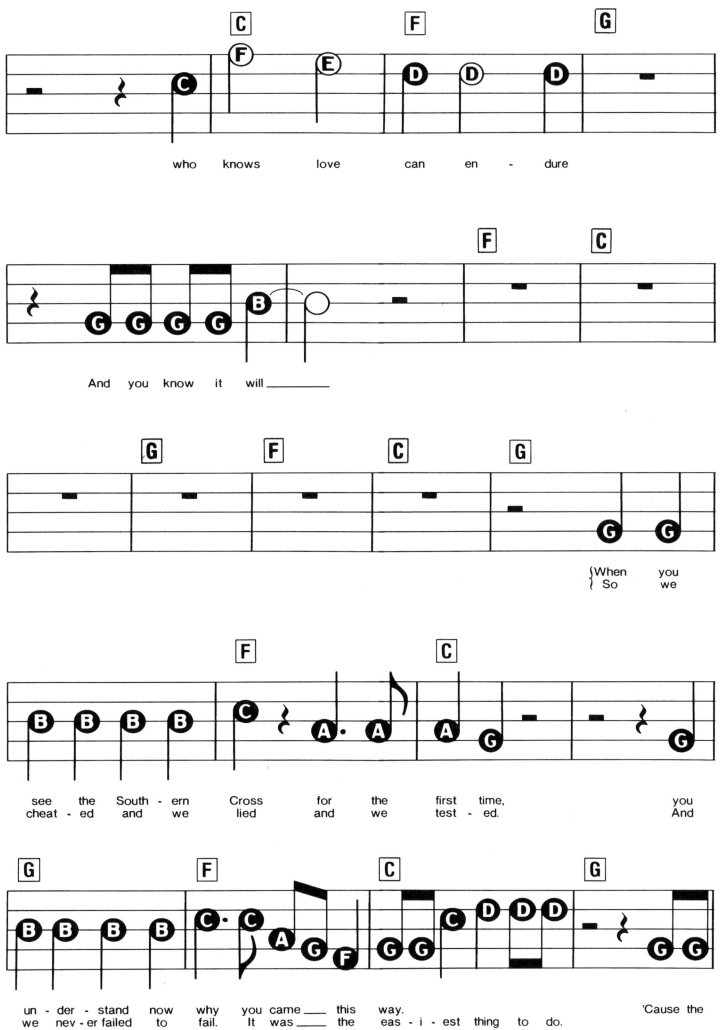

152

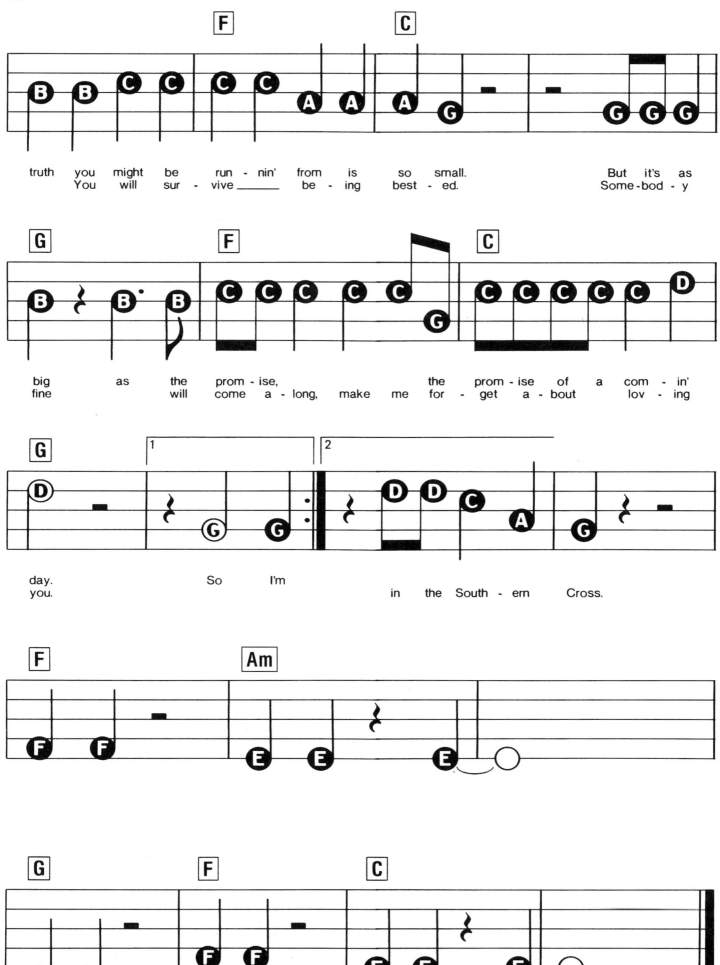

Toes

Registration 4
Rhythm: Country Rock

Words and Music by Shawn Mullins,
Zac Brown, Wyatt Durrette
and John Driskell Hopkins

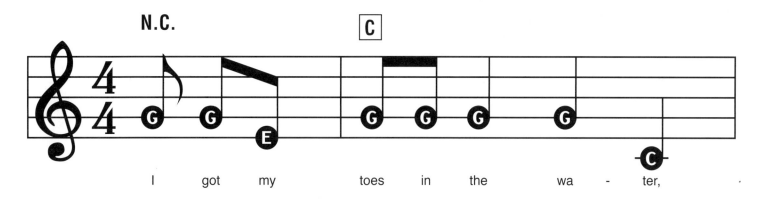

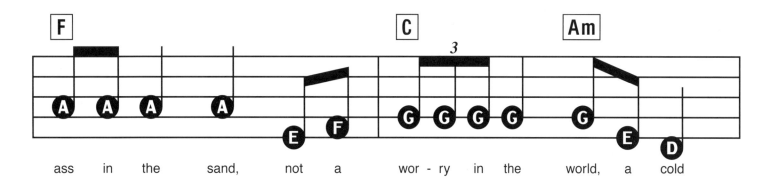

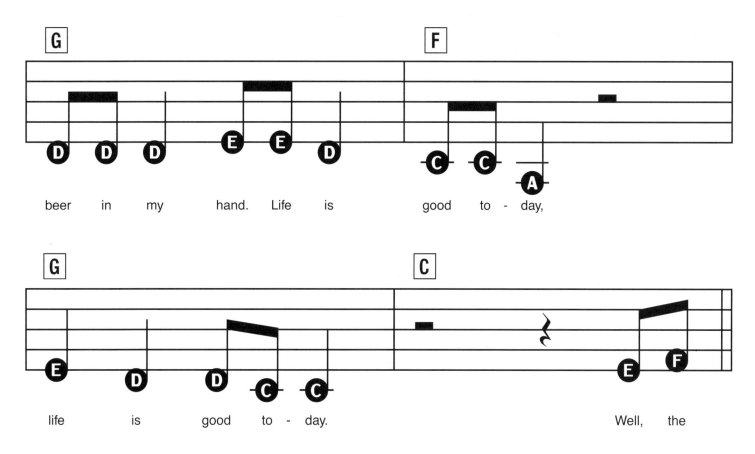

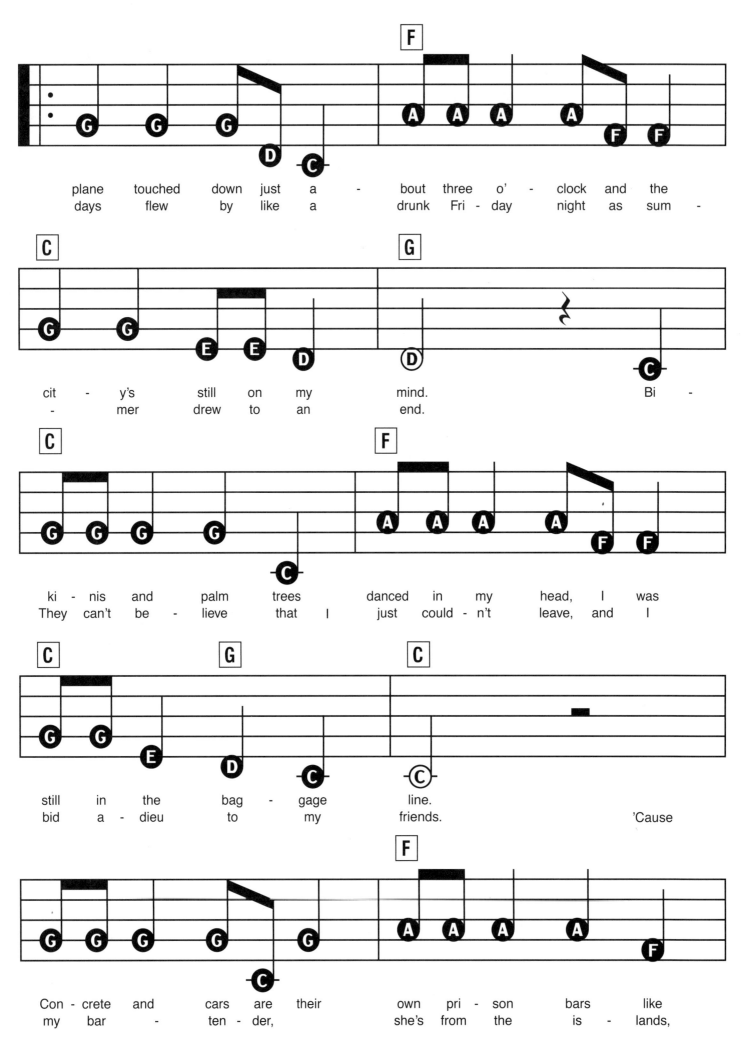

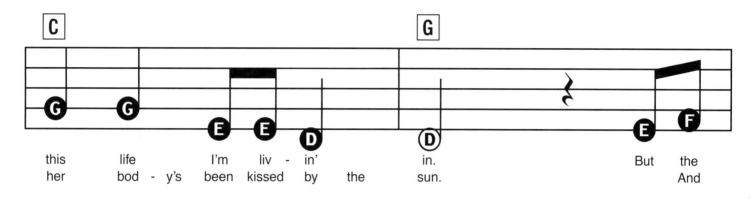

this life I'm liv - in' in. But the
her bod - y's been kissed by the sun. And

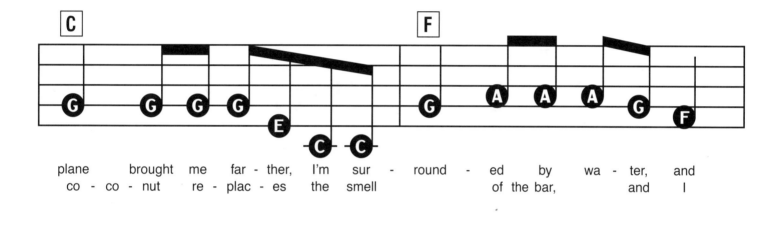

plane brought me far - ther, I'm sur - round - ed by wa - ter, and
co - co - nut re - plac - es the smell of the bar, and I

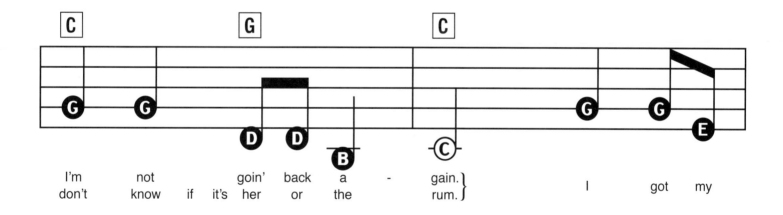

I'm not goin' back a - gain. } I got my
don't know if it's her or the rum. }

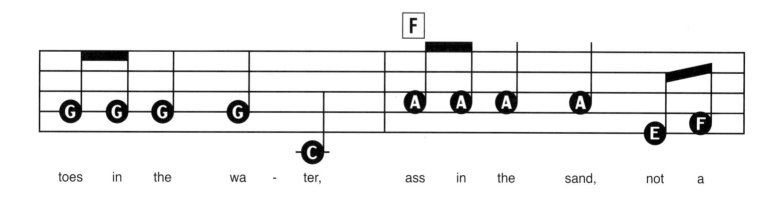

toes in the wa - ter, ass in the sand, not a

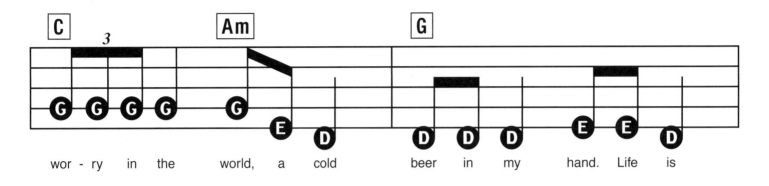

wor - ry in the world, a cold beer in my hand. Life is

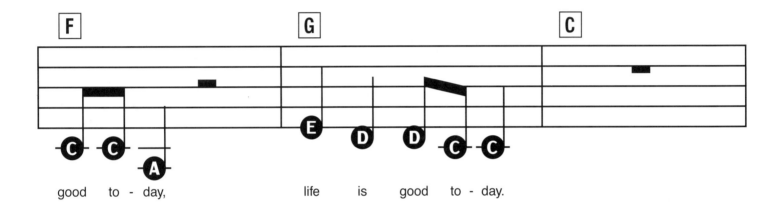

good to - day, life is good to - day.

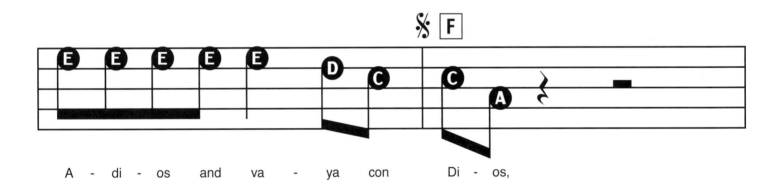

A - di - os and va - ya con Di - os,

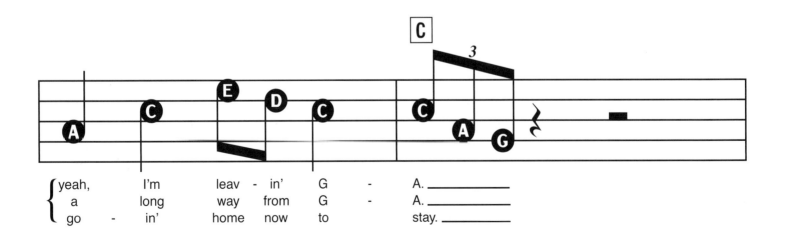

yeah, I'm leav - in' G - A. _____
a long way from G - A. _____
go - in' home now to stay. _____

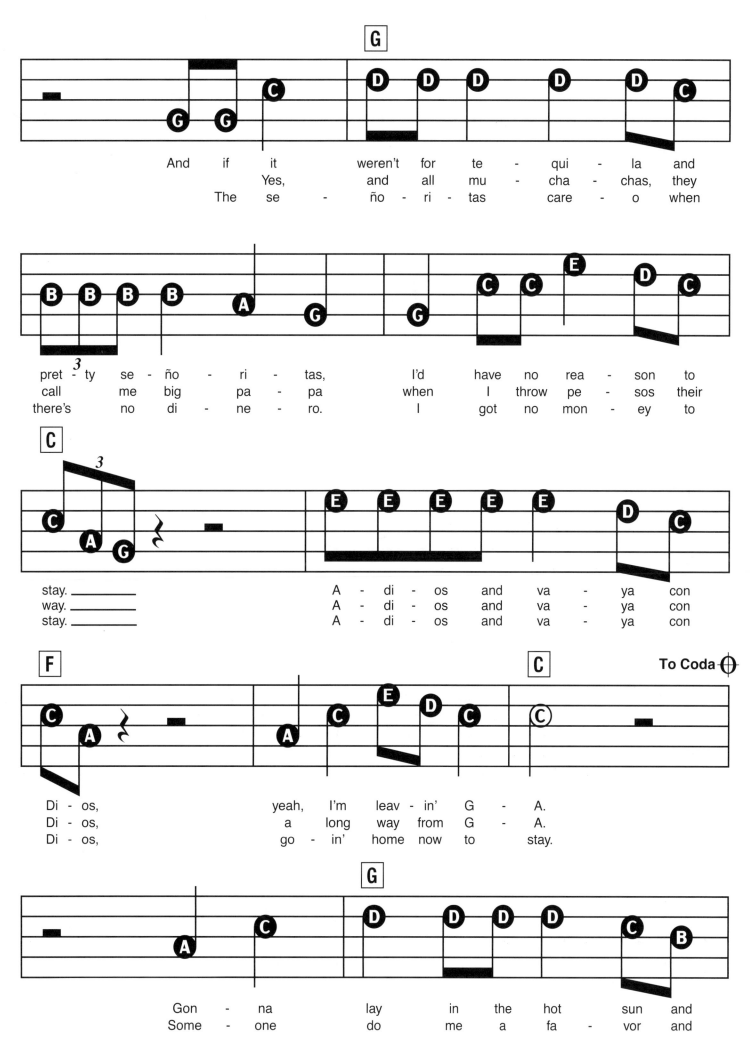

158

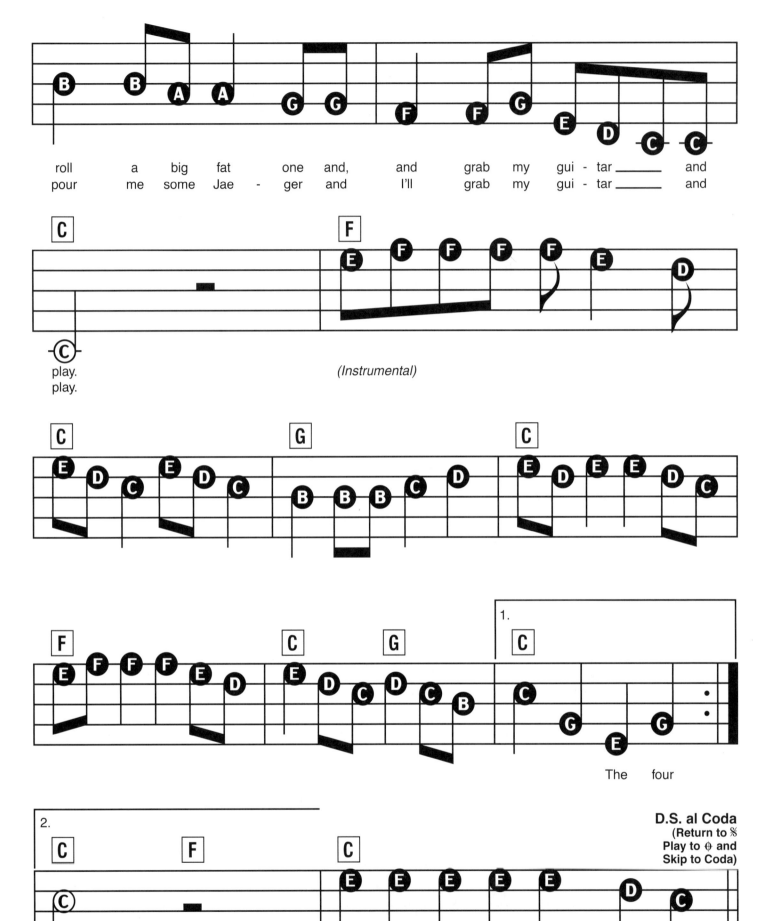

roll   a   big   fat   one and,   and   grab my   gui - tar_____ and
pour   me   some Jae - ger and   I'll   grab my   gui - tar_____ and

play.
play.

(Instrumental)

1.

The   four

2.

D.S. al Coda
(Return to 𝄋
Play to ⊕ and
Skip to Coda)

A - di - os   and   va - ya   con

CODA
G
C
(Spoken:)
Just gonna drive up by the lake and put my ass in a lawn chair,
F
C
Am
3
toes in the clay, not a wor - ry in the world, a P - B -
G
F
R on the way. Life is good to - day,
G
C
F
C
life is good to - day.

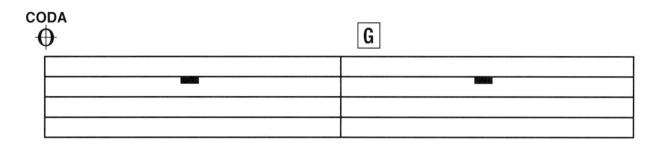

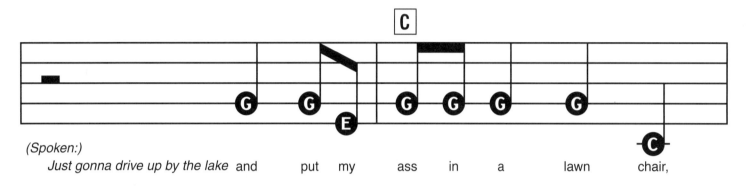

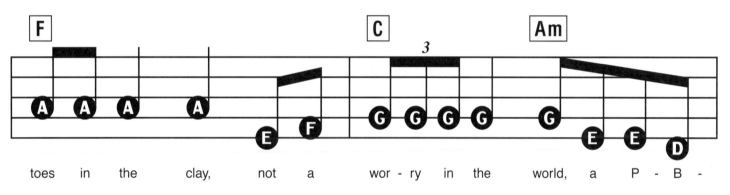

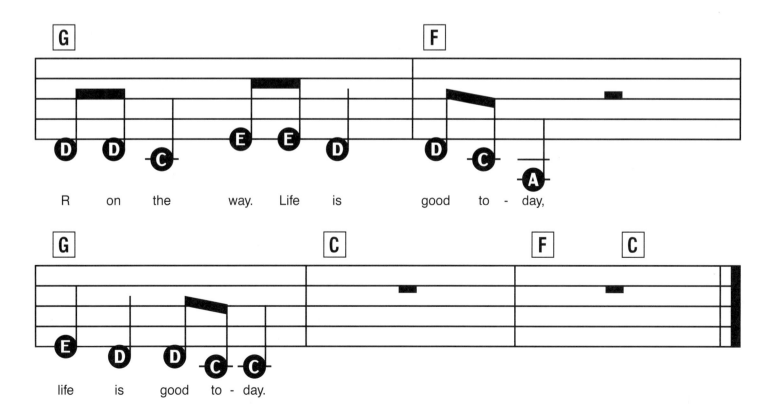

Sunny

Registration: 3
Rhythm: Fox Trot or Ballad

Words and Music by
Bobby Hebb

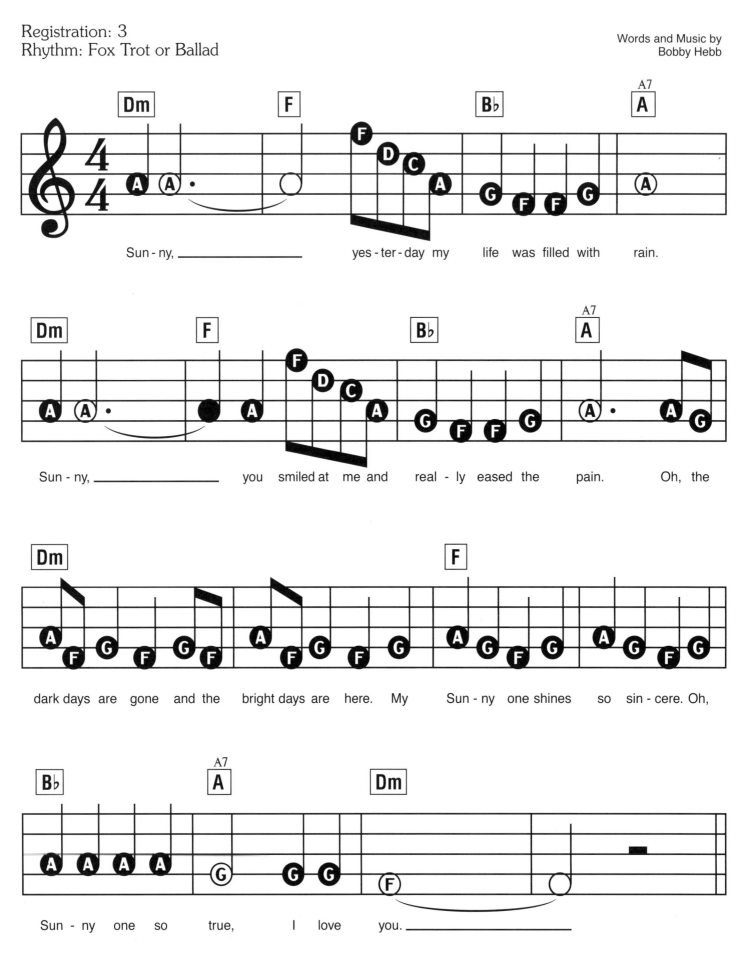

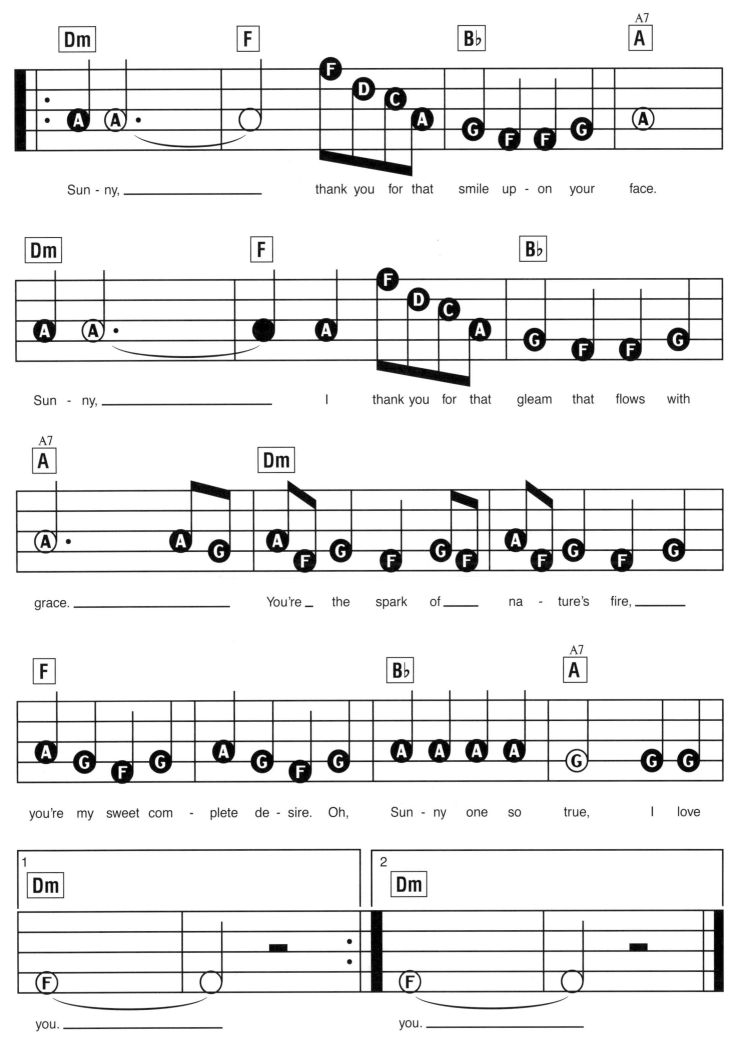

Superman
(It's Not Easy)

Registration 8
Rhythm: Pop or Rock

Words and Music by
John Ondrasik

C   **G**   **Am**

E E C G   D   F E C D

I can't stand to fly.   I'm not that na - iy -
wish that I could cry.   Fall up - on my

F   **C**   **G**   **Am**

D   F E C G   D   C   F E C D

ive.   I'm just out to find the bet - ter part of
knees.   Find a way to lie 'bout a home I'll nev - er

F   **C**   **G**

D C C D E G C C D E G G A C C

me. I'm more than a bird. I'm more than a plane. I'm more than some
see. It may sound ab - surd, but don't be na - ive. E - ven

Am   **1.**   **F**   **C**

F E C F F   E C A C D C   E E

pret - ty face be - side a train. And it's not eas - y to
he - roes have the right

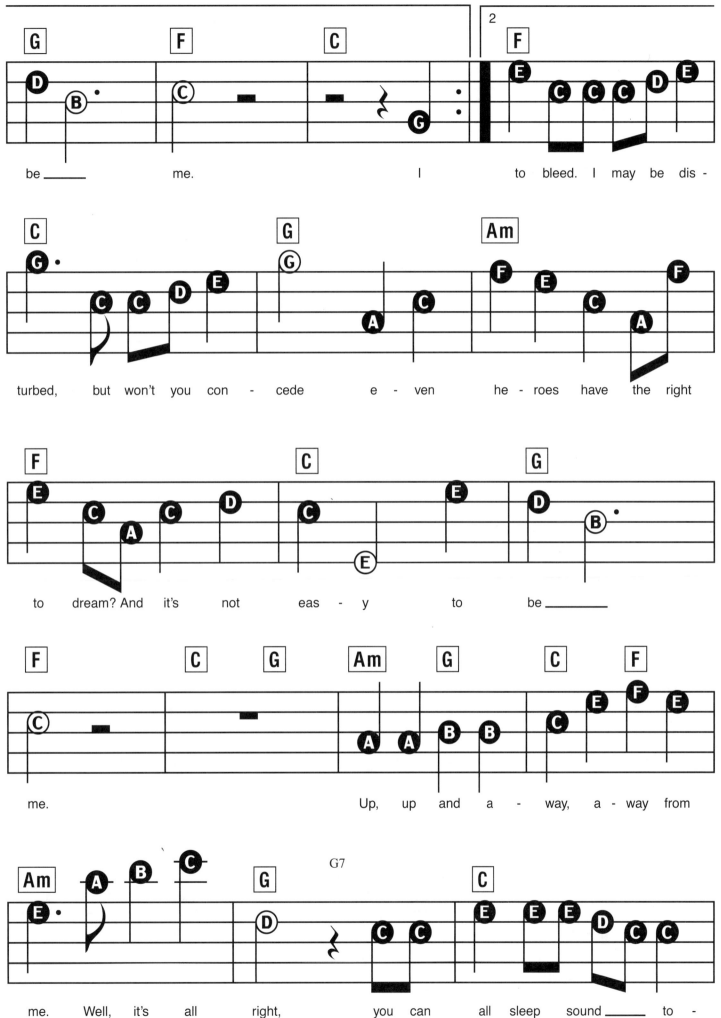

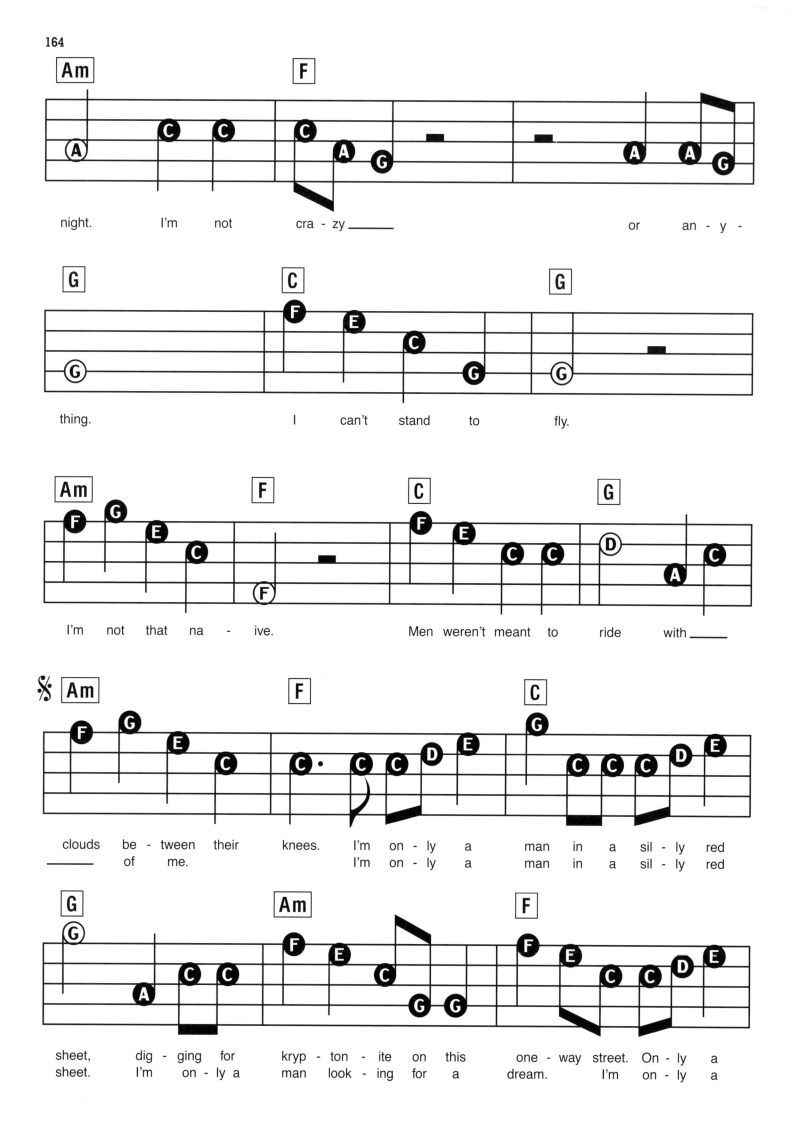

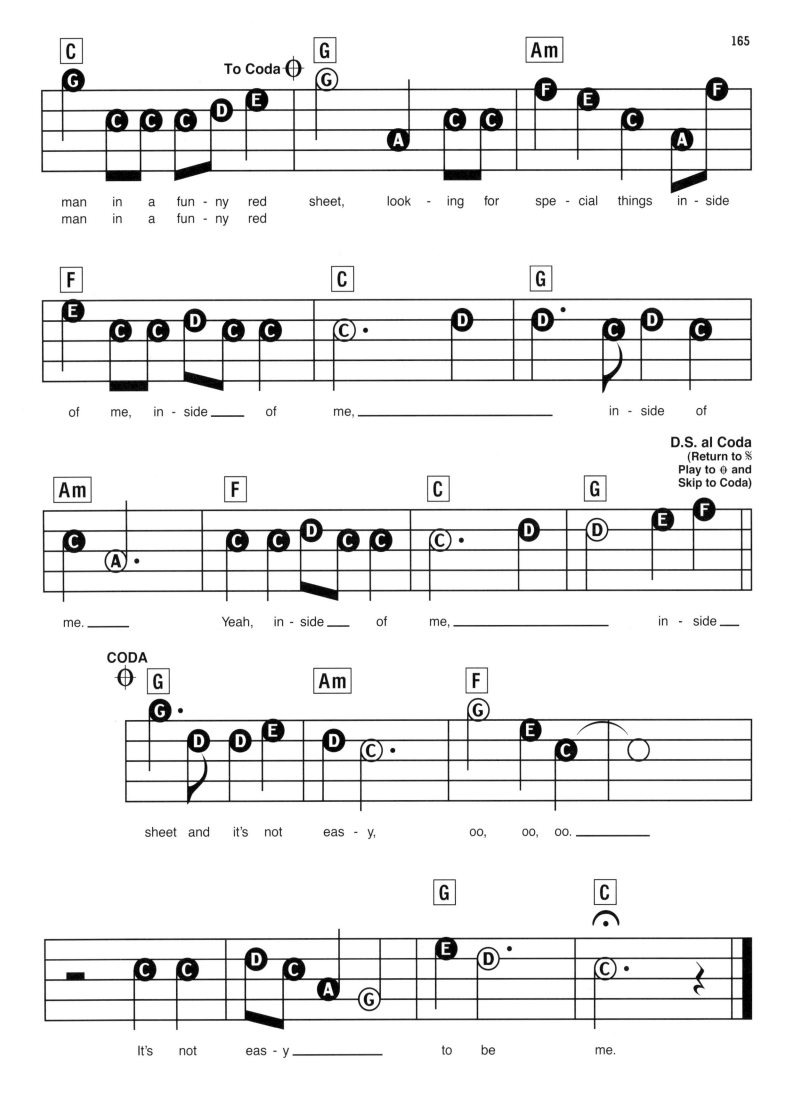

Viva La Vida

Registration 3
Rhythm: Rock or Pop

Words and Music by Guy Berryman,
Jon Buckland, Will Champion
and Chris Martin

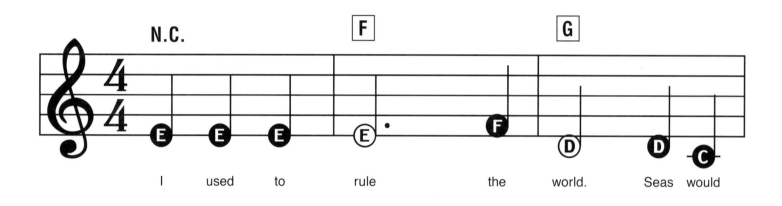

I used to rule the world. Seas would

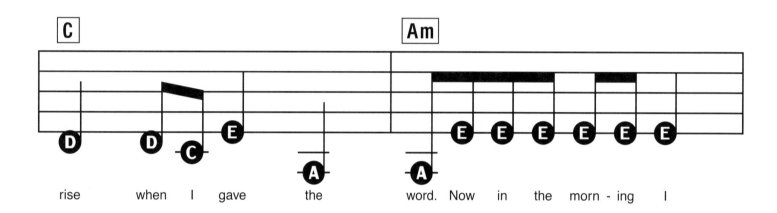

rise when I gave the word. Now in the morn - ing I

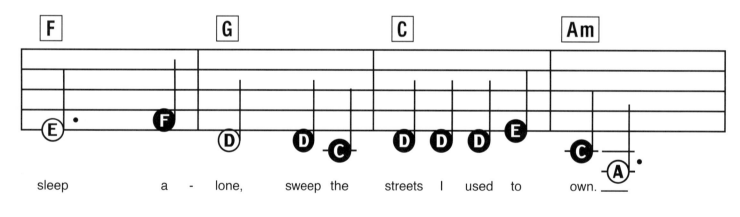

sleep a - lone, sweep the streets I used to own. ___

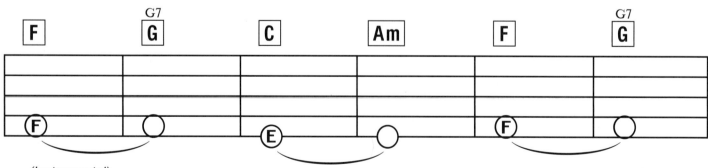

(Instrumental)

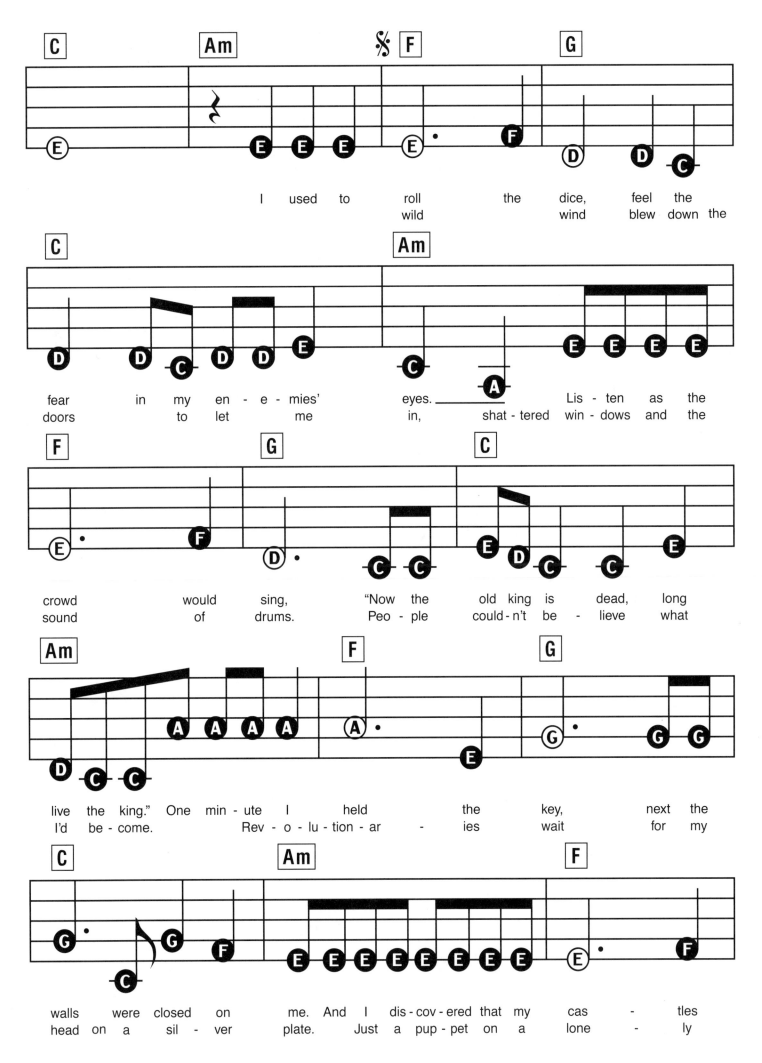

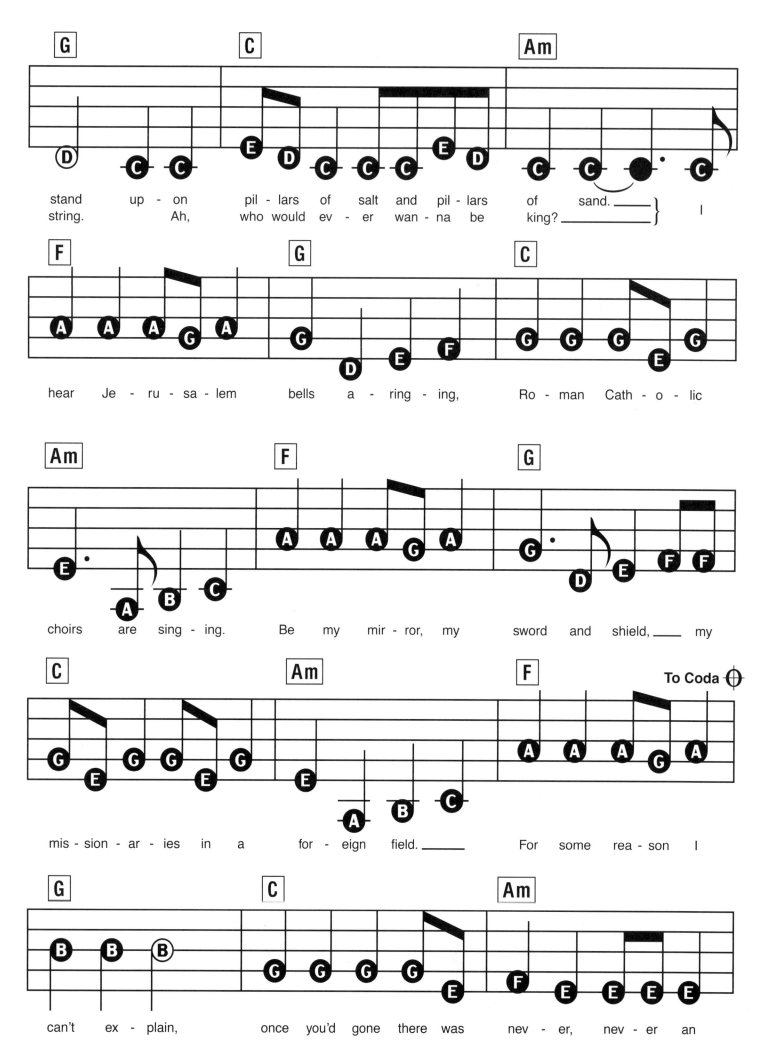

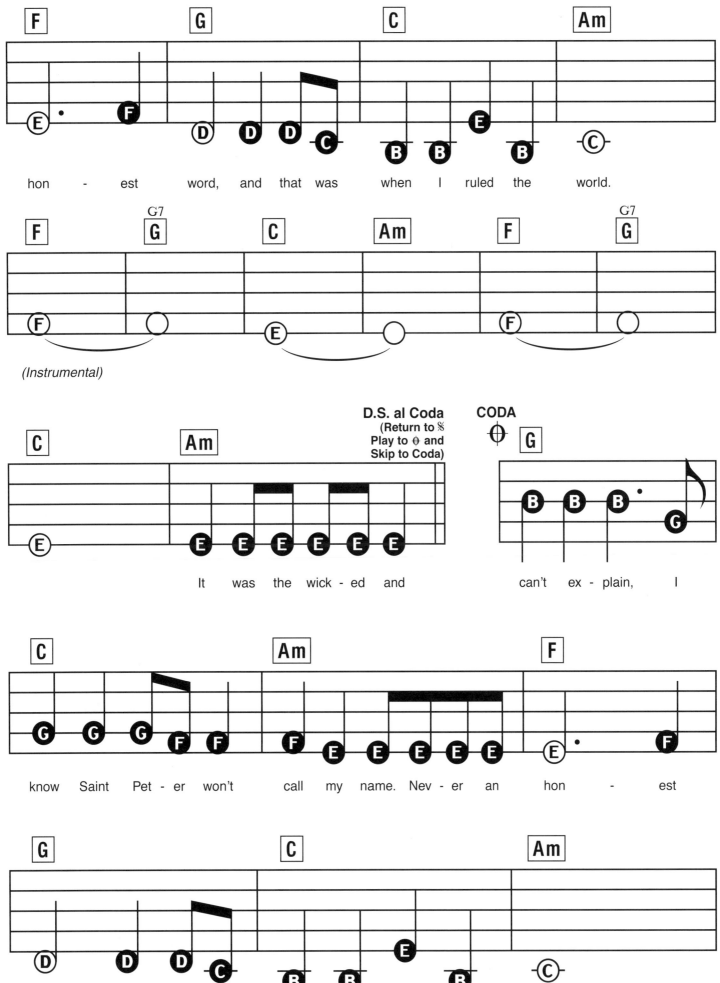

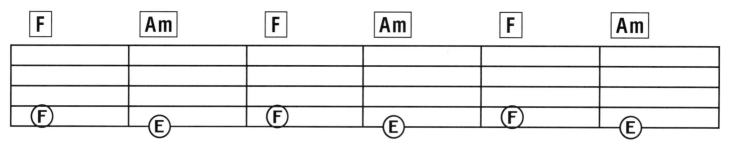

(Instrumental)

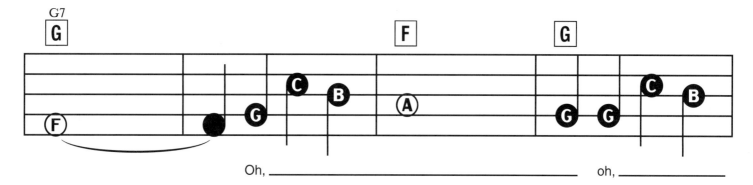

Oh, _____ oh, _____

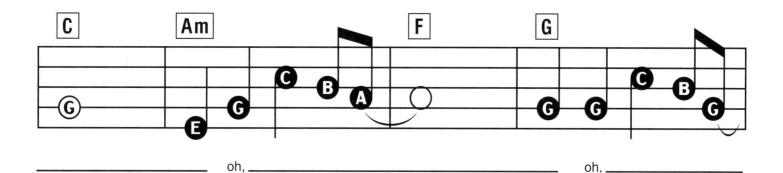

_____ oh, _____ oh, _____

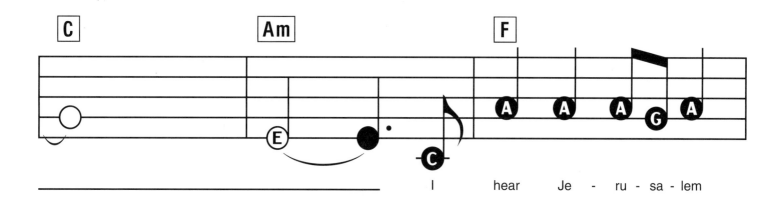

_____ I hear Je - ru - sa - lem

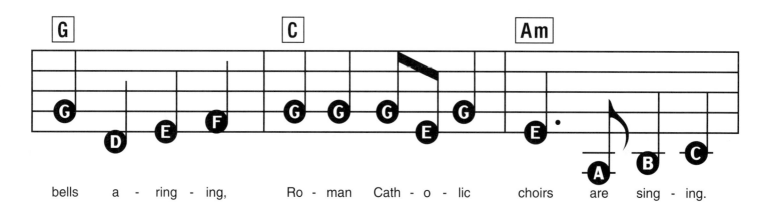

bells a - ring - ing, Ro - man Cath - o - lic choirs are sing - ing.

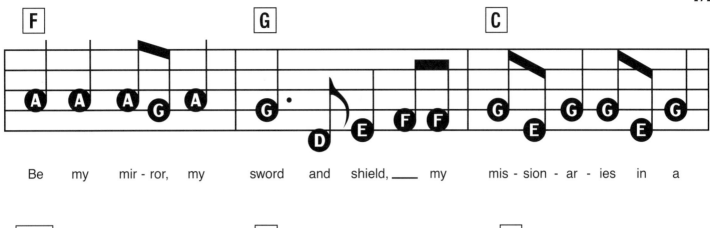

Be my mir-ror, my sword and shield, ____ my mis-sion-ar-ies in a

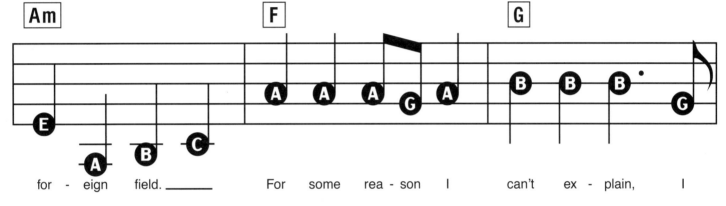

for - eign field. _____ For some rea - son I can't ex - plain, I

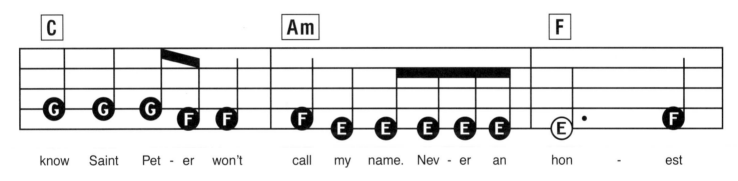

know Saint Pet - er won't call my name. Nev - er an hon - est

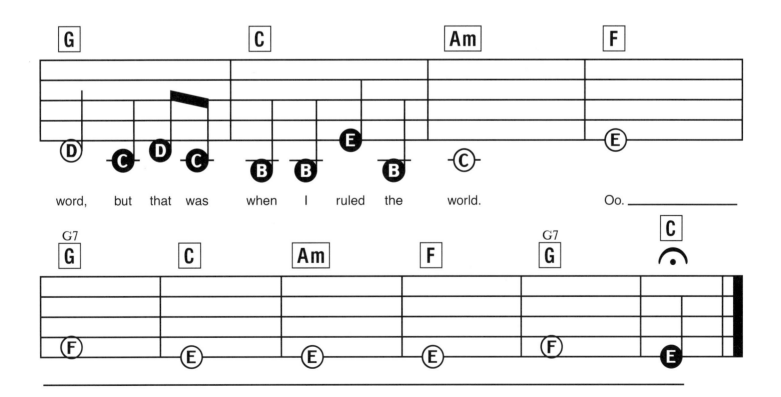

word, but that was when I ruled the world. Oo. _____

Who'll Stop the Rain

Registration 4
Rhythm: Rock or Pop

Words and Music by
John Fogerty

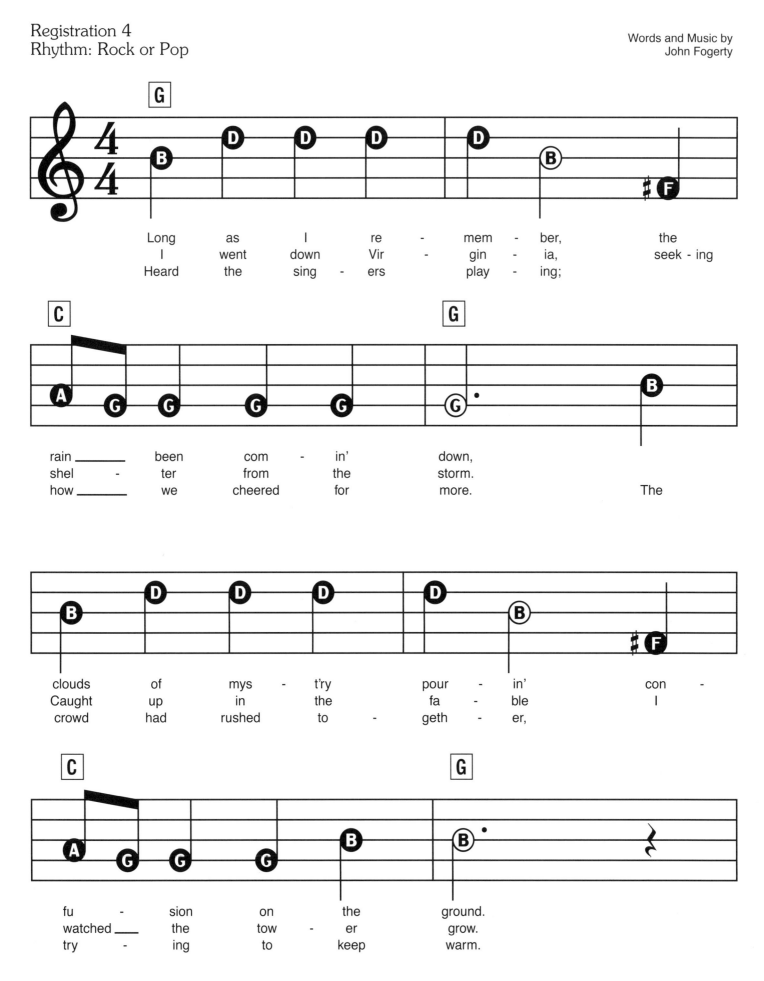

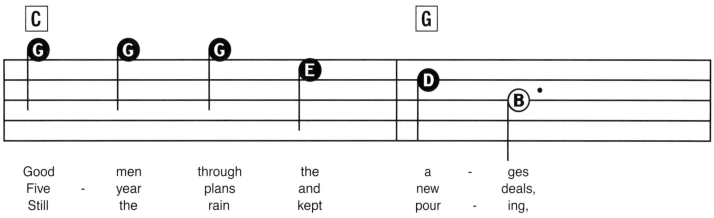

Good men through the a - ges
Five - year plans the and new deals,
Still the year rain kept pour - ing,

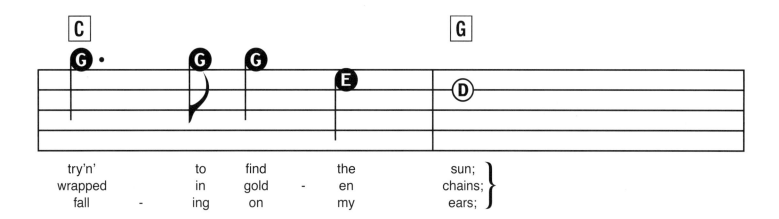

try'n' to find the sun;
wrapped in gold - en chains;
fall - ing on my ears;

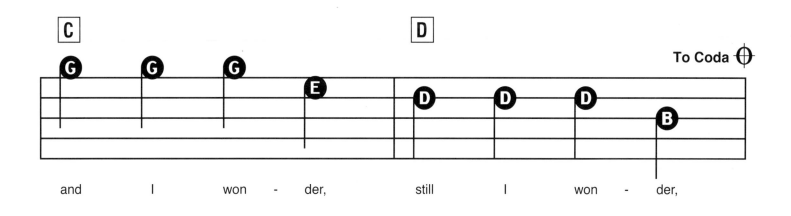

To Coda

and I won - der, still I won - der,

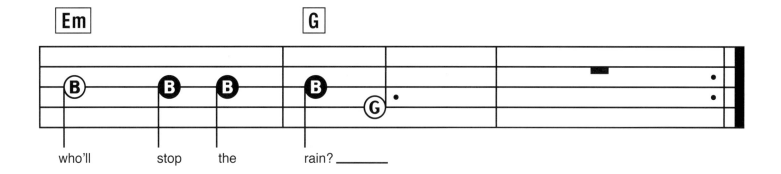

who'll stop the rain? _____

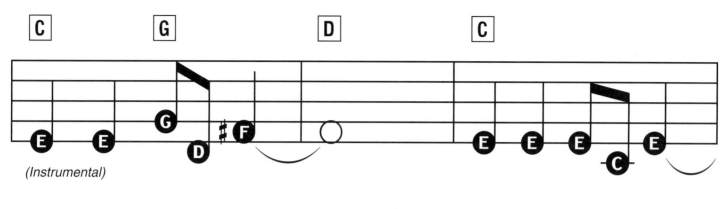

(Instrumental)

D.S. al Coda
(Return to %
Play to ⊕ and
Skip to Coda)

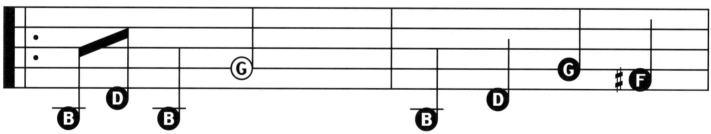

CODA
⊕

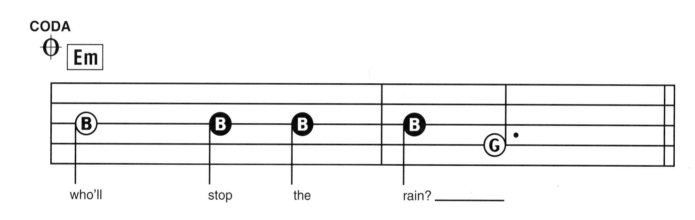

who'll   stop   the   rain? _____

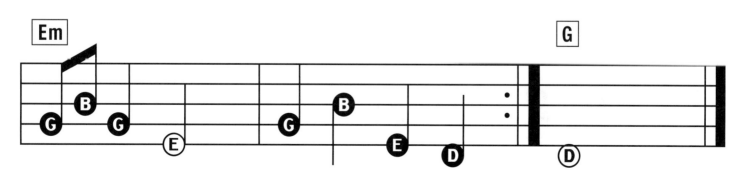

(Instrumental)

Wonderful Tonight

Registration 4
Rhythm: Pops or Rock

Words and Music by
Eric Clapton

It's   late   in the eve - ning;
We   go   to a par - ty,
It's   time   to go home   now,

she's   won - d'ring what clothes to   wear.
and   ev - 'ry - one   turns to   see
and   I've   got an ach - ing   head.

She   puts   on her
this   beau - ti - ful
So I   give   her the

make - up
la - dy
car   keys

and   brush - es her   long blonde   hair.
is   walk - ing a - round   with   me.
and she   helps   me to   bed. _____

And   then she   asks   me,
And   then she   asks   me,
And   then I   tell   her,

"Do I   look   all
"Do you   feel   all
as I   turn   out the

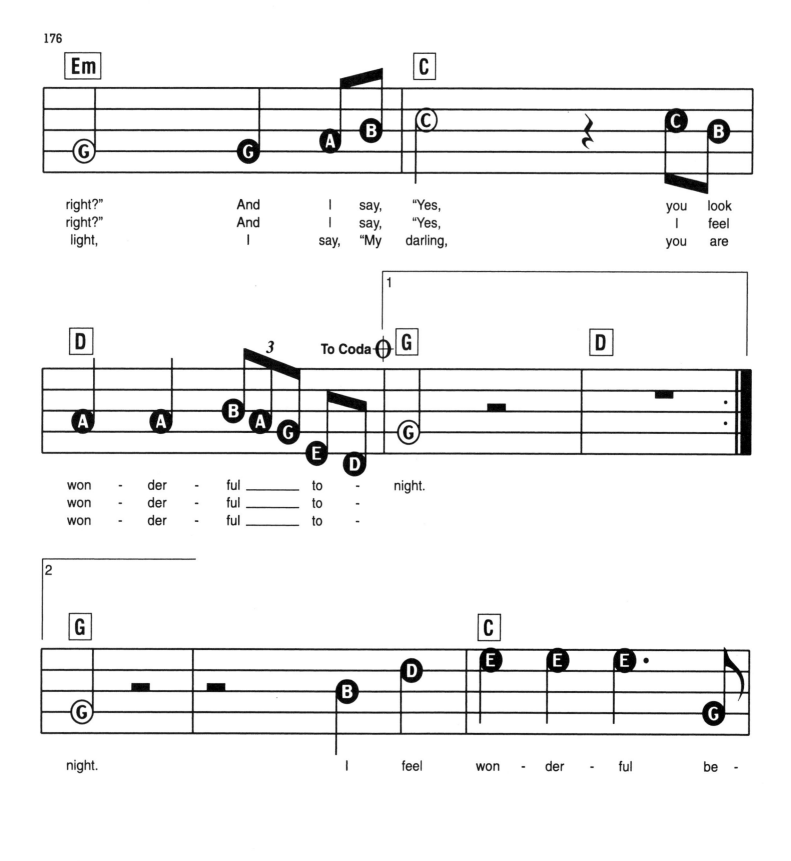

right?"   And   I   say,   "Yes,   you   look
right?"   And   I   say,   "Yes,   I   feel
light,   I   say,   "My   darling,   you   are

won - der - ful _____ to - night.
won - der - ful _____ to -
won - der - ful _____ to -

night.   I   feel   won - der - ful   be -

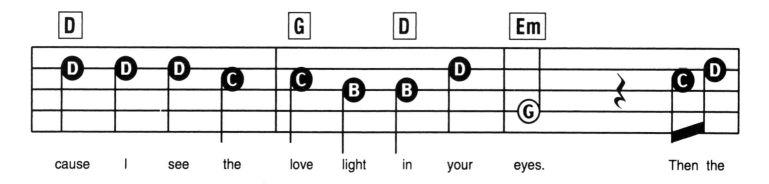

cause   I   see   the   love   light   in   your   eyes.   Then the

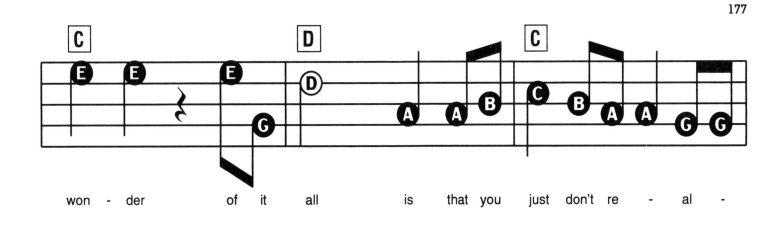

won - der   of it   all   is   that you   just don't re   -   al -

D.C. al Coda
(Return to beginning
Play to ⊕ and
Skip to Coda)

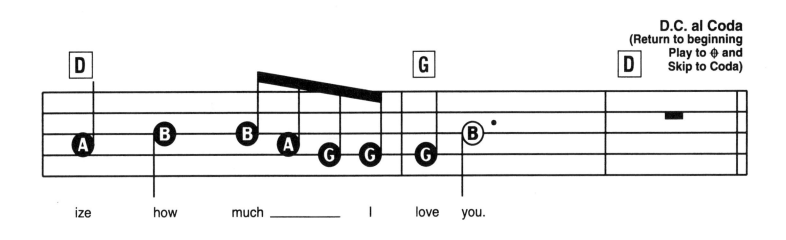

ize   how   much _____   I   love   you.

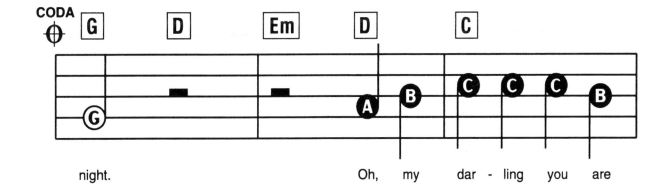

night.   Oh,   my   dar - ling   you   are

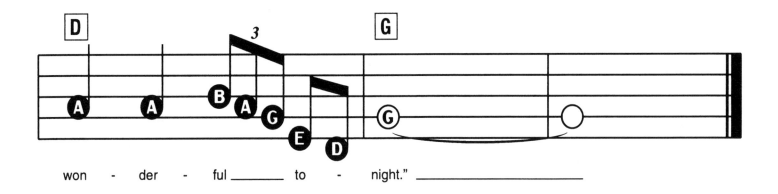

won - der - ful _____ to - night." _____

With or Without You

Registration 4
Rhythm: Rock

Words and Music by
U2

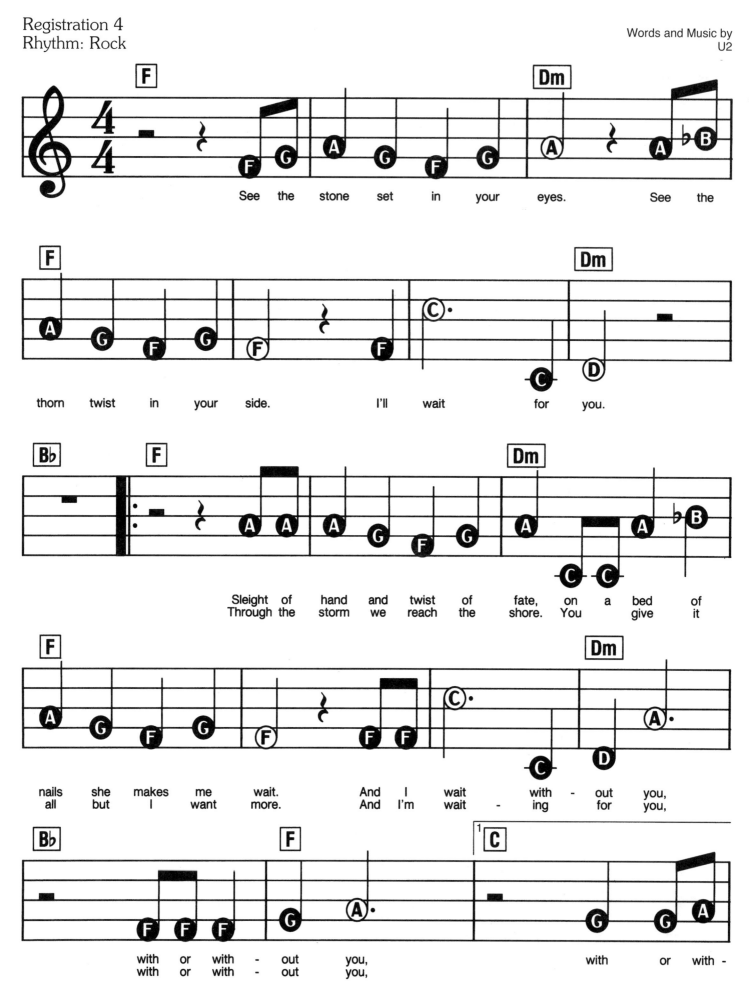

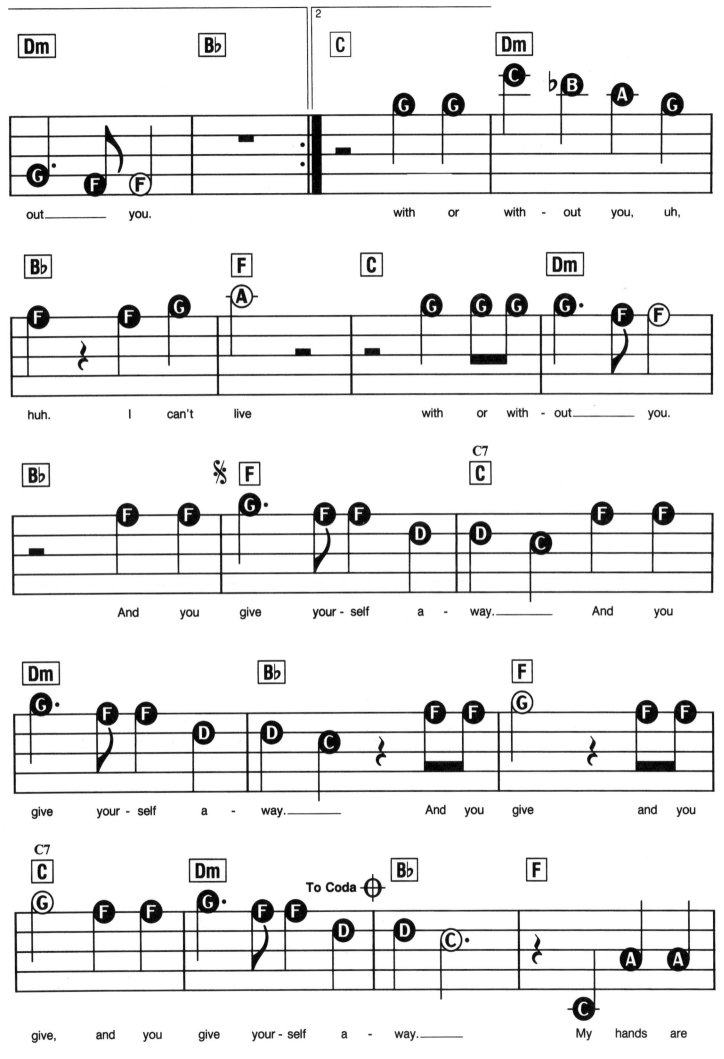

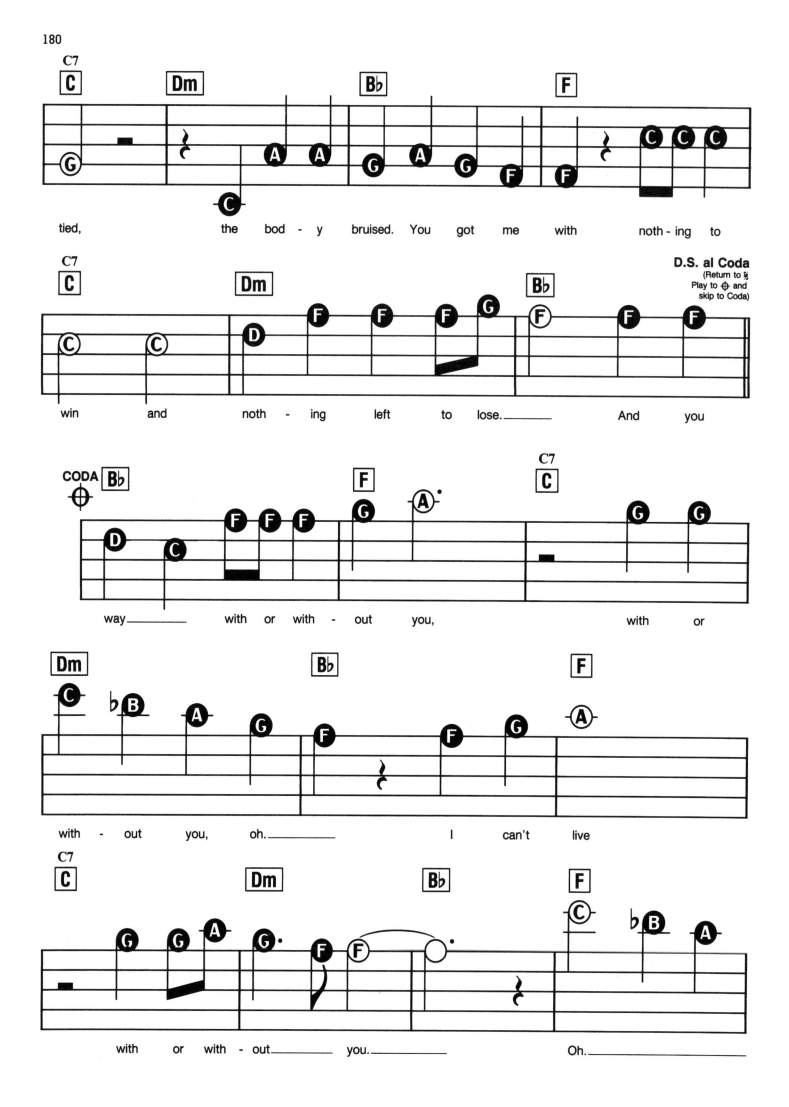

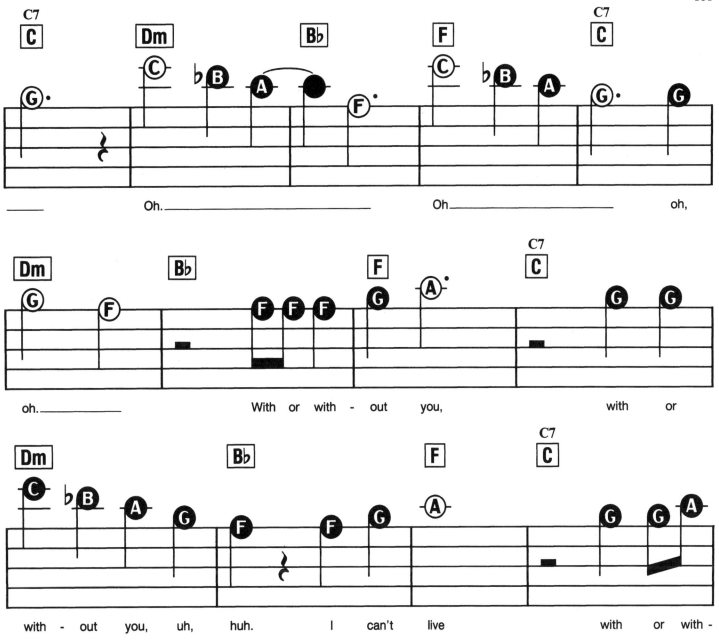

Oh. Oh oh,

oh. With or with-out you, with or

with-out you, uh, huh. I can't live with or with-

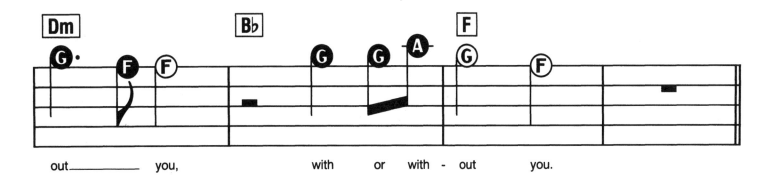

out you, with or with-out you.

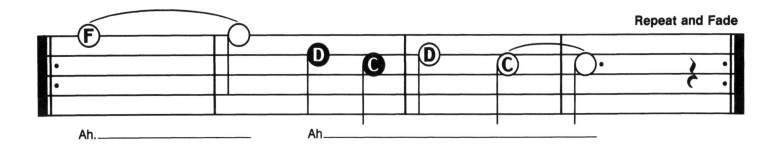

Repeat and Fade

Ah. Ah

You Raise Me Up

Registration 3
Rhythm: Ballad

Words and Music by Brendan Graham
and Rolf Lovland

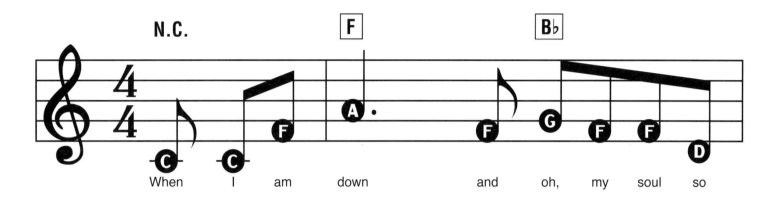

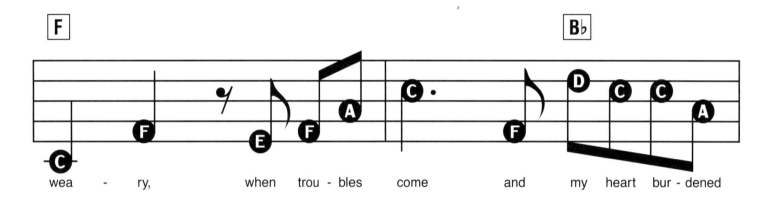

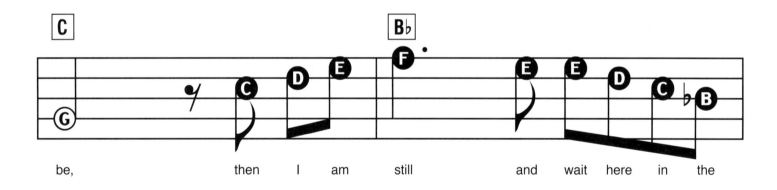

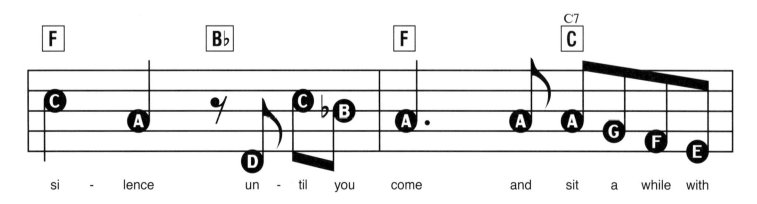

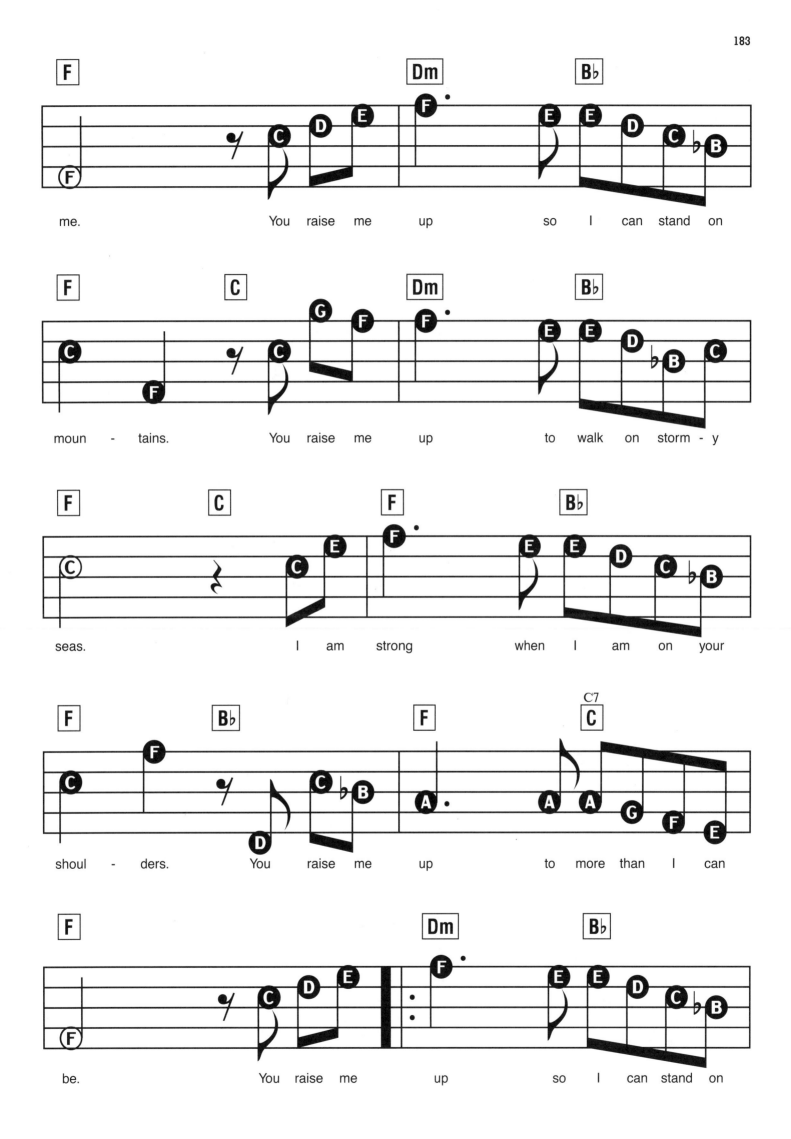

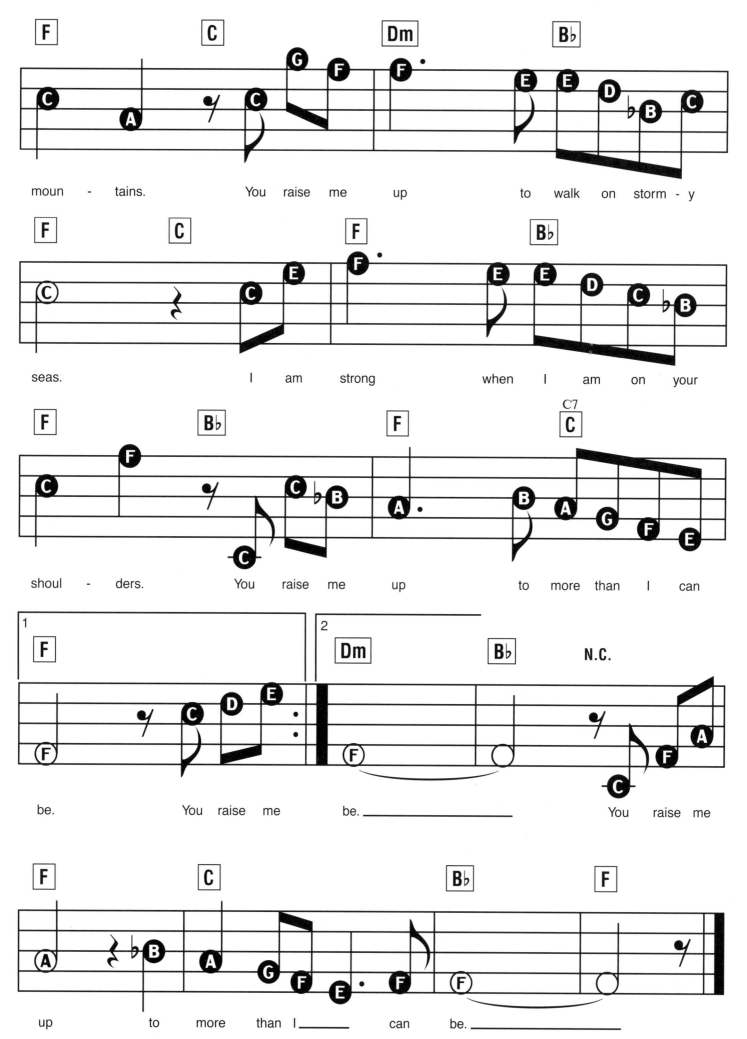